SURVIVE!

Essential Skills and Tactics To Get You Out of Anywhere—Alive

LES STROUD
with Michael Vlessides
Photography by Laura Bombier
Illustrations by Beverley Hawksley

COLLINS
An Imprint of HarperCollins*Publishers*

Published by Collins, an imprint of HarperCollins Publishers Ltd

FIRST EDITION

All photos by Laura Bombier, with the exception of those on the following pages, which are by Les Stroud: 35, 79, 94, 102, 109, 144, 149, 152 (top), 160 (left), 164, 166, 279, 341.

Illustrations by Beverley Hawksley.

This book has been carefully researched, and all efforts have been made to ensure its accuracy. However, readers use at their own risk any of the information and advice the book offers, and they should carefully study and clearly understand the material before any such use. The authors and publisher assume no responsibility for any injury or loss suffered in connection with use of the book.

HarperCollins books may be purchased for educational, business, or sales promotional use through our Special Markets Department.

HarperCollins Publishers Ltd
2 Bloor Street East, 20th Floor
Toronto, Ontario, Canada
M4W 1A8
www.harpercollins.ca

Library and Archives Canada Cataloging in Publication Data is available upon request.

ISBN 978-0-00-200886-0

Printed and bound in the United States
RRD 10 9 8 7 6 5 4 3 2 1

Contents

Introduction

It was decidedly fate. Soon after quitting the music industry and resolving to live a life of outdoor adventure at the age of 25, I opened the newspaper one morning and saw a small ad for a wilderness survival course. Not long after, I found myself on my first solo outing: curled up in my shelter, boots sticking out the entrance, rain teeming down . . . and I was giddy. I realized then and there that I was reliving my boyhood days of building shelters behind our family cottage, only this time I could stay out *all night*. I was hooked, and since then, wilderness survival has figured prominently in my life.

In *Surviving the Extremes*, Dr. Kenneth Kamler writes, "Human beings are the only animal whose emotions, spiritual imperatives and lust for adventure override our survival instincts. We get into trouble because we have an insatiable desire to explore. We know very well we have assumed risks when we travel in an extreme environment and that our decisions could have fatal consequences." My own insatiable lust for adventure has seen me voluntarily place myself, time and time again, in survival ordeals or extreme adventures. I used to do it for fun, and I guess I still do.

I have always channeled my creative energy toward filling voids, doing things that nobody else has done. Creating a survival series for television was no different. I had seen lots of survival films; they seemed dry, boring, and of little interest to anyone but the hardest-core survivalists. What was missing was the drama that unfolds in real-life situations. I realized that to *really* show how to survive you need to go out and actually do it—and film the experience. Out of this thinking, my idea for producing a television series, eventually called *Survivorman*, was born.

From the get-go, I vowed not to let *Survivorman* make a mockery of survival by incorporating games and challenges, or by cheating my way through it by staying in hotels every night or bringing along a makeup artist to help me look dirty. There would be no camera crew to offer me food and assistance. I needed to be out there, alone, just as I had for years trained to be, actually surviving, or at least coming as close as I could to simulating that experience.

Dr. Kamler notes, and I agree, that there are four forces at work in the struggle for survival. *Knowledge*—well, you've got a good start by reading this book. *Conditioning*—an often-overlooked aspect of preparation for wilderness adventure. *Luck*—my dad would have called it "dumb" luck; hopefully you've got some! And the single most important force of all: *the will to live.* Without it, people have perished beside packs of supplies. With it, others in similar situations have survived seemingly impossible ordeals. To this list I would add *survival kit.* Certain gear can make a huge difference in your struggle to survive.

Snowmobiler Chris Traverse certainly had most of these forces when he got lost on his way home from a fishing trip in northern Manitoba in March 2008. To reach safety, he had to endure five days of walking through waist-deep snow without supplies. I was humbled when Chris credited *Survivorman* with helping him survive.

Stories like Chris's are a large part of what led me to write this book and to make sure that, like my TV show, there is nothing phony about my work. The field of wilderness survival is cluttered enough with information. I stick to tried-and-true methods, providing the background and explaining the skills that I know can help you to survive. The skills are ones that anyone can easily learn and use, and that should work anywhere, anytime. I also provide essential checklists, which you'll find at the end of the book; photocopy these and use them to plan your next adventure. Preparation is everything.

Yet no matter how prepared you may be, you should never lose sight of the fact that a survival situation is an *emergency.* It may seem fun on a survival-skills weekend when you're fully fed, guided by an instructor, and surrounded by a group of like-minded students, all smiles and dirty faces. But in a real-life ordeal, "fun" is not part of the equation.

Survival is not about smelling the pines and feeling the breeze on your weathered and tanned face. Survival is not fun. It's not pretty. It's never comfortable. It may involve eating gross things, enduring pain and deprivation, and battling fatigue and loneliness. It may involve danger. It's about life or death. If you want to learn how to *survive*, read on. . . .

Chapter One

TRIP PLANNING AND PREPARATION

In everyday life, planning for survival isn't an issue. Our societies have created extensive systems designed to bail us out in times of emergency. Should you be unfortunate enough to be involved in a car accident, chances are high that an ambulance will soon arrive and take you to an emergency room.

Well, there's a big difference between waiting on the side of the highway for an ambulance and shivering on the side of a remote river in northern Canada with all your food and supplies washed downstream because you just wrecked your canoe running a Class IV rapid. Dialing 911 is *not* going to help you. The ambulance is *not* going to come. This is where trip planning and preparation come in.

I'm talking about more than just menu planning here. It's great to know that you're going to eat dehydrated chicken teriyaki with rice on the third day of your paddling trip, but what will you do if all your food is gone? That is a completely different situation, and one in which trip planning and preparation *with an eye toward survival* can make all the difference in the world. The most common cause of death in the wilderness is unpreparedness. Most people do some preparation before their adventures. *Not* to prepare would be the height of foolhardiness. But beyond arranging route, destination, camping spots, and meals, too few outdoor enthusiasts actually plan for the possibility of a survival situation.

Why? I suspect there are several reasons. Most people don't consider the possibility of finding themselves in such a situation to start with, which can be a grave mistake. Others probably think they have enough survival skills, knowledge, and training, and therefore don't need to contemplate the specifics of a particular trip. Some may feel that thinking of worst-case scenarios is pessimistic, and that it takes the fun out of anticipating a trip. But it's not pessimistic to anticipate emergencies. It's just good bush sense.

And the importance of planning and preparing for your *particular* trip can't be overstated, because every region is different, sometimes in subtle ways. You could dramatically increase your chances of making it through a survival situation by getting just a few tips about the locale.

The more experienced you are in wilderness travel, the more likely you'll have developed your own list of must-haves to bring on your adventures. Remember that each person is responsible for his or her own survival!

Do Your Research

PLANNING AND PREPARING FOR YOUR ADVENTURE BEGINS with research, a fairly easy undertaking in today's information-rich digital age. Between the Internet and the countless books available in public libraries, the foundation is there for anyone to begin to build a location-specific store of knowledge for just about any region on earth.

Printed publications offer other benefits too, aside from the significant information they can yield. First, you can carry small guidebooks and pamphlets with you and—assuming they haven't washed down the river with your canoe—refer to them along the way. Second, reading about your destination ahead of time gets you excited about the trip and empowers you with information that might save your life.

One thing to keep in mind when reading books or online materials, though, is that while they may describe, for example, the types of plants that can be sources of water in a specific area, you cannot be 100 percent sure that you'll be able to identify a plant unless someone has personally taught you how. In this book, for instance, I note that you can find water in the chevron of the leaves of most banana trees. That's all well and good, but you may need someone to show you a banana tree, and teach you how to distinguish it from similar-looking plants.

Ideally, anyone going on a backcountry wilderness trip should take the time to train in that region with a local expert, one who can offer such vital advice as which plants are edible and which ones will kill you. Take the time to find an expert, and try to dedicate at least one day with him or her on the land. The training and teaching may even be available in your own area. The first survival courses I ever took (to prepare me for northern Ontario) were offered in a city . . . Toronto.

Although local experts obviously know the best ways to build shelter, make fire, gather food, and locate water, I often find that it's not the big lessons they teach that ultimately help me the most but the little nuggets of wisdom they throw out in passing. For example, when a native Costa Rican taught me how to eat mussels, he shared a tip with me: if the water that drips out of the mussel is green, it's poisonous; if it's clear, then it's good to eat. That information was nowhere to be found in any of the books on the region, but it could have saved my life. On another occasion, a Kalahari Bushman taught me how to catch small weaver birds by hand by walking up to their nests at night and simply plucking them out of their holes. This is the kind of tip that you can't find anywhere else, but that may prove invaluable if you're stranded . . . and starving.

I realize that spending time with a local expert takes time and money. Most people have only one or two weeks off work and can't dedicate time for training or education while on vacation. But if you can, it will make you more self-reliant, enhancing your trip in ways you never thought possible, even if you never get caught in a survival situation.

Ask the Right Questions

Now that you've committed yourself to learning about the area, your next question is this: What should I be looking for?

First, you should be intimate with your route and destination. Outdoor adventurers can spend hours looking at maps. It's kind of like, well . . . map porn.

Carefully study your maps to get a feel for the land before you see it. As you come to understand an area's features, you will begin to visualize

Had I not taken the time to learn from Kalahari Bushmen, I would have missed out on a plentiful—and easy-to-catch—source of food: the weaver bird (which, as shown here, I am attempting to pull out of a nest).

the terrain in your head. Later, when you're out there, nothing will surprise you. Beyond this, here are the vital things you should always know about any region you plan to visit:

- What kind of vegetation, trees, or plants can you expect to find?
- Which, if any, of these are edible?
- Where are the water sources?
- What kinds of animals are there, and which are dangerous?
- What's the worst possible weather for that area and season? (Checking the weather forecast is a must, as well: if conditions look bad, maybe you should postpone your trip for a while.)
- What will the day and night temperatures be?
- When do the high and low tides occur, and what are the levels?
- Who are the local people, what are their customs or taboos, and are they friendly?

People can play a bigger part in your wilderness adventure than you may think, and unfriendly people may prove a significant hurdle to overcome, even where I live in Canada. There is a river in northern Ontario

There is no substitute for local knowledge. Here, I pick up the finer details of making fire with a hand drill from desert expert David Holladay in Nevada.

that flows through a region that was once rife with controversy, part of the old "loggers versus tree-huggers" chestnut. At one point, the local logging community decided to take out their anger on anyone who traveled the river. More than once over a three-year period, groups of paddlers and anglers reached the parking lot at the end of their trips to find their tires slashed. Imagine if the campers had emerged with a time-sensitive casualty in tow!

Learn to Use a Map and Compass

THIS BOOK OFFERS AN EXTENSIVE CHAPTER ON WILDERNESS NAVIGATION, but nobody should venture into the wild without at least the basic skills to interpret a topographical map and use a compass. You don't play hockey without learning how to skate; you don't go sailing without learning how to sail; and you don't fire a rifle without learning how to shoot. So don't venture into the wilderness without learning how to navigate. There are numerous local college courses available on the subject. Take one!

Always carry a map, whether you're on your own or with a guide. If you're with a guide but have neglected to bring a map, ask to see your guide's as often as possible. Familiarize yourself with it, as well as with the route you are traveling. Your guide should not be annoyed by this, but rather pleasantly surprised that someone else on the trip is willing to become knowledgeable in case the worst should happen. After all, what would you do if your guide became incapacitated?

In preparing yourself by reviewing a route map, you may notice, for example, that a road runs parallel to the river or trail you're traveling on. This is good to know should you run into trouble: *A half day's walk due east will put me onto a road and into the path of possible rescue.* You may also see landmarks such as bridges, buildings, or even small towns. You would never have known that if you hadn't looked at the map *before* it got lost or washed down the river.

Rely on Yourself, Not Your Guide

I'VE OFTEN FOUND THAT PEOPLE ARE FAIRLY GOOD about researching a trip if they're going by themselves or in a small group. Where they get lazy is when they go with a guide. Assumptions are made that the guide a) knows what he or she is doing, b) knows the area really well, and c) has made all the necessary provisions in case of emergency.

Trust your guide, but don't rely on him or her. In other words, you must be self-reliant. Remember that your guide, like you, is human. Guides have been known to make errors—whether out of lack of experience or bad judgment—that lead their parties into otherwise avoidable survival situations. And some of the grimmest survival stories ever told are borne of the fact that people blindly relied on their guides. Your guide will be grateful if you take responsibility for yourself, and you'll feel empowered by doing so.

STROUD'S TIP

If you're traveling in a group, share your survival knowledge and skills with your partners *before* disaster strikes. Make sure that everybody has a basic understanding of the steps they should take in an emergency. Remember, if you have an accident and are facing possible death, your travel companions are the ones you'll have to trust to see you through to safety.

Get in Shape and Know Your Limits

AS WITH ANY PURSUIT THAT PLACES PHYSICAL DEMANDS UPON THE BODY, you'll stand a better chance of making it through a survival ordeal if you already have a baseline level of physical fitness. How far you can trek in a day, how well you can build a shelter under extreme weather conditions, how effectively you can dig a hole for a solar still—all are directly related to your strength and conditioning. And with physical fitness comes greater self-confidence and self-esteem, both of which are critical to maintaining the will to live.

In general, the more we human beings focus on good nutrition and attain a high level of physical fitness, the more capable we are of accomplishing tasks, the more focused we are in our thoughts, and the more clear-headed we are. These are all attributes you'll need if you find yourself struggling to survive.

For me, the importance of being physically fit is magnified when I venture into the wild. I am accepting the risk of undertaking these activities, and I have a responsibility to myself, my travel partners, and my family to be properly prepared. This isn't to say you *can't* trek into the wilderness if you're not fit. But if you do, you're putting yourself at a disadvantage from the start.

As part of physical preparation, consider seeing to any nagging or chronic health (including dental) conditions that may impede you. In the Hollywood movie *Cast Away*, Tom Hanks's character, Chuck Noland, was marooned on an island with a painfully abscessed tooth. To me, that was one of the most realistic parts of the film, because these things *can happen*. If you are traveling in a group, it's also a good idea to know what health issues your partners have, in case you need to look after them.

If you suffer from a chronic condition such as diabetes or high blood pressure, take this into account when planning your trip. And always carry enough medication to last you for longer than you expect.

Finally, if you're planning to travel to an exotic or tropical location, make sure you receive any vaccinations you may need for diseases such as yellow fever, malaria, cholera, typhoid, hepatitis, smallpox, polio, diphtheria, and tuberculosis; an anti-tetanus injection is also a must. Failure to get the proper vaccines may leave you vulnerable to diseases prevalent in the area. Note that some vaccinations must be administered over the course of several months, so look into this well ahead of your departure.

Test Your Mental Fitness

Though often overlooked, mental preparedness is an important part of the survival equation. And the best way to prepare yourself mentally for an outdoor adventure is to gain *knowledge*. Knowledge really is power, and it brings you the confidence you need to survive should disaster strike. Review the suggestions outlined in this chapter to help guide you through the research process. Before you leave, you should do the following:

- gather as much information as possible from printed sources
- contact a local expert who can inform you about the specifics of the destination: its flora and fauna, dangers, and any benefits or advantages (such as shelters, escape routes, or water sources) offered by the terrain
- receive at least basic training in wilderness survival and navigation skills
- gage your level of fitness and determine that you're ready for your trip
- prepare a region-specific survival kit

If you've completed all the above tasks, you'll know that if you find yourself in an emergency, you are as prepared as you can possibly be.

The other thing you can do to prepare mentally for a trip—and for any survival situation in which you may find yourself—is to accept that the worst *can* happen. If you head into any outdoor adventure with the notion that "It can't happen to me," you're deluding yourself.

You should think exactly the opposite: "It *can* happen to me. I *could* end up in the middle of this wilderness alone, even though I'm rafting in a group of 12," or "I *could* get turned around and lost, even though it's just a Sunday hike and there are 75 other people out here today." Once you accept the fact that an emergency *could* happen to you, the next logical step is to prepare so that it's less likely to happen and so that you're ready to handle it if it does.

Choose the Right Gear

It is important that any equipment you bring on an outdoor adventure is up to the task: strong and versatile. Don't ask yourself if it will function under the *best conditions*, but rather, will it do so under the *worst conditions*? If not, do you want to stake your life on it?

Your equipment preparation is almost entirely dependent on your destination. Again, I recommend that you speak with someone local or, alternatively, talk to another traveler who has done the same sort of activity in the same place. They will help you to determine what equipment you need.

You can also learn about equipment by meandering around local outdoor stores that are tailored to the activity you'll be doing. These are great places to meet people, especially other customers, who may have experience that could help you. Also consider posting a notice on a board in stores like these, to get in touch with other adventurers who may have knowledge to share.

STROUD'S TIP

Do not select your equipment based solely on what's suggested in books and other print materials; these sources may contain too many errors and omissions, or may be out of date. It is important that you learn from other travelers' personal experiences.

Assuming that you now have all the right equipment for your excursion, the next step is to make sure you *know how to use it*. Don't make the mistake of thinking that you will have the chance to learn about your gear *during* your adventure. Your survival ordeal could take place within the first few hours of the trip, and you might panic because you don't know, for example, how to set up your tent in a storm. So get yourself out in the backyard, on the deck, or even in the living room, and spend a few hours acquainting yourself with your gear. Practice setting it up and taking it down. Even more important, figure out how to fix it if it breaks; it may have to last you for a lot longer, or under more difficult circumstances, than you think!

Equipment planning and preparation pertains to clothing as well, yet another category in which a little local knowledge goes a long way. Don't always trust the salespeople at your local outdoor store. I've seen many cases where a clerk has recommended the wrong item of clothing just because he's been told to push a particular brand. Again, try to speak with other travelers who have been to where you're going. Remember, poor clothing choices won't make much of a difference if everything goes right, but they can sure go a long way toward making you miserable should things go wrong.

Wind, rain, cold, poisonous creepy crawlies, and extreme heat are some of the elements you may face. Your clothing should be able to withstand all of these. Make sure it fits well and is not too restrictive. You want clothes that will keep you dry and warm but that also offer enough ventilation to prevent overheating (see "Clothing," Chapter 12).

STROUD'S TIP

Think of your clothing as your first shelter. Proper clothing should enable you to withstand extreme elements without building a shelter. So whether you're surviving in the bitter cold of the Arctic or in a torrential downpour in the jungle, you should be able to stand still in only your clothing and survive.

While in the Canadian Arctic, I was outfitted with a caribou parka and pants, traditional Inuit gear. In temperatures as low as –58°F (–50°C), these enable the wearer to stand in a blizzard, impervious to the cold. Now that's a great shelter!

Inform Others of Your Plans

TELLING PEOPLE WHEN AND WHERE YOU'RE GOING is a vital aspect of trip preparation. Unfortunately, people sometimes get lazy in this regard. Don't. If you do, you may find yourself in the same situation as Jennifer and James Stolpa, a young couple who, along with their five-month-old son Clayton, got lost in a blizzard in northern Nevada in the early 1990s.

While driving to a family funeral in Idaho, they found their planned route closed by a snowstorm. They decided to take a detour but didn't tell anybody about the change. Their truck later became stuck in the snow, and they found themselves stranded 40 miles (64 km) from civilization.

The Stolpas spent the first four days of their ordeal in their truck's camper-shell. When nobody came along to rescue them (nobody knew where they were), they decided to attempt walking to safety, towing Clayton in a makeshift sled. When Jennifer could no longer walk, James found a cave for her and Clayton to stay in, while he continued on in search of help. Over the next 60 hours, James slogged almost 50 miles (80 km) in his sneakers before stumbling, incoherent, into the view of a passing motorist, who then helped rescue his wife and son.

Could this emergency situation have been avoided? I believe so. First of all, the Stolpas didn't execute the best judgment in traveling against weather advisories and taking a back route to Idaho. But where they really went astray was in failing to inform anyone of their plan, a mistake that cost them their toes (lost to frostbite) and nearly their lives.

So anytime you're undertaking a backcountry adventure—or any journey that takes you into remote areas—make sure that at least two different people (including local authorities) know, when appropriate:

- the nature of your activity
- when you're starting out
- when you're scheduled to finish
- your route
- how they can communicate with you
- how they can find you if there's a problem

Fortunately, technology has come a long way in making wilderness travel safer. Websites such as SendAnSOS.com will allow you to enter your own personal travel plan. If you don't sign in to the site after your return date, it will automatically send an SOS message to your contacts. Devices such as the SPOT satellite messenger not only allow others to keep track of your progress but also send an SOS message to your contacts when you push the Help button.

If you take advantage of all the planning resources and fail-safes available to today's outdoor enthusiasts, you will radically increase your chances of making it through any survival situation.

Chapter Two

SURVIVAL KITS

Preparation and planning arm you with the tools you need to make it through a crisis alive and well, not to mention that they strengthen your psychological state. And among pre-trip tasks, none is as crucial as putting together your personal survival kit.

Most people take the time before heading into the backcountry to obtain the necessary basic equipment such as proper clothing, a tent, and a stove. But you may not realize that your basic survival kit could be the single most important thing you carry with you on any expedition. At various times, I've ventured into the world's most remote areas with different sorts of survival gear: fully stocked survival kits, basic "whatever I can carry" survival kits, and sometimes even no kit at all. Survival items have dangled from my belt or hung around my neck. Sometimes they've been in fanny packs I barely noticed and other times in fanny packs so heavy I would have preferred not to carry them at all (but did anyway).

How you set up your kit is limited only by your imagination. Why not fill the hollow end of your fishing rod with a lighter and some kind of ignitable tinder such as cotton balls? Or if you're a mountain biker, pop off your handlebar grips and fill your handlebars with a few items, such as fire starter, some cord or rope, or a multi-tool. Once I even had a kit that was drilled into the stock of a rifle.

Take Responsibility for Your Own Survival

WHILE TEACHING SURVIVAL COURSES, early in the week I would announce to my students that we were going for a wilderness hike the next morning. When they asked me what they should take along, I would casually tell them, "Whatever you think you need for a hike in the bush."

The next day, midway through the hike, I would stop and ask everyone to show me what they had brought. There was always one person armed to the teeth with survival gear. A few more would be carrying a few basic survival items, and others would be carrying almost nothing.

I was often struck by how many people would go out *not* expecting the unexpected. Here they were, hiking into the bush, and most were carrying very little to help them if disaster struck. When you're in the wilderness, you never know when or where or how an emergency may occur. Disaster often strikes in mysterious ways. And you may be separated from your travel companions at any time. Just as you shouldn't rely completely on your guide, you shouldn't rely completely on your partner or partners.

This kind of wrong-thinking was never more obvious than when *couples* took my course. They were usually proud to show off their *one* very well-equipped pack, invariably carried by the husband. In those instances, I would pull the wife aside and say, "So, now . . . what do *you* have?" Only then would it occur to her that she had nothing that would help her in a survival situation. She was relying on her husband, not on herself.

Creating a survival kit is a personal undertaking and one that should never be left to someone else, no matter how close you are to them. To be left alone without a few basic survival items is to court death.

Make It Yourself

WHEN IT COMES TO SURVIVAL KITS, most of us are faced with two options: buy a prefab kit at our local outdoors store, or make it ourselves. To my mind, there is no question which route to go: Make your own.

There are a few reasons I feel this way. First, the primary motivation for the company that makes the prefab kit is *profit*, not necessarily your survival. They're going to try to cut costs wherever possible. This means the kit may not contain the best of everything. Something in there is going to be cheap or unnecessary, and take up precious room and weight. It might be the flimsy plastic whistle that cracks the first time you drop it, or matches that snap when you try to strike them. With a prefab kit, something is bound to let you down when you need it most.

Second, most people who buy a prefab kit never become acquainted with the proper use of its contents. Some never even open the kit before setting off on their adventure. Why? Because they trust it. They just throw it into their day-pack and forget about it, feeling sure they have done the right thing just by bringing it. I've seen people walk around with a flint striker on their belt or a compass in their pocket that they've never tried and haven't a clue how to use.

Third, I have yet to see a prefab kit that contains all the necessities from top to bottom.

Your personal survival kit should be based on the suggestions I make in this chapter, but even more important, it should be your own creation—one that takes into account the *region* you'll be traveling in, the *season*, the *weather*, and your anticipated *activities*. If you are leading others, the kit's contents should also reflect the fact that you may have to help others in the group survive.

My recommendation is that you purchase your kit items individually so that you know what you've bought will stand up to the rigors of a survival situation. The mere fact that you take the time to select the items increases the chances that you're going to check them out, make sure they work, and get to know how to use them.

Your Personal Survival Kit

A *personal survival kit* isn't a separate pack that you carry in addition to the everyday gear on a wilderness expedition. In fact, your personal survival kit is not really a "kit" at all but the most important survival gear you should carry with you at all times—on your belt, in your pockets, or around your neck. Why? The answer is simple: You may leave a fanny pack behind on a portage or when you stop for a snack. It happens all the time. But you'll never leave a pocket behind.

Your *personal survival kit* starts with a sturdy belt knife, which has a multitude of uses. Consider it a survival kit unto itself. The biggest benefit of a belt knife is its strength, which allows it to be used to pry and twist objects you might not otherwise be able to manipulate. Used properly, a belt knife will split wood. It will easily whittle and shape wood components for traps, snares, and shelters.

Don't underestimate the importance of keeping your knife sharp. If you're not overloaded in terms of weight, carry a sharpening stone in your *complete survival kit* (which we discuss later in this chapter). In a pinch, however, you can sharpen your belt knife on just about any smooth stone you find in the bush. Sandstone is quite effective, and quartz and granite also work well.

Here is a list of the personal survival kit items that you should carry at all times, whether you stash them in your pockets or wear them clipped to your belt or around your neck. Each member of a group should have his or her own

- bandana
- compass
- flashlight (small, LED)
- garbage bags (2, preferably orange, large)
- lighter (my preference is a butane lighter that works like a little blowtorch)
- matches (strike-anywhere type) in a waterproof metal case (with a striker, just in case)
- magnesium flint striker (hey, I like fires!)
- metal cup (folding; for boiling water)
- multi-tool or Swiss Army–style knife (make sure it has a small saw blade)
- painkillers (a few)
- parachute cord or similar rope (about 25 feet [7.5 m] of 1/4-inch [0.6-cm] cord)
- protein bar (e.g., PowerBar)
- sharp belt knife
- solar, or "space," blanket (small)
- whistle
- Ziploc bag (medium or large)

This may sound like a weighty list, but remember that you can also carry a couple of these items, such as the whistle and magnesium flint striker, on a piece of rope or parachute cord around your neck. Remember, too, that when everything is spread out on your belt or among your various pockets (obviously, wearing clothes with lots of pockets is helpful) you'll hardly notice them at all.

Your Complete Survival Kit

Now that you've ensured your survival by strategically stowing a few basic—yet supremely helpful—items on yourself, it's time to build your *complete survival kit.* Just because you're carrying the same thing on your body (a lighter in your pocket, for example) doesn't mean you shouldn't put one in your complete survival kit. The items in your pockets are your fail-safes; *always* double up on these items between your personal and complete survival kits. When building your complete survival kit, keep in mind that the heavier and bulkier you make it, the more likely it's going to be a hindrance rather than a benefit. And as soon as your kit becomes a burden, you increase the chances that you won't take some of the items with you in the first place or that you'll leave them behind during a trip. If it's a screaming hot day and I'm climbing a mountain, do I want to be carrying around 20 pounds (9 kg) of extra gear? You have to strike the balance: the kit needs to be large enough to carry certain essential items, but small enough that it doesn't become a nuisance. Leave the gear hording to the gear geeks; your job is not to impress your partners but to enjoy your trip or adventure . . . and to survive if you need to.

You can choose any sort of carrying case into which your survival gear will fit, but you want the container to be large enough to hold items of various sizes, easy to stow and carry, durable, and, if possible, waterproof. I like using a coffee can with a lid as my survival kit because it holds almost all the items I need and can also be used to boil liquid or cook food. Assuming the lid fits snugly, I can even use it to carry water or hot coals.

What follows is a list of the items essential to any kit (some can be used for more than one purpose). You can gather all of them quickly by consulting the Complete Survival Kit Checklist on page 354 before setting out on your adventure. Remember that you will have to modify this list depending on your particular destination, season, weather, and activity:

Bandana: This multi-purpose garment will protect your head from the sun, but it can also be used as an emergency bandage or, when dipped in water, as a cool compress.

Belt knife (with sharpening stone): If you happen to lose your knife, having a backup in your survival kit could be a big help.

Candle: A candle can help you get a fire going if you light it and allow the wax to drip into the tinder.

Cup (metal, collapsible): A cup can be used for drinking or to boil water.

Dried food: Most survival kits contain everything under the sun *except* extra food. I realize dried food adds to the weight and bulkiness of your kit, but nothing will give you a physical and psychological boost like knowing that you have an energy bar or two on hand. Fat is important. Peanuts are an excellent and compact source of fat and protein.

Duct tape: The wonders of ultra-durable and super-sticky duct tape have long been lauded in the outdoor community, with good reason: it can repair just about any kind of outdoor equipment. And it can also be useful in bandaging wounds and other minor injuries. Just make sure you use it in conjunction with a piece of cloth; don't apply it directly to a wound.

Recent years have seen the introduction of colored duct tape. And while you may have a problem with patching your gear with pink or yellow, keep in mind that it'll stand out more than battleship gray. Duct tape is also excellent as a fire starter; it holds the flame the way a candle would.

Fire-starting devices: Fire is one of the most beneficial things you can have with you, no matter where you find yourself. It doesn't matter if you're in the desert or the jungle, for even in the world's hottest places, fire makes all the difference to survival. Fire-starting devices should be a priority in your kit.

I am always asked what my favorite fire-starting method is. Is it flint and steel? Magnesium flint striker? Fire and piston? What I can tell you is that making fire *without* a fire-starting device is extremely difficult, so

STROUD'S TIP

Some people think it's a good idea to waterproof their matches by dipping them in wax. Leave that to the gear geeks. Instead, buy solid strike-anywhere matches and invest in a good waterproof container.

make sure you give yourself options. I love knowing that I have several options with me and that I'm prepared for almost any situation.

My preference is a butane lighter, the kind that shoots a flame like a propane torch. These work upside down and in the wind, two great advantages. A lighter will eventually run out of fuel, but only after a few hundred fires. Furthermore, in a survival emergency, the first fire is the most important.

Always carry a high-quality lighter, because depending on where you are, it may well be a challenge to keep your fire going. You don't want to add the stress of fire-starting to your list of worries.

In addition to a lighter, I like to carry a magnesium flint striker (which in a pinch can be used as a signaling device), a fire piston (if weight is not an issue), and some solid strike-anywhere matches *with a striker* (just to be sure) in a waterproof container such as a film canister. Note that plastic containers can be unsafe to keep matches in because, though a remote possibility, static electricity can ignite the matches. A metal container is best.

Just make sure—as with everything in your survival kit—that you know how to use these fire starters. Take the time to practice making a fire with them *before* disaster strikes. I recommend that you carry at least one of these fire starters on you, as part of your personal survival kit (for example, in a pocket), and a couple more in your complete survival kit. See "Fire," Chapter 6, for more on this topic.

Fire-starting tinder: There are a few different types of commercially available tinder, including pellets, pastes, and shavings. I like having three or four wax-and-cotton fuel wads. A small piece of this added to the tinder you collect in the bush will flame up from a simple spark and keep going like a candle flame until your fire is roaring. You should also add bits of tinder, such as birch bark or dried grass, to your survival kit as you come across them during your travels.

The wax-and-cotton cube, one of the best commercially available tinders you can buy, holds a flame for a long time.

First-aid kit:

- antidiarrheal tablets and painkillers: If you get diarrhea on vacation in Mexico, you're disappointed. Get it in the jungles of Borneo and you could be dead. Pain, on the other hand, won't necessarily kill you, but painkillers such as ibuprofen or acetaminophen can increase your chances of survival if you have to make your way down a mountain with a small injury or even a pounding headache. For a really nasty injury such as a broken leg, powerful painkillers such as Demerol (meperidine) can save an injured person from slipping into fatal shock. Pack all medicines in waterproof, airtight containers.
- antihistamines: They are handy for allergies, as well as for insect bites and stings.
- bandages and antiseptic ointment: An "ouch" kit can help prevent infection.
- butterfly sutures: These will hold together deeper and more serious wounds.
- prescription medicine: Always bring extra.

- surgical blades: Light and small, these are for more than just dressing wounds. They can be used for whittling, cleaning fish, or skinning and gutting game.
- triangle bandages: Use these as wound dressings or as slings.

Fishing lures (3), hooks, sinkers, a leader, and fishing line: As a rule, you're better off keeping heavier line in your survival kit. The weight and volume difference between 10-pound and 30-pound test is nominal, but the difference in strength is significant. Most people avoid lures, but they don't add much weight to your kit and can significantly improve your chances of catching dinner. Throw in a leader as well, just in case you want to try for "the big one."

Flares: You want to be found, right? The more compact the flare, the better. They can also be used to start fires.

Flashlight (small, LED): These little lights can be very bright, which makes them good not only for locating things at night, but for signaling too. You might also consider packing a couple of extra batteries. When you buy a flashlight, make sure you get one with a white, yellow, green, or blue light (red LEDs are not very bright).

GPS (Global Positioning System), in *addition* to a map and compass: The GPS has revolutionized wilderness travel. The beauty of a GPS is that it provides you with precise, real-time information regarding your location, at all times and in all weather conditions. As long as it has enough battery power, a GPS will determine your latitude, longitude, and altitude.

Garbage bags (2, orange, large): Garbage bags can make the difference between life and death because of the multitude of purposes for which they are useful. They fold down to practically nothing, don't weigh much, and fit easily into a pocket. But make sure you get the 45-gallon (170-L) orange ones (which can be readily seen), not green bags (which can't).

You can turn a garbage bag into a raincoat, or a makeshift jacket to protect you from cold and wind, by tearing or cutting a hole in the top for your head and holes in the sides for your arms. You can signal with it because it's bright and highly visible. Your wondrous, orange plastic sheet can also act as a rain-catch if you need water or be used in the construction of vegetation and solar stills (although the best type of bag for a vegetation still is a clear plastic one. See "Water," Chapter 5).

My favorite use for garbage bags is as waterproofing for a shelter. No matter how adept you are, it is exceptionally difficult to build from scratch a shelter that is completely waterproof. If you have a garbage bag on hand, just cut it open so that it forms a single sheet (the 45-gallon ones will be 4 feet x 6 feet [1.2 m x 1.8 m]) and you have a ready-made roof.

Hand lens (small): A small hand lens such as a Fresnel lens is essentially a magnifying glass that can be used to start fires or inspect small injuries.

Map and compass: Topographical maps are your best source of detailed information in the backcountry; carry them whenever possible. If you are carrying one, you owe it to yourself also to carry a high-quality compass that you know how to use. There are many excellent books and college courses on compass use and map reading. See "Survival Travel and Navigation," Chapter 9.

Marker or "surveyor's" tape: Bright red or orange tape can be hung from your shelter to help attract rescue or be used to mark a trail.

Money: A $20 or $50 bill won't help you procure water in the wilderness, but it sure comes in handy when you eventually make your way out to a highway. Once you scramble out of the bush, the money in your kit will allow you to buy something to eat and drink, and take care of any immediate needs. You may also want to put a credit card in your kit.

Multi-tool: When I set out for a week of survival, I believe there's nothing more crucial than a multi-tool. A twist on the classic Swiss Army–style knife, the multi-tool takes things to the next level with the addition of an integrated set of pliers, which has many uses in the wilderness. I often use the pliers on my multi-tool to take a pot of boiling water off a fire.

Make sure that the multi-tool you choose includes a saw blade. You won't use it much for felling trees, but a saw blade is excellent for making traps and snares. Scissors also come in handy in a survival situation, so make sure your multi-tool has a pair. And remember, quality counts! Don't buy a cheap model or you will regret it.

Needle and thread: It's a good idea to carry a needle and thread, yet in all the years I've been participating in survival-related activities, I think I've used these only once, to mend a torn canoe pack. Bring a needle with a very large eye so that it can be threaded with thick materials, such as sinew and coarse thread. Perhaps the best use for the needle is in first aid, to remove splinters and slivers.

STROUD'S TIP

You can magnetize a needle by rubbing it in one direction on a magnetic item, such as the speaker of a radio. When you float the magnetized needle in water, on a leaf or on a piece of paper, the needle will point north/south. Once you determine which end is north, color that end of the needle with a marker.

PLB (Personal Locator Beacon) or EPIRB (Emergency Position-Indicating Radio Beacon): While these units do not contact your family *at the same time* as they contact search and rescue organizations (the way SPOT does), they are excellent for notifying emergency personnel or the military, and have saved many lives.

Parachute cord or similar rope (about 50 feet [15 m] of 1/4-inch [0.5 cm] cord): As romantic as it may sound to make rope out of bark and roots, the fact is that the process is slow, tedious, and often difficult. On the other hand, having a good spool of parachute cord can make a tremendous difference in a survival situation. You can use it to make shelters, fire bows, signals, snares or traps, and for countless other purposes.

I've singled out parachute cord here because it is legendary for its strength. Constructed of an outer sheath surrounding seven inner strands, true parachute cord is one of the strongest and lightest ropes you can find, and it's rated at 550-pound test.

Parachute cord can be bulky in large quantities, however, so it helps to come up with innovative ways to carry it. Some travelers wrap it around the handles of their belt knives; others use it in lieu of shoelaces, as every little bit helps when it comes to lightening your load.

Pencil and notebook: Use these to write your personal survival log, in which you take note of efforts and discoveries you've made. It will help boost your morale, act as a reference guide, and support your memory should it begin to fail. Perhaps its most important use is in leaving a note for potential rescuers if you move on, to let them know where you have gone.

Safety pins: These are helpful when making repairs to clothing and other gear. Safety pins can also be used as fish hooks.

Saw (folding): Here's an item I really love, although admittedly a folding saw is bulkier and heavier than most items you'll see in a typical survival kit. Nevertheless, it's worth its weight in gold, because it completely transforms how you can build shelters or keep a fire going, both of which are crucial (physically and psychologically) in a survival ordeal.

It used to be that you could get only poor-quality folding saws, but they've come a long way in recent years in terms of quality and durability. My favorites are the one-piece units with a blade that folds into the handle. When folded they're about 10 inches (25 cm) long.

Signal mirror: When choosing a signal mirror, you have a couple of options. Personally, I prefer hand mirrors that are designed to act as signaling devices. You can distinguish these by the small hole in the middle, which is used for sighting passing aircraft.

Like any item in your survival kit, your signal mirror can also serve other functions, such as grooming or first aid. If you get something in your eye (which happens more often than you'd think), a little mirror is invaluable. Something as seemingly innocuous as a pine needle in your eye can cause intense pain if you can't get it out. A good signal mirror can also serve as a fire starter by reflecting the sun's rays.

Snare wire: Like parachute cord, snare wire has a multitude of uses, the most important of which is catching your potential dinner! Snare wire meant for rabbits is the most appropriate.

Solar or "space" blanket (small): A solar blanket reflects your own body heat back to you, which is effective if you need to get warm in a hurry. Granted, it doesn't feel warm and cozy, but it works better than anything else you can get for the weight.

The potential danger with solar blankets is that they do not breathe or permit perspiration to escape, so they have the potential to leave you damper and colder than when you started. Don't roll up in one or use it as an under-layer inside a jacket; simply wrap it around you.

Solar blankets are terrific reflectors and can be used for signaling if necessary, as a makeshift tarp to waterproof your shelter, or as a rain-catch. While surviving in the Canadian Rocky Mountains outside of Revelstoke, British Columbia, I used one as a roof, and it made for the warmest shelter I can remember. Be careful with solar blankets around fire, however. They can melt within seconds when touched by flames.

SPOT satellite messenger: The SPOT enables you to send e-mails by satellite, and includes your latitude and longitude coordinates. It will even track you and send your coordinates to 10 contacts by e-mail or text message every 10 minutes. The SPOT goes beyond a GPS to the next level of safety. A GPS will tell *you* where you are. The SPOT will tell *your rescuers* where you are.

Water purification tablets: Each iodine-based water purification tablet will purify 1 to 2 quarts (1 to 2 L) of water, depending on the level of contamination.

Iodine-based tablets can also be used in first aid. Simply crush one tablet and add about a teaspoon of water. This will yield a strong topical solution of iodine, which can be used to disinfect wounds.

Water-purifying straw: A relatively new innovation, the water-purifying straw uses a combination of iodine and resin to purify water as you drink. Each straw is good for 20 to 25 gallons (75 to 95 L) of water, depending on how dirty the water is. Some of these nifty little straws claim to reduce bacteria and viruses by as much as 96 percent!

Whistle: Get the sturdiest, loudest, brightest, and most obnoxious one you can find. My favorites are manufactured by Fox 40.

Ziploc bags (large): In a pinch, these bags have many uses, including storing and carrying water. Ziplocs can also be used for keeping sensitive items, such as fire-starting tinder, dry. You can even fill them with snow and put them under your coat to melt the snow into a drink of water.

Your complete survival kit items should help you make it through almost any situation, provided you know how to use them.

A well-planned, complete survival kit will help you make it through the toughest situations.

Tailor Your Kit to Your Destination

THINK OF YOUR COMPLETE SURVIVAL KIT as something that should evolve and change according to your needs, rather than as something that you assemble once and toss into your pack each time you travel. The complete survival kit I've listed above should help you through most emergencies, but survival is situation-specific, and certain tools that may help you in the Arctic or the boreal forest will do you little good in the desert or jungle.

And as you'll soon see, different forces are at work in different areas. Ignore them at your peril. If I'm going tripping in the boreal forest of northern Ontario in the middle of May, the first thing I know I need is bug netting, which is specific to that region and time of year. Do I need to pack bug netting if I'm skiing across the Arctic tundra in the middle of November? Nope. It's important that you take these factors into consideration before every trip.

Arid Regions, Deserts, and Canyons

Acquiring water is paramount when traveling in these areas, so your survival kit should address this critical fact. Make sure you carry a clear garbage bag in your kit in case you need to construct a solar still or vegetation still. A long, thin drinking tube is useful too. You might also consider carrying a small trowel or collapsible shovel to make digging for water easier.

Boreal and Other Temperate Forests

Blackflies and mosquitoes were reputed to have driven many of the early Canadian explorers insane. So I highly recommend bug netting for any region where you expect to be dealing with insects. Why netting as opposed to bug spray? Several reasons. Bug spray is bulky and heavy, whereas netting is light and can be folded to take up very little space. Also, while you will eventually run out of bug spray, your netting will last indefinitely, provided it doesn't tear (and even then, you can repair it).

You may also consider taking along a bug shirt and bug pants, a variety of which are now on the market.

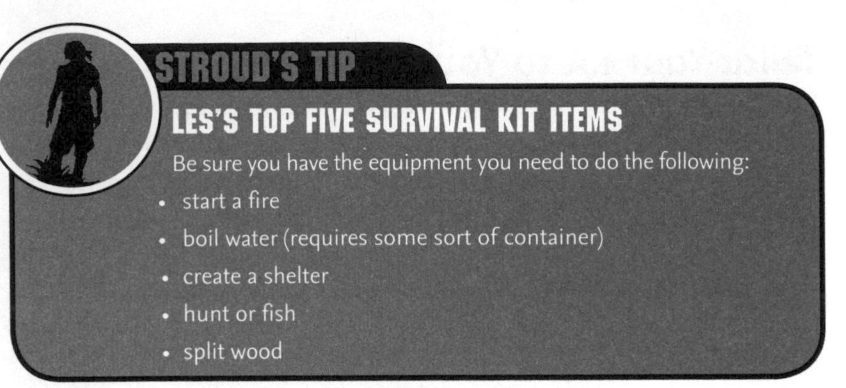

The Arctic and Polar Regions

Most of the drinking water you'll find in the world's polar regions comes from snow and ice, which is notoriously devoid of vital mineral content. This deficiency won't hurt you over short periods of time, but over the course of a few weeks it can begin to seriously affect you. You can offset this problem by carrying mineral tablets, which can be either chewed, or dissolved in drinking water.

In summer, bug netting is a vital addition to your survival kit. And in the spring, sunglasses will protect your eyes from snowblindness, which can result when the sun reflects off the snow all day and all night.

On the Sea or Open Water

As in arid regions, the most important aspect of survival on open water is procuring drinking water. For this reason, it is essential that you carry a desalination or distillation device. Clearly these are too bulky to carry in a standard survival kit, but you will need one or the other nonetheless.

Jungles

One of the most critical—yet frequently overlooked—items you need in the jungle is foot fungus medication. The constant rain and humidity of the jungle environment is murder on the feet, and foot fungus is inevitable. Let it become too severe and it can impede your ability to walk, which could threaten your life. And always carry more than one pair of socks.

Shelter is crucial in the jungle, so take an extra garbage bag or two. Insects can be a huge problem in certain areas and at certain times of year, so take bug netting too.

Coastal Regions

You'll greatly increase your chances of eating well in coastal regions if you add a small, folded fishnet to your survival kit. This will also come in handy if you expect to be near a river or lake.

Your Vehicle Survival Kit

Ranking high in the most-ignored-but-most-needed category of survival equipment is a vehicle survival kit. *Every* driver should have one, but it is even more important if you live in (or travel through) areas of remote wilderness, or places prone to extreme weather, such as snowstorms and thunderstorms, where the risk of finding yourself in a survival situation is greater. Regardless of how well stocked your vehicle survival kit may be, make sure you bring additional food and drink with you on any extended journey.

As a rule, if you get into trouble, you should stay with your vehicle until help arrives, especially now that you'll have a well-equipped vehicle survival kit. And if you've got gas, then you have a source of fuel for firestarting. Your primary concern, however, should be to get your vehicle back on the road and let it carry you to safety.

If you decide to leave your vehicle, do so only when the weather permits and if you feel confident in your ability to travel by land. And don't leave your car or truck without cutting, ripping, and tearing anything and everything out of it that you think may help you in your quest to survive. One day you will be able to buy a new vehicle; buying a new life is not an option.

I once had the privilege of re-creating for television the survival scenario faced by James and Jennifer Stolpa, the couple who became lost with their car (and baby) in a mountain blizzard. In my re-enactment, I made sure I used everything the vehicle offered before I bade it farewell, a strategy the Stolpas failed to employ, even though they had no winter gear with them and only casual shoes. For instance, I cut the foam from inside the seats of the truck, covered it with the vehicle's seat covers, and secured it to my feet with seat-belt material. The result was a set of warm makeshift boots that allowed me to travel on top of the snow, rather than through it, as if I were wearing snowshoes. It may seem like overkill, but it saved my feet from frostbite. The Stolpas were not so lucky.

Your vehicle survival kit should have an appropriate case. If budget is a consideration, any backpack or duffel bag will suffice. Ideally, you should get something that is both sturdy and waterproof. Always keep the kit stowed in your vehicle. See the complete Vehicle Survival Kit Checklist on page 355.

Your vehicle survival kit should include all of the items in the complete survival kit *plus the following:*

Cell phone: The problem with a cell phone is that if you're stuck in a remote area, chances are you won't have cell coverage. You can, however, carry speaker wire. Secure the wire to the highest point you can reach (or climb to) and attach it to your phone's antenna. You might not get enough coverage to make a call, but because text messaging operates on a weaker signal, the wire may bring help.

Clothing (warm) and blankets: Pack an extra set of weather-appropriate clothes, including socks, gloves, and hats for every passenger, as well as blankets, sleeping bags, sleeping pads, and a solar or "space" blanket.

Cook set: Cook sets (also known as "mess kits") are compact sets of pots and/or pans. They allow you to boil up a hot brew, or cook food.

Cook stove and fuel: This is a luxurious extra, to be sure, but one that will greatly increase your chances of survival if you're stuck for any length of time.

Drinking water: Make sure there is enough room in the bottle to allow for expansion should it freeze.

Flares: These are great for signaling but can also be used, if necessary, to start a fire. You will likely have just a few of these, so use them only when needed.

Flashlight (small, LED) with extra batteries: Also available are flashlights you can crank by hand, which never need batteries. Some of these even come with sirens and cell-phone chargers. Make sure the one you buy is compatible with your phone.

They're not pretty, but boots such as these—which I made from the foam of a truck's seats and some seat-belt webbing—might just save your feet from frostbite.

Food, including MREs: MREs—or Meals Ready to Eat—are available at most camping stores and Army & Navy supply shops. This stuff lasts forever and often comes with its own fuel source for heating. Energy bars are also a good option; look for ones that pack the most calories. Many people ignore the importance of salt in their diets. Carry some with your extra food or take along powdered energy drinks high in sodium to replenish electrolytes.

Road maps (local): Make sure you carry maps of regions in which you travel frequently, and before traveling to a new area, add a map of the region to your kit.

Snow shovel (collapsible or folding) and tire chains: You likely won't need these if you live in Florida, but freak snowstorms have killed people in places where snow hadn't been seen in years. If your vehicle gets stuck in the snow, you can use your hands to dig, but a shovel will do the job faster and better. Tire chains can help you when road conditions are slippery.

Tarp: Throw in an orange one, for visibility, sized roughly 8 feet by 9 feet (2.5 m x 2.7 m).

Toilet paper: It's an often overlooked item, but toilet paper can sure come in handy—not just for the obvious purpose. It can be stuffed into your clothes to increase their insulating power, and it can be used as tinder for fires.

Tools: Useful tools include a screwdriver, pliers, a wrench, a hatchet or axe, and jumper cables.

Chapter Three

PSYCHOLOGICAL ASPECTS OF SURVIVAL

You're stranded, stuck, likely alone, in a place that a few moments ago was a wonderland of adventure but now has become a living nightmare. Your next move is crucial to your survival.

But surviving in the wilderness is about more than knowledge and skill. It requires clear-headed, rational thinking, mental toughness, and a positive attitude. It requires a never-yielding *will to live.*

This will to live, which stems from a positive attitude, is what will keep you going and get you out alive. It's what gets you up in the morning. It's what makes you put one foot in front of the other when you're completely exhausted. Fuel and maintain your will to live and you stand a very good chance of making it home. Lose it and your survival hinges on nothing more than dumb luck.

Although it may seem like some people have a genetic disposition for it, the will to live is a conscious decision. I *will* make it out of this. I *will* live. I *will* survive. You may be without the comforts of home, but you can work to make yourself more comfortable. You may be scared of being alone in the dark, but you can make a fire to keep the fear away. You may be hungry, but you can identify at least one or two things in the area to eat.

The importance of the will to survive is illustrated in the many tales of people with little training who have managed to see themselves through harrowing ordeals. The story of Aron Ralston is one of my favorites. Aron was an experienced outdoorsman and mountaineer, but he had had almost no survival training when, during a canyoneering trip in Utah's Blue John Canyon in 2003, his hand and forearm got trapped under a massive boulder.

With very little water and food to sustain him, and his hand and forearm crushed, Aron spent five days trying to lift, pry, and chip away at the boulder that held him captive. Nothing worked. To his credit, he realized that the only way he would ever live to see his family and friends again was to snap the two bones in his forearm and cut his arm off, which is exactly what he did.

In that crisis, Aron had nobody to count on but himself, and his book, *Between a Rock and a Hard Place*, vividly describes the emotional roller coaster he experienced. In the end, it was his intense will to live that saved him. I wonder how many other people would have made it through such an ordeal.

For each story like Aron's, however, there are many sad tales of individuals who, though they were knowledgeable about the ways of the wilderness, panicked and died. It wasn't their skill that abandoned them; it was their ability to think straight under the most stressful of circumstances. If you can maintain your composure and your will to live, you will make it through virtually any survival situation.

You can bolster your will to live in many ways, first and foremost by thinking about the people you love and for whom you want to survive. Some turn to spirituality or religion in times of great stress; you may derive comfort, confidence, and strength from prayer and meditation. Studies of survivors show that having a goal may empower them. The *goal* to see their loved ones again. The *goal* of revenge. The *goal* of telling of the event. Having a goal and keeping it in sight is a driving force in survival.

Make no mistake about it: when you find yourself in a survival situation you will confront stresses that can break the resolve of even the toughest individual. If you fail to anticipate these stresses, they can turn you into a mass of indecision waiting for the end to come, or worse, a panic-stricken lunatic wasting precious energy on tasks that don't increase your chances of surviving. In survival, as in life, your attitude will affect your outcome. If you play the victim, you will be one. If you imagine yourself the hero, you will be one.

A very able-bodied woman once told me that she knew she could never handle being alone in the wilderness, and, in fact, would likely kill herself should she end up in such a situation. Clearly, she was defeated from the start. She would be much better off thinking something like this: *If this trip falls apart, I know I can make it out of here. Heck, I'll be a hero and even write a book about it!* Now that's confidence.

Stress and Stressors

MOST OF US HAVE UTTERED THE WORDS "I AM SO STRESSED!" at one point or another. Stress is a given in the modern-day world, but there are few stressors felt as acutely as those you'll face when alone in a survival situation.

Despite the pressure it heaps upon our shoulders, stress can sometimes be a beneficial force. Stressors can stimulate us to perform at our peak level, giving us the chance not only to take advantage of our strengths but to work on our weaknesses. But stress can be as destructive as it is constructive. Too much of it can lead to distress, an unhealthy condition that may turn to panic.

Like the emotions I discuss later in this chapter, the key to succeeding in a survival situation is confronting and managing the stressors you may face. These are many and varied, and include injury and illness, hunger, thirst, the environment, cold or heat, lack of knowledge, fatigue, or negative group dynamics, boredom and depression, loneliness and isolation, a general lack of control, and of course, death.

Each of these needs to be acknowledged, confronted, and dealt with. Remember that when you're fighting for your life, you don't want any disadvantages at all. If there are any facing you, you can't sweep them aside. In a survival situation, there's no ignoring and no procrastinating.

Now What? Assessing and Prioritizing

YOU MAY BE STRESSED, SCARED, PANICKY, UPSET, LONELY, and perhaps even humiliated. Don't worry; this will pass. Let it pass *right now*. Relax and know that you have what it takes to get through this. Don't focus on what is beyond your control.

Before doing *anything* else (assuming you've removed yourself from any immediate danger), you need to stop. Sit down, take a deep breath, and calm yourself. Do not move until you have allowed yourself enough time to assess your circumstances and formulate a plan. There may be no return from a silly mistake. Do not give in to feelings of panic-producing fear, guilt, and frustration. What's done is done and cannot be undone. Recognize that you are now in a survival situation and must keep your wits about you if you are to make it back to safety.

Indeed, your brain is one of the most important tools you can rely upon. Use it!

Relieve Fear Through Knowledge

BEGIN BY ASSESSING YOUR BODY FOR ANY INJURIES and deal with those as soon as possible. Once you have taken care of yourself, assess your environment and the specifics of your emergency.

- Who knows where you were going?
- Is anyone expecting you? If so, when?
- Is it possible to walk out of your current location on your own, or will you need to be rescued to get out?
- Are you certain of the way out?
- What do you have to keep you alive?

To answer the last question, figure out what you have at hand that will help you survive. This could be equipment that you carried with you—such as a tent, a knife, and food—or aspects of your environment, such as a cave or a lake. If it's physically possible, lay out all your immediate resources on a tarp or blanket or even the ground to get a good mental picture of what you have available. Seeing it spread out may spark ideas as to how items could work together or what you can make out of your supplies. In making these assessments, you're providing yourself with one of the most important tools in your survival kit: knowledge.

Armed with your increasing base of knowledge, you can begin to make a plan to deal intelligently and systematically with your needs. The

Keeping a positive frame of mind is essential to survival, especially if you find yourself suddenly alone. Stay focused on how you can improve your situation and you'll find the strength to go on.

time you take to assess and prioritize will go a long way toward reducing your stress and any possible negative emotions, as you break your situation down into individual hurdles or challenges and see how your worst-case scenario improves:

Worst-case scenario: I'm going to freeze to death out here.

No, wait: there's an old trapper's cabin over on that hill with a stove inside it and dead trees around. So now the worst-case scenario is that I'm left out here to die alone, but at least I'll be warm.

No, wait: my family knows that I had to be out of here within two days, and they know where I am. So now my worst-case scenario is that I'm going to be stuck for a few days alone in a cabin. But there's wood, and I can melt snow and drink water, so I'll be all right.

Focus on the tasks at hand and follow your plan, but also stay flexible enough to revise your plan if it isn't working, You may need to improvise. Adaptability and ingenuity are keys to survival.

When it comes to improvising in the wilderness, you need to look at the world anew. Don't think of objects in your surroundings in the traditional way but in terms of how they will help you on your journey to safety. That tree may be a rotting birch, but peel the bark off and you've got yourself one terrific roof shingle for a shelter.

On one occasion, my sister Laura and I were paddling a canoe on a pristine lake in northern Ontario. I prefer paddling close to shore, where all the action is: beaver houses, animal tracks, birds. We came to this one particularly dense section of forest. To me, it seemed enchanted, and I imagined an inspiring time walking through it and breathing in its smells. My daydream was interrupted by my sister, who mentioned how intimidating she found the thought of being left alone in such a dark and imposing-looking forest. The difference between us, of course, was our knowledge and experience. I already had a fair bit of survival knowledge, had spent time in such forests, and viewed them as a second home.

After three days of survival instruction, Laura had grown immeasurably in her comfort level with such places.

There's also some benefit to talking out loud, whether to yourself, to nearby animals, or to the trees and the rocks. Verbalizing your predicament can help clear your head and put you on the road to survival. Remember the movie *Cast Away*? Tom Hanks's character, Chuck Noland, turned a simple volleyball into his companion, "Wilson," with whom he could talk, share his emotions, and even work out plans.

Here are the mental keys to surviving:

- Maintain the will to live.
- Confront and manage the situation.
- Acquire knowledge.
- Adapt and use ingenuity.
- Go with the flow of nature.

Prioritize

ONE OF THE MOST COMMON QUESTIONS I'm asked about survival is this: "After calming down, what should I do first?" Certain essential elements will be your primary focus during any emergency: shelter, water, fire, food, and a rescue signal. But it's impossible to say which of these you should first focus your energies on, for it changes with every situation.

I take a three-pronged approach to prioritizing my needs:

1. **Deal with any emergencies:** Your situation is the emergency. But if there are pressing safety and/or health concerns, deal with them immediately. In some cases, the weather presents an emergency, so building a short-term makeshift shelter is critical.

2. **Signal for rescue:** Why is this number two? Survival is about getting *home*, the sooner the better. Rescue is crucial, so start making a signal as soon as possible.

3. **Plan for long-term survival:** I classify everything after those first two steps as long-term survival. Why does this come third? Well, you wouldn't want to go to the effort of making a shelter and gathering cattails to eat, only to see a plane fly overhead and realize you could have been rescued if you'd built a signal fire to attract attention.

Whatever tactic you choose, you will improve your chances of success if you're realistic about your prospects for rescue and set an appropriate time frame for your ordeal in the wilderness. Don't lay the groundwork for what may become bitter disappointment by telling yourself you're going to be rescued in two days when more likely you'll be on your own for two weeks. The old adage "hope for the best, prepare for the worst" is a valuable one to keep in mind. You'll find it much easier to adjust to pleasant surprises than to unpleasant ones.

Reacting to a Survival Situation

HOW WILL YOU REACT TO A WILDERNESS EMERGENCY? The answer to this all-important question is as individual as you are. It's impossible to predict exactly how you will react. Don't feel weak, ashamed, or guilty for having conflicting feelings! If anything, these responses help illustrate your humanity, and it's that humanness that will give you the tools to survive.

It may even help you, in the long run, to break down for a short time and release destructive emotions. Most grown men (even the macho ones) will admit to crying at some point during a survival ordeal. And all of them recognize afterwards that shedding those emotions enabled them to "give their heads a shake" and pick themselves up, ready to carry on. Sometimes a good screaming or crying fit is all you need to turn your dejected mental state into a determined ("enough of this feeling sorry for myself") state.

In fact, these emotions, while initially disconcerting, may actually motivate you to find a way out of your situation. Some people have been embarrassed by the mistakes they made that left them in a life-threatening situation but used that feeling—and the desire to make up for that mistake (and possibly to regain their good name)—to get themselves to safety.

Of all the emotions that prove motivational, none is as powerful as love. With love set squarely in your sights, you *will* make it through your ordeal, to see your spouse, children, family, and friends again.

Panic

Panic is a common yet debilitating reaction that affects many, particularly in the early stages of survival ordeals. Panic can be especially dangerous in a group setting, since it's contagious and spreads rapidly.

Physiologically, it can be a motivating force in that it speeds up our body processes. But panic can also use up incredible amounts of energy, which is why people invariably feel exhausted after these episodes.

The most common response to panic is to move *now* and move *fast*. So you start thrashing through the bush, running in the sand, or paddling feverishly up the river hoping to come across something familiar to you. These are dangerous reactions, however, unless you have to get out of that spot immediately for safety reasons.

Instead of fleeing instantly, stop, calm yourself down, and assess. And then make a plan. Knowledge is power. When you assess your situation, you're giving yourself knowledge and therefore the power to control your fate. Resist panic; it will do nothing to help you.

Fear and Anxiety

Fear and anxiety are close cousins of panic, but with important distinctions. Unlike panic, which tends to overwhelm a person like a wave, fear and anxiety take slightly longer to cultivate. No matter how tough you may be, there will likely come a point during a survival situation where you will be scared and/or anxious.

Remember that fear is a normal reaction and can be helpful if kept under control—it adds a dash of caution to circumstances where recklessness could lead to injury or mistakes. But allow it to overcome you and it can be a paralyzing force, impeding your ability to perform the essential tasks of survival. It can send you running through the woods blindly looking for a way out of your living nightmare. Make every effort to keep fear from turning into panic.

Anxiety may actually help to motivate you since it sets in motion an instinctual drive to "make things right." Focusing on survival-related tasks will reduce your anxiety little by little, increasing your sense of well-being and decreasing your fear.

STROUD'S TIP

In a survival situation the following symptoms are more likely signs of panic than of a heart attack. They will subside once you begin to gain control over your situation:

- dizziness and blackouts
- racing heartbeat
- sweaty palms
- back and neck pain
- headaches
- shaking
- hives

For most people in survival situations, fear strikes in the middle of the night, when complete darkness has fallen and the area around you is filled with strange, discomforting sounds. One of the little tricks I've come up with to minimize my fear is to prepare for it.

In the few hours before dusk, I take time to scan my surroundings, imagining what they will look like once darkness falls. Later that night, I realize, "I'm in the exact same spot with the exact same surroundings, only they're dark." It may sound like a simplistic solution, but it works for me, and I'm in the dark a lot out there!

The key is not to let fear and anxiety take control of you. Acknowledge your fear and anxiety—and the normalcy of your reaction—but stop there. Don't give in to them. Recognize that with every effort you make toward your own survival, your fear and anxiety will diminish. Bravery and courage are based not on fearlessness but on healthy fear.

Anger and Frustration

I am fortunate in that I do not get terribly frightened in survival situations, but I can't claim I don't feel my share of anger and frustration. These emotions almost always come from the awareness that I've made mistakes or haven't anticipated events. When I feel anger or frustration coming on, I remind myself to back off and reassess, because there is always another answer.

The danger in succumbing to anger is that it makes you lash out. You take your anger out by breaking a branch against a tree when you should be dealing with your immediate survival needs. Not only will you waste time by lashing out, you'll waste valuable energy and perhaps sustain an injury as well. Frustration and anger tend to result in impulsive reactions, irrational behavior, and poorly thought-out decisions. In some cases, these emotions might even cause you to throw up your hands and declare, "I quit!"

To deal with these feelings, take the same tack as with most of the other emotions we're discussing here: stop, calm down, and dedicate your physical and emotional energy to formulating a plan for getting yourself out of the emergency.

Having said that, for some, there is a benefit that can be derived from anger, assuming that they can keep their anger level at a minimal,

Stay Calm, Stay Alive

Necessity really is the mother of invention. This is a lesson Jonathan Clement, a 13-year-old Calgary teenager, learned the hard way. Little did he know that when his father, Gerry, took him on his first bow-hunting trip, a freak accident would harm his dad—but that Jonathan's own quick thinking would save his father's life.

Gerry and Jonathan had set out to explore the headwaters of Oldman River in Alberta's Rocky Mountains, but soon after their adventure began, Jonathan accidentally launched an arrow into his father's leg. When Gerry looked down at his thigh, it was spurting blood "like in a horror film. I knew [the arrow] had hit an artery and I was in major trouble, but my little guy, almost immediately, kicked into survival mode."

Though Jonathan had inadvertently caused the injury, his actions afterward demonstrated his steady resolve to set things right. Upon seeing the fountain of blood, he instantly removed one of his dad's socks and created a makeshift tourniquet to stem the flow. When asked how he'd known what to do, Jonathan said he'd seen the technique on TV: "I knew because I watched a show called *Survivorman*, where a guy's out in the wilds for days." I'm sure that Jonathan's father had never suspected television could be so educational!

With the tourniquet in place, the young teen helped his father walk back to their campsite, which was over a mile away. As relieved as they were to get behind the wheel of their pickup truck, misfortune soon struck again. During their drive for help, the truck's undercarriage got stuck in the rocky terrain, and Jonathan and Gerry were forced to make their way back to camp on foot. Gerry was still losing a lot of blood, so his son carefully guided him back to their site.

Soon after they arrived, Gerry fainted, hitting his head as he fell. All the while, Jonathan remained calm, though he admits he was worried about his father's condition. "Once we got a fire going, it was better," the boy recalls. "My dad was pretty cold, but I was okay." »

The two spent a grim night by the campfire, hoping that the bleeding would slow down and that someone in the area would spot the smoke. As his father dozed, Jonathan took it upon himself to wake up every few minutes and check on his dad, to "make sure he was snoring."

At daybreak, with no help in sight and his father's condition worsening, Jonathan set out for help, knowing full well that he'd be crossing the heart of bear country. Despite the danger, he traveled on foot for over three miles before eventually stumbling upon other campers, who were able to help him and his father to a hospital.

Jonathan's poise under frightening circumstances helps show that survival isn't about macho gestures but about staying calm and using your head. Gerry Clement, a proud father whose life was saved by his son's good judgment, says his boy was "an absolute hero."

simmering level. They use anger to fuel their will to live: they're angry with the person responsible for getting them into the situation and want to get back at them. There's the story of Hugh Glass, an early American fur trapper whose two travel companions left him to die after a grizzly bear attack. Fueled by his hatred of the men who abandoned him, Glass traveled some 200 miles (322 km)—with a broken leg—to safety.

Loneliness, Boredom, and Depression

Let's face it, if you're alone in the wilderness doing nothing for days on end, it can get very, very boring in no time at all. Boredom can then bring on negative, introspective thoughts, which in turn can lead to depression.

When people feel depressed, they start to give up. Their focus shifts from improving their situation to convincing themselves that there is nothing to be done. The problem with these two emotional states, and depression in particular, is that they are insidious—they creep up on you. Add to the mix the fact that you're probably hungry and tired, maybe injured and scared, and it's easy to see how depression can take hold. Don't let it, for it will only eat away at your will to live.

Remember that it's normal to feel miserable in a survival situation, especially during the first few days. Your success in defeating this misery rests squarely on your ability to be proactive and do something, *anything*, to better your situation. Even if it's only adding one bough to the roof of your shelter, *add it*. Even if it's making just one deadfall trap a day, *make it*.

Activity bars the mind from negative thoughts, staving off loneliness, boredom, and depression. There will always be something new and helpful you can do to improve your circumstances, and planning and completing each task will help to break the monotony of your ordeal. Each successive accomplishment will better your attitude.

Having said that, be careful not to go to the other extreme and try to take on the whole world at once, which may be overwhelming. Take one step at a time. There is surprising comfort in tucking into a little shelter at night with a flame nearby, knowing your world to be only that which exists a few inches in front of your face. Pull your coat over your head and face and know that for the moment, that is your own small world. You control it and it is safe.

Guilt

Guilt is a common response in a survival situation, especially in the case of an accident that has resulted in loss of life. As one of the survivors (or the only survivor) of an accident, a person undoubtedly will be burdened with guilt over being spared while others died. It is natural to feel this way.

But guilt, like most of the other emotions I describe in this chapter, can be channeled for the betterment of your situation. Use it as motivation to try harder. Perhaps you were spared for some greater purpose in life. Live to carry on the work of those killed, or to tell their stories to their loved ones.

Man Versus Nature

SOME PEOPLE LIKE TO CHARACTERIZE THE QUEST FOR SURVIVAL in a wilderness setting as a battle between man and nature. Others like to anthropomorphize nature as an omniscient and benevolent woman that will look after them as long as you give her the proper respect. These are the same people who say you should try to "become one" with nature. At best, "becoming one" with nature is a bad cliché. At worst, it leads you into a passive mind-set, which can get you into real trouble.

Several years ago, my wife, Sue Jamison, and I spent an entire year living in the bush and replicating life as it was lived 500 years ago: no metal, no matches, no plastic, and no nylon. While we hunted, fished, and foraged, and lived in a way similar to that of native peoples hundreds of years ago, we *never* felt like we were one with nature. It's just not like that out there. Survival can be harsh at the best of times. If you become one with anything or anyone while you are trying to survive out there, it is with yourself.

Nature is neutral. It doesn't want to help you, and it doesn't want to kill you. Yet there is a positive energy in the wilderness that can be emotionally and spiritually uplifting, and can fill you with strength to carry on and complete the tasks that you need to, even in the worst survival scenarios.

Survival is not about "man versus wild." Nor, at the other extreme, is it about "becoming one" with nature. The key to survival is the middle ground of "going with the flow" of nature. There is a time to push against the rain and a time to wait it out. There is a time to travel hard and a time to hunker down. There is a time to let go of emotions and there is a time to buck up and straighten your back against your troubles.

But make no mistake about it. Nature must be respected, watched, listened to, and considered constantly, if you expect to survive.

Group Versus Solo Survival

Most aspects of survival are easier when more than one traveler is present, but the group dynamic may well prove most beneficial when it comes to the psychological aspects of survival. You can derive significant comfort from the presence of other people in what may be the most trying moments of your life. And you can boost your feelings of self-worth and confidence by comforting those in your group who need support.

Of course, there's another side to this. Not everything is rosy within a group. Panic is frighteningly contagious and can spread like wildfire.

The solution is to acknowledge a strong and effective group leader. Most groups will not be proactive enough to actually elect a leader; one typically emerges naturally. A strong, competent, and confident leader will help quell the fears and doubts the group may be feeling, and will focus each individual's efforts on the tasks necessary for survival.

Chapter Four

SIGNALING

The irony of survival is that for all the planning and preparation you do to stay alive in the wild, all you really want is to *go home.* Survival instructors tend to romanticize survival by teaching the many excellent, sometimes advanced skills that will help you live as long as possible in remote areas, but the bottom line in a true survival situation is that you're scared, hungry, tired, and cold. You just want out of this nightmare. Signaling can be key to getting you home, and sooner rather than later.

Debate continues as to which aspect of survival should take first priority, but I believe that once you've established your immediate safety and if there is no urgency about shelter, your next step should be getting signals ready. And since you never really know when a potential rescuer may appear, you need to be ready to signal *immediately* and *at all times.* It would be nice to be saved quickly, but the reality is that it could be hours, days, or even weeks, before somebody spots your signal.

Signaling devices fall into two categories: *targeted signals* that need to be seen or heard by someone passing by, and *technological signals* that send information about location or situation to someone a greater distance away.

Targeted Signals

TARGETED SIGNALS ARE SIGNALS that need to be seen or heard by a target—a person on foot or in a plane or boat, for example—to be effective. There are those that are ready to use and those that you need to make yourself.

If you are using a visual signal that you want to be seen by passing aircraft, locate it in a clear, flat area on the highest possible terrain. Know that if you are spotted by an aircraft, it will probably not land immediately. Look for the pilot to acknowledge your signal by flying low, dropping a message, dipping the plane's wings, or flashing lights.

No matter what type of signal you make, know how to use it and be ready to get it going on short notice. You may have only seconds, and a missed opportunity could cost you your life.

Ready-to-Use Signals

Ready-to-use signals are the easiest ones to employ in the wilderness because they're typically the product of some sort of technological innovation. At least one of these devices should be in your complete survival kit.

Signal mirror: A signal mirror's reflection can be seen as far away as 50 miles (80 km) on a clear, sunny day. Signal mirrors can also work on overcast days and with moonlight, although with less range.

True signal mirrors come with an aiming hole in the middle, but any mirror or reflective material (like a square of tinfoil) can be aimed at its target. Face the target and stretch out your arm so that your hand is just beneath the target. With your other hand, hold the mirror near your head and aim the reflected light directly onto your hand. Tilt the mirror up and down rapidly. Given the range of the signal mirror, you should flash any airplane you see, no matter how far away it may seem. The internationally recognized *SOS* signal is three short reflections followed by three longer ones followed again by three short ones.

Generally, the larger the mirror the more light it will reflect. Glass mirrors reflect better than any other material, but also are the most easily broken; metal mirrors (including stainless steel), on the other hand, scratch easily and are also subject to rust, particularly in saltwater environments.

Using a Signal Mirror with a Sighting Hole

1. To effectively use a signal mirror with a sighting hole, hold the mirror fairly close to your face. Through the hole, you should be able to see a bright glow.

2. Align the glow so that it covers your target; this is where the sun's reflection will shine.

Using a Signal Mirror Without a Sighting Hole

1. Face the target and stretch out your arm so your hand is just beneath the target.

2. Tilt the mirror rapidly up and down.

3. Aim the reflected light directly onto your outstretched hand as shown.

Chemicals: Potassium permanganate is an example of a chemical that can be used to make a temporary sign on water or a more permanent one in snow (it dyes the snow purple) to signal for rescue.

Chemical lights: Although some companies make chemical lights for survival situations, these are not very bright and usually can't be seen from more than a mile away. Chemical lights are most easily seen when swung in wide arcs or sweeps; all have a limited storage life that runs out quickly after exposure to air.

Flares: Flares are an effective way to signal someone and they have saved lives all around the world. They work only for a short time, however, so don't use them until you're sure they'll be seen.

Flashlight: These don't have the same range as signal mirrors but work in the same way and are very useful at night. Be careful not to waste battery power; there's no point dangling your flashlight in a tree all night unless there's a chance someone may see it.

Laser flares: Take flashlights one step further, with a more powerful, colorful, and visible beam and you've got the laser flare. Another benefit of laser flares is that they're compact and long-lasting.

Signals You Make Yourself

If you're not fortunate enough to have a ready-to-use signal on hand, there are still a few signaling options available. These can be as effective as the ready-to-use variety, but require more effort and are subject to the vagaries of your environment.

The Signal Fire: Signals fires must be built in a wide-open space. Timing is everything; they must be ready for the moment when a plane passes overhead. Stay with a signal fire once you have lit it, in case the pilot attempts to communicate with you.

During the day, the most visible part of a signal fire is the smoke, so you will also want to have items on hand that create as much of it as possible. Rubber and plastic work well (producing black smoke), as do fresh (green) branches and boughs, which produce white smoke. Moss or punky wood also work well.

Given the choice, go for black smoke, since it is not likely to be confused with a campfire. Either way, smoke is most effective on clear, calm days. Wind, rain, snow, and clouds disperse or shield smoke, significantly decreasing the chances it will be seen. In addition, smoke is not nearly as important at night, when the flame itself will be more easily spotted from above.

Some survival guides say you'll have a better chance of attracting attention if you prepare *three* signal fires and position them in the shape of a triangle, a commonly recognized distress symbol. I tried this during a winter survival course. On the day that the plane finally flew over, the temperature hovered near –40°F (–40°C), and I had been surviving for seven days and had little energy left.

When I heard the plane approaching, I had to run with burning bark from my survival fire to the signal fire, which was about 60 yards (55 m) away, in the middle of a frozen lake. When I got the first point of the triangle lit, I had to run the 40 yards (37 m) to each of the other points to set them burning as well. My hands felt frozen, I nearly put out the bark I was running with, and I taxed my remaining energy reserves doing all that running.

The pilot saw my signal fires and came down to rescue me. Once we were in the air, though, I was shocked to see that the triangle I had made—which had seemed so big and spread out on the ground—looked surprisingly small from the air. In the end, one very large fire would have served the same purpose and would have saved me a lot of energy—and firewood.

Making a Signal Fire

1. To make a signal fire, begin by making a tripod of three trees.

2. If you have extra rope, weave it across the base of the tripod to make a platform. Fill the platform with dry, quick-burning materials such as birch bark. On top, place smoke-producing materials, like damp moss, punky wood, rubber, or plastic.

3. Ignite the signal fire when you believe a plane will see it.

STROUD'S TIP

Bush pilots have told me that if they see *anything* that looks out of the ordinary on the ground—whether it appears to be a signal fire or even just a tarp laid flat in the middle of an open space—they will stop to check it out, regardless of whether it's an "official" distress signal such as a triangle or the letters *SOS*. Don't overlook the value of a simple signal as well. A coat hung on a tree has saved more than one life.

The Tree Torch: A variation on the signal fire is the tree torch, which involves setting a single tree on fire. Although standing dead trees will light most easily, live trees can also be set on fire, particularly ones that bear sap. Paper birch trees are also very good tree torches; their thin bark lights easily.

To make a tree torch, place dry wood in the lower branches and light them. The flame will flare upward and should ignite the leaves overhead. When creating a tree torch, select an isolated tree so you don't start a forest fire!

Although signal fires are the most common type of signal you make yourself, there are other everyday (perhaps unexpected) items you can use to signal and improve your chances of being found.

Clothing and rag signals: You can attract attention to yourself by wearing bright-colored clothing that stands out against your surroundings (fluorescent orange works best). If there's no risk of them getting wet or blown away, drape some of your extra clothing on nearby branches. Tie a brightly colored rag or piece of clothing to your shelter too.

Ground signals: When making a signal on the ground, pick an open area that can be seen easily from overhead. Remember that things are a lot smaller when viewed from overhead, so size matters. Go as big as you can.

Those orange garbage bags in your survival kit have so many uses; they make excellent ground signals since they usually provide stark contrast against earth tones. Lay them flat in a highly visible area and secure them with rocks to attract the attention of passing aircraft. If you don't have one of these bags, try orange surveyor's tape, aluminum foil, or anything bright or reflective. Spelling out *SOS* or *HELP* is internationally recognized but can be labor-intensive. If you don't have the materials or energy to do so, a large V or X should do the trick.

If you have nothing in your kit with which to make a traditional signal, you can use natural materials to attract attention to yourself. Use rocks, logs, brush, seaweed, or branches formed in words or arrows or any obvious marking. If you don't have any of these materials on hand, you can still make a signal by clearing away or burning bushes and other ground cover, or even tramping down snow.

Vehicle wreckage signals: In some cases, your survival situation may include a vehicle (car, snowmobile, plane, or canoe). Your vehicle is big and conspicuous and will attract attention. Stay with it if you suspect rescue may be on its way. If you can fashion your vehicle into your shelter, all the better. Now it's serving *two* purposes.

In addition, you may be able to use parts of the vehicle to attract attention. Arrange them in a way that makes them conspicuous. Your vehicle's lights and horn are also powerful means of attracting attention.

If you can get a tire off your car (or have a spare), add it to your signal fire. Burning rubber creates thick black smoke. (Burning a tire is not the most environmentally friendly option available, but when it comes to life or death, that is not an issue. Your goal is to live; you can dedicate yourself to environmental causes when you return to safety.)

Oils and fuels are also good for creating smoke, especially when rags are soaked in them.

Audio signals: Although audio signals aren't effective in alerting aircraft, they can work well for signaling to ground-based rescuers and passersby. Even if you're not sure that someone is looking for you, it can't hurt to make as much noise as possible.

One audio signal that does not work very well in the wilderness is your voice; it doesn't carry far enough. A survival whistle, however, is excellent, and the better commercial ones can be heard more than a mile away. Gunshots are also audible from a great distance, though you will have to balance the need for ammunition for other survival uses with the chance of someone hearing your shot.

STROUD'S TIP

No matter what type of noise you are making, the international signal for distress can come in handy. Whether you're clanging pots together, blowing on a whistle, or blasting from an air siren, repeat the sound *three straight times*, which indicates you're in need of help.

Technological Signals

UNLIKE TARGETED SIGNALS, WHICH NEED TO BE SEEN OR HEARD by someone in your direct vicinity to be effective, technological signals carry your message over greater distances. If technology shines anywhere during a survival situation, it's in signaling. Cell phones, satellite phones, two-way radios, and PLBs have saved the lives of countless stranded adventurers.

EPIRBs (Emergency Position-Indicating Radio Beacons), ELTs (Emergency Locator Transmitters), and PLBs (Personal Locator Beacons): Among a class of devices known as tracking transmitters, these beacons all function by sending a distress signal that allows search-and-rescue personnel to locate your position almost immediately. EPIRBs commonly signal maritime distress; ELTs signal aircraft distress; and PLBs are for personal use.

Although the basic idea behind all these devices is to get the person rescued within 24 hours of activation, this is not always the case, particularly in developing nations. I once made a survival film off the coast of Belize. My sailboat captain explained the reality that the authorities there probably would not act if I set off a locator beacon, and that they might not even know what it was. He dared me to set mine off and see what happened. I did and . . . nothing.

SPOT satellite messenger: First implemented by SPOT Inc., the satellite messenger is one of the greatest technological innovations to hit the world of outdoor adventuring—and surviving—in recent years.

The SPOT device is a hand-held unit that serves as a distress beacon like a PLB but does much more, primarily through one-way text messaging and e-mail. SPOT will send a pre-programmed distress message (with your exact GPS location) requesting help from up to 10 programmed contacts, each of whom will read your message on their computer or phone. It will also inform your contacts of your location (using Google Maps) and let them know you are okay. The device will even allow your friends and family to track your progress using Google Maps. But for a real emergency, you press the "911" button, which informs local search-and-rescue teams of your need for help.

Cell phones and satellite phones: Your cell phone will transmit information about your location, even if there is no service in your area—so keep it on as long as possible. Text messaging has greater range than your cell phone may indicate, since it works on a different signal.

In years gone by, satellite phones were bulky, weighed a ton, and had questionable coverage. With technological innovation, however, they have become cheaper and more compact. On the downside, satellite phones have a limited battery life.

STROUD'S TIP

By far the best devices you can have with you are the SPOT satellite messenger and a satellite phone. With these, when you send a message, you can be sure that somebody is receiving it. With any other form of communication, you *hope* people get the message.

On the Move

IF YOU DECIDE TO LEAVE YOUR EMERGENCY LOCATION, it's important that you give potential rescuers as much information as possible about your journey. If you have paper and pencil available, leave a detailed note in a safe, dry, and conspicuously marked location. Let them know when you left, where you are going, how you are traveling (by boat or on foot), your physical state, how many of you there are, and the extent of your supplies. You should also mark your direction of travel with an arrow. Rocks and branches can be laid on the ground to point rescuers in the same direction, or you can use your knife to cut directional signs into trees.

When Rescue Arrives

WHAT DO YOU DO IF YOUR SIGNAL ACTUALLY WORKS? Assuming you are now in the clear can be a big mistake.

If you are being rescued by an aircraft such us a light plane or helicopter, remove all loose materials from the landing area to prevent them from being sucked into propellers and rotors. Sometimes a helicopter may not be able to land where you're stranded, so they may need the aid of a device to lift you from the ground. In all cases, follow the instructions of your rescuers to the letter.

Group Versus Solo Survival

ONE OF THE BENEFITS OF BEING IN A GROUP is that you have more eyes and ears trained on the possibility of rescue, and more people available to attract attention when the time comes. You can also build more and bigger signals, and, if necessary, spread them out over a greater area.

As in all aspects of survival, adaptability and ingenuity are paramount when it comes to making a rescue signal. Some victims have cut or burned down a hydro pole. When hydro workers eventually came out to fix it, the lost were found.

Set fire to a small island if you have to. If it were me, I wouldn't hesitate if it meant seeing my family again. I could live with myself if I had to take drastic measures to be rescued. How about you?

Chapter Five

No fire. No shelter. No food. Except in the most extreme cases, doing without these won't kill you . . . at least not quickly. But nothing compares in seriousness to the lack of water. So while I always seek out locations with good supplies of firewood, shelter material, and food sources, I would trade them all for a constant supply of clean water. Always try to conserve what you have, and start looking for an alternative source as soon as possible.

You can live for more than three weeks without food, but you likely won't make it much past three days without water. Granted, in a crisis, some people have survived as long as 10 days without water, but their ability to function will have been radically reduced after the third day. And depending on your circumstances, in as few as 24 hours you could start suffering the harsh effects of dehydration, particularly in a hot, dry, and windy location such as the desert. First the migraines and headaches kick in, followed by a rapid drop in energy. Now let's see you get that fire going, build that shelter, or make a bunch of scorpion traps!

After only 24 hours surviving in the Kalahari Desert, the lack of water in my body brought on terrible headaches. On my fifth day there, with temperatures in the sun and on the sand pushing 140°F (60°C), my water ran out altogether. Over those five days, I had urinated only once, and that was after having drunk a gallon (about 4 L) of water for each of the first four days.

On the fifth and sixth days, the few ounces I made by chewing plants and distilling my own urine still didn't suffice. Even the act of eating the plants used up water in my system needed for digestion. The very act of chewing in extremely hot weather used up energy I didn't have to spare. Sometimes doing nothing is better than trying something that doesn't work.

Fortunately, I could walk out of the desert. But what if you can't? Our bodies need 2 to 3 quarts (2 to 3 L) of water each day. Throw in heat, cold, stress, exertion, or diarrhea, and you need much more. To survive in the wilderness you need to know how to find water, make water, and even prevent your body from losing water.

One thing that people get hung up on with water (assuming they're lucky enough to find it) is whether it's clean enough to drink. They aren't sure whether to drink it at all, for fear of getting sick. I go over this in greater detail later in this chapter, but for now, learn this mantra: *Drink, drink, drink*. You will die a lot faster from dehydration than from the effects of drinking untreated water. In fact, in all but the rarest circumstances, drinking untreated water won't kill you. Even if you do contract parasites, most of them won't hit you for at least a week, if not longer. Should you make it out alive, you can treat most of them (albeit with powerful drugs).

STROUD'S TIP

After drinking questionable water, crush up some charcoal and place it in a rag. Strain water through the rag and drink the black liquid. It can prevent stomach upset. Make sure you use charcoal from non-poisonous wood sources!

And water in remote areas usually *is* safe to drink. Sure, if you're downstream from an African village or just outside a town that happens to use the stream as its septic system, you're probably going to ingest pathogens. Then again, if you're that close to civilization, you're not in a survival situation at all! I've been infected with giardia, a nasty parasite that wreaks havoc on your bowels, after drinking from a seemingly pristine lake. I've suffered horrible bowel cramps after drinking from a seemingly pristine river. But I lived to tell the tales. And I *haven't* died of dehydration.

I happen to be a huge fan of adventure races, events lasting anywhere from eight hours to two weeks, where contestants bike, run, paddle, and take on many other types of adventure travel through remote wilderness. The first one who makes it to the finish line, even if it is a week later, wins. During one such race, organizers had warned contestants not to drink the water along the route without first treating it, for fear of ingesting giardia.

The first stretch of the race was a slog through miles of thick bush during the height of mosquito and blackfly season, with temperatures cresting at 86°F (30°C). The race leaders took 24 hours to complete that stage. Many other teams, including mine, took nearly twice that.

At the first checkpoint in the race, a station where you can stop, check your time, and even eat a bit of food, most teams arrived looking terrible and suffering from the dry heaves. Not mine, though. Why? At every stream, river, or swamp—even the muddy ones—I forced myself and them to drink, because I knew that otherwise, under those extreme conditions, dehydration would soon shut us down. So when we finally made it to the first checkpoint (even though we were one of the last teams to get there), it was noted that we were in better shape than any other team.

It seems all the other teams were scared to drink untreated water, and none of them wanted to commit 15 minutes to treating their water for fear of losing ground in the race. So they ran on, hurting themselves in the process through dehydration. Not only did my team feel fine but none of us got sick, even though we drank from dozens of streams and swamps without filtering.

That said, *never* be cavalier about water. It is quite possible to drink from contaminated water sources and within hours find yourself knocked down from pain and diarrhea, only making your ordeal even worse. Your best bet is to assume that all water *is* contaminated and to purify it if you can do so.

But if your choice is between drinking untreated water or dying of dehydration . . . drink.

Rationing and Preserving Water in Your Body

Almost as important as procuring water to drink is the ability to preserve the water stores in your body. The best way to do this is to minimize your exertion, if at all possible. With this in mind, I have one simple rule from my friend Dave Arama: If you don't have to stand, sit; if you don't have to sit, lie down. You also lose more water when you talk than when you don't, and when you breathe through your mouth as opposed to your nose.

Of course, when you're in a survival situation and trying to build a shelter, gather food, find water, or just get out, you don't have the luxury of sitting around. Nevertheless, there are measures you can take to keep your body's water loss to a minimum.

First, although you will have to work, try to keep your workload to a consistent level that minimizes perspiration. After all, through sweating, one of your body's primary methods of cooling itself, you lose moisture through your pores. In hot, windy conditions, you may find yourself tempted to strip down to all but the bare minimum of clothing. Don't! One of the fastest ways to have water sucked from your body is through convection: those warm breezes will only serve to dehydrate you more. So wear a loose-fitting shirt to slow the process, and get out of the wind if you can. You also lose a fair bit of moisture through your head, so cover it to help slow the loss of moisture, as long as you can do so without overheating.

What about rationing any water supplies you have on hand? Like many topics I cover in this book, this one is bound to spark debate among survivalists. Let's say you have enough water to drink 8 ounces (237 ml) a day for one week, but you think you may be on your own for two weeks. You have a couple of choices: Drink the water in a week and hope you find another primary water source in the meantime, or cut your daily intake down to 4 ounces (118 ml) and stretch it out for two weeks.

Some survivalists argue that you're better off drinking the 8 ounces a day, thus keeping the water in your body and your organs fully hydrated. But I believe that if you're stuck for a long period of time and are unable to find an ample water supply, having those 4 ounces every day can be an incredible physical and psychological boost. Although I can't prove that physiologically this is the best strategy, personally I would opt for rationing.

STROUD'S TIP

Make sure you have enough water for yourself, given the situation. Make sure everyone in the group has enough water for themselves. Repeat these two lines over and over!

Physiology

To appreciate the importance of water for our well-being, let me remind you that you should drink a minimum of a gallon (about 4 L) each day, even if you're sitting in the shade doing *nothing*. Water is constantly being used by our bodies through normal processes such as breathing. Throw in the extra stress of surviving in the wilderness—which may entail extreme physical activity, perspiration, vomiting, diarrhea, and bleeding as a result of injury—and you can see how the situation can become dire. Even digestion, particularly after eating foods that are sweet or spicy, as well as those high in salt or protein, uses up precious stores of water in our system.

From everything I've read, death by dehydration is horrible and painful. In fact, you can start to feel the many adverse physical and mental effects of dehydration after dropping your body's water supply by as little as 1 percent. In addition to the headaches I noted above, nausea, poor judgment, and depression are all symptoms of dehydration, symptoms you don't want to be dealing with anytime, let alone when you're trying to survive in the wild.

Thirst is not a good indicator of your body's need for water: you may not notice when you need more. While surviving beside a lake in Canada's boreal forest during a heat wave, I forced myself to drink about 8 ounces (237 ml) of water every hour, whether I felt thirsty or not. This simple act kept me feeling refreshed and even helped mask the hunger pains I otherwise would have suffered, as I had little food at the time. Oh, I was still hungry, but drinking regularly, almost constantly, seemed to take away the pain.

So in a survival situation, setting a mandatory time to drink each day, especially in the winter (when you don't normally *feel* like drinking), will help you get past your mind's lack of attentiveness, itself another symptom of dehydration. If you are not alone in your ordeal, then you have the added responsibility (and sometimes advantage) of looking out for the others in your group. The buddy system used by underwater divers should be used in survival as well. Check others for red or pink skin and excessive sweating, two sure signs of overheating. A dehydrated person will often be slow, clumsy, or withdrawn, and show poor judgment (I must have a lot of chronically dehydrated friends!). This simple test also works well: pinch the skin on the back of the hand. If the pinched skin returns very slowly—that is, does not "snap" back quickly—to its original shape and form, the person is suffering from dehydration. Another sign is urine color. Dark yellow indicates dehydration. And if you are not peeing at all, you are not drinking enough water, period.

Some guidebooks distinguish between mild, moderate, and critical levels of dehydration. Don't get bogged down in semantics. Dehydration is a quick killer and preventing it should remain among your highest priorities.

Finding and Collecting Water

Regardless of your location, keep this in mind: Almost *every* environment has water present to some degree. Your ability to survive will likely depend on your ability to find and collect it. The more proficient you are at identifying indicators of nearby water, the better off you'll be.

I separate water-finding and water-collecting methods into what I call *primary sources* and *last-ditch efforts*. The amount of water the human body needs to *thrive* is much more than what you can get by licking dew off leaves or peeing in a hole and distilling the condensed water. If you are going to make it out of the wilderness alive, you will need, often desperately, to find a primary water source.

Locating Primary Water Sources

The best primary sources of water are those that flow. These include rivers, streams, and creeks. If these aren't available, you have to move on to progressively more stagnant bodies of water. Lakes and ponds are the next best primary sources, followed by swamps, marshes, fens, bogs, et cetera. Snow, slush, and ice are also primary sources of water.

To locate a primary source, your best bet is to study the topography of your surroundings. You need to understand the different indicators of water around you and react to them.

Look at the water source you have found. Scan the shoreline or check upstream for contaminants such as dead animals. The higher the altitude of your source (such as a mountain stream), the purer the water. Remember that even the sweetest-smelling and freshest-looking mountain streams may have an upstream contaminant you can't see.

Walk Downhill: There are subtle differences among regions, but walking downhill is usually an effective strategy for locating water because it is a sucker for gravity. Valley bottoms are great places to find water.

Observe Changes in Vegetation: Be on the lookout for changes in vegetation, which may indicate availability of water. If you see a place where vegetation is darker or denser than in the surrounding area, there's a good chance you'll find water there, even if you have to dig for it.

Watch the Sky: Another small trick that I've often used in survival situations (but it takes a seasoned eye) is to look for subtle changes in the color of the sky. Typically, the sky directly over a source of water will look bluer than the rest of the sky, reflecting the water source. And early in the morning, due to moisture content and temperature differences, low-lying clouds and fog tend to congregate directly over a body of water.

Follow Animal Trails: Animals need water too, and their trails may lead you to a life-giving source. If you see numerous game trails, they may even make a formation, much like a series of veins (or like a river system on a topographical map). Where the sections join and create a V, the point of the V will indicate the direction of water. But be warned that following animal trails can sometimes lead you nowhere.

Follow Birds: Birds congregate near water, and the direction of bird flight in the early morning or late afternoon might indicate a source. Grain-eating birds are never too far from water; when they fly straight and low they are *usually* headed for water. But note that these are subtle indicators and following them doesn't guarantee you'll find a source.

Bear in mind too that most wild creatures urinate and defecate in the same place they drink. So once you've located a primary source of water, move at least a couple hundred yards from the spot where the game trail meets the water, preferably upstream. Giardia cysts tend to sit closer to the surface of a lake, so if you can weigh a vessel down and send it to the lower depths you have a better chance of retrieving uncontaminated water. A weighted jar or can with a rope tied to it works well. Once you're sure the vessel is full of lower-level water, pull it up quickly to minimize the amount of surface water that gets in.

Track Insects: If you see insects (especially bees or ants) going into a hole in a tree, there may be water in the hole. Plastic tubing can be used to siphon the water, or a cloth can be stuffed in the hole to absorb it. The presence of swarming insects also indicates that water is near. Bees are never more than a few miles from a water source, although they have irregular watering times.

Use Ice, Snow, and Slush: If you find yourself trying to stay alive in a part of the world or during a season of the year when ice, snow, and slush are present, you have a good source of water at your fingertips, particularly if you are able to make fire. As with many aspects of survival strategy, however, opinions about eating ice, snow, and slush are subject to debate; mine don't jibe with the prevailing sentiment.

Many instructors will tell you that you should avoid eating snow, largely because it will reduce the temperature of your body, which will then consume precious energy during warming. This is true, but given the vital role that water plays in survival, I believe the opposite. Eating snow and ice will cool your body down and may slightly abrade the inside of your mouth. But if it's the morning and you're working hard to assure other aspects of your survival, eating snow can help to maintain an optimal body temperature. And the fact is, you need that liquid.

You have to be careful about eating ice and snow later in the day, though, when you're tired and the air is cooling off. Eating snow when your defenses are down can do you more harm than good. This applies not just in the dead of winter, but in springtime too—anytime you are eating snow.

The ideal is to be able to melt the ice and snow and even heat it before you drink it. If I don't have a fire available, I like to fill a water bottle (or similar vessel, or even a Ziploc bag) with snow, and slip it inside my clothing during the day while I work or in my sleeping bag (not touching my body) at night while I sleep. It takes a while for the first bit to melt, but once that's done, the rest melts quickly. If I can manage to do this overnight without chilling myself, it's great to wake up to find the water melted and ready to drink.

Water from snow (or rain, for that matter) is very low in salt and minerals, which we need to survive. But that is a longer-term concern that should not affect your decision to eat snow, if you need to, during a survival ordeal. Add edible plants and grasses to your melting pot to help supplement these missing nutrients.

Last-Ditch Water Sources

If you have exerted your best efforts to find a primary source of water and have come up empty, you need to turn to last-ditch water sources, those that may not keep you thriving but will at least keep you alive for a while.

Collect Rain: Most of us have heard about the ravages of acid rain, but this isn't a concern when it comes to survival: you can drink rainwater anywhere on earth. To harvest enough to keep yourself going, you need to use as big a catchment area as possible and contain the water in some sort of receptacle. If you don't have a suitable container on hand, dig a hole in the ground. This should hold water for a while, but you will need to line it with clay, plastic, or some other impermeable material, and keep it covered.

Collect Dew: Heavy dew has been known to provide water for wilderness survivors, and there are various ways to procure it.

If you find yourself in an area of long grass, heavy with morning dew, you can make like native Australians and tie rags or tufts of fine grass around your ankles while walking through the dew-covered grass. As the rags or grass tufts absorb the dew, wring the water into a container. Don't

STROUD'S TIP

My friend and survival companion Allan "Bow" Beauchamp has a couple of unique water-collection methods that are very effective: Moss cups can collect large amounts of rainwater. Here's what to do. Cut a large square sheet of green moss and lay this on the ground moss-side up, or, best-case scenario, right on a flat rock. Then, using rocks and dirt, bank up the sides of the moss sheet until you have what looks like a square moss "cup." Using one large piece is the best and will retain the most water. You can also collect punky wood and leave it out on the ground for the night. When you wake up in the morning you'll find that dew will have settled in these dry pieces of wood. Simply pick them up and wring them out.

underestimate the effectiveness of this procedure! It is surprising how much you can get. If there's no long grass in the area, the only source of dew you'll have is on leaves, which you can lick. Here you'll run a significant risk, however: some leaves contain oils or toxins that might aggravate your system or cause diarrhea, resulting in you feeling worse than when you started.

Make a Vegetation Still: Vegetation stills can be used in many parts of the world and require only a few simple components, though collecting the water does demand patience. It can take as long as 24 hours to obtain up to 1 quart (1 L) of water, and that's under ideal conditions.

You will need some green, leafy vegetation—gathered from trees, bushes, shrubs, or grasses—along with a clear plastic bag and a small rock. Choose a sunny location with a slope on which to place the still, and follow these steps:

1. Fill the bag with air by turning the open end into the breeze or by "scooping" air into it.
2. Remove from your gathered vegetation any sticks or spines that might puncture the bag. Fill the bag half to three-quarters full of the vegetation (or tie the bag onto the end of a branch). Do not use poisonous plants; they will produce poisonous liquid.

3. Place a small rock in the bag to weigh it down.
4. If you have a piece of tubing, a small straw, or a hollow reed, insert one end into the mouth of the bag before closing (remember to tie off or plug the tubing so that air will not escape). This will allow you to drink the condensed water without untying the bag. Then tie the bag securely shut as close to the end as possible; it's important to maximize the amount of air space in the bag.
5. Place the bag on a slope in full sunlight. The mouth of the bag should be positioned higher than the base of the bag (which contains the rock), to keep the bag from slipping or blowing away and to keep the water dripping to the lowest point.
6. To drink: If you don't have a tube to draw the condensed water from the still, loosen the tie around the bag's mouth and drain. Retie the mouth securely and reposition the still to allow further condensation.
7. Change the vegetation in the bag after extracting most of the water from it, to ensure a regular supply of water.

If you can't fill a bag with vegetation, tying it to the end of a branch with lots of leaves will do the trick. Just make sure it's in a sunny spot. If this tree had been poisonous, the water it produced could also have been poisonous. Don't take chances unless you're sure of the source tree or bush.

Make a Solar Still: I'm always leery of survival skills that require the effort of digging a hole. Nevertheless, the solar still can be an effective method of collecting water, particularly in a very dry location such as a desert. To make a solar still, however, you need four components: a sunny spot, a receptacle in which to catch the water, a clear plastic sheet approximately 6 square feet (.5 m^2), and some type of weight to place on top of the plastic. You'll also need to dig a hole, so a shovel or trowel would be useful.

You can build a solar still without digging a hole if you are lucky enough to have a large container like a barrel. When surviving on a small tropical island off the coast of Belize, I had at my disposal one half of the large plastic container that my life raft had come in. Using this container saved me a great deal of digging.

Solar stills can take a couple of hours (or more) to make, and their yield is not very high. How much you get depends largely on the ambient temperature, the types of vegetation you include, and access to direct sun. A still such as this may produce water for two to four days depending on the moisture content of the soil or sand itself, and must be moved every so often. The added bonus, however, is that the outside of it also serves as a great dew or rain-catch. You'll likely need at least three solar stills to meet your daily water-consumption needs.

Here are the steps for building a solar still:

1. Select a sunny site where you believe the soil contains the most moisture. The lower and damper the spot, the better.
2. Dig a bowl-shaped hole about 3 feet (1 m) around and 2 feet (.5 m) deep.
3. If possible, fill the hole with non-poisonous vegetation. Pour salt water, water contaminated with bacteria or urine into and onto the sides of the hole.
4. Place your collecting receptacle (the wider the better) at the bottom of the hole, preferably in its own small hole. Do not let any impure water, salt water or urine get in the receptacle (cup).
5. If you are lucky enough to have a drinking tube (or can fashion one out of available materials), settle it into the receptacle and stretch it out so that it terminates above ground. The tube allows you to step up to the still and drink from it without disturbing it.

6. Cover the hole with the plastic sheet; the sheet should be anchored around its perimeter with rocks or other heavy objects. Place a small rock or other weighted object in the center of the plastic sheet, ensuring that the lowest point of the sheet is now directly above the receptacle.

The idea behind a solar still is that solar energy heats the air, soil, and vegetation (if available) in the hole by passing through the plastic sheet. Moisture from the soil—all soil has moisture—evaporates and condenses on the low point in the plastic. Added vegetation (non-poisonous!), such as leaves, grasses, or seaweed, can help speed up the process, and since solar stills also purify water, the condensed water that collects on the underside of the sheet will be fit to drink.

Creating a Solar Still

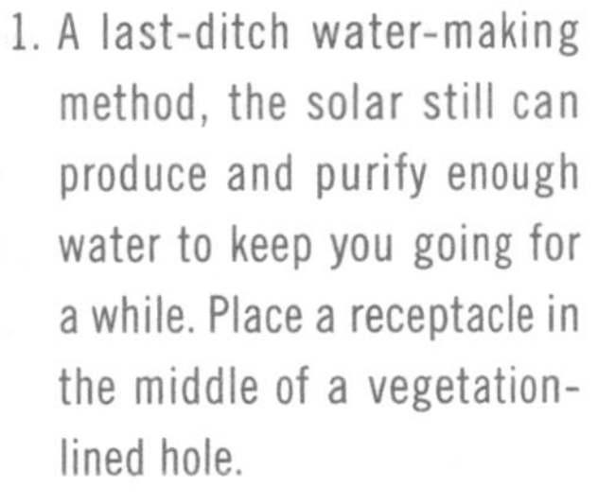

1. A last-ditch water-making method, the solar still can produce and purify enough water to keep you going for a while. Place a receptacle in the middle of a vegetation-lined hole.

2. Put a plastic sheet on top of the hole, with a stone over the receptacle. The receptacle under the plastic catches and collects the droplets that condense from the vegetation.

Water from Plants

The Bushmen of the Kalahari Desert live where heat extremes are a part of life. In adapting to this harsh climate, they have mastered the art of extracting water from plants. They are able to travel long distances, seeking out roots along the way, which they cut into chunks and mash. The water they squeeze out and drink helps to replenish them.

The Bushmen know that where there is vegetation, they can find water. But in most cases, the process is painfully slow and produces only enough liquid to wet the mouth. What's more, for you or me to be able to locate and correctly identify a water-bearing root or plant requires instruction from a local expert. Even then, the chances of finding one of these plants are slim, making it not worth the effort for most people.

Despite my hesitation about relying on plant innards to provide water, there are a few notable exceptions to the rule. Green bamboo is an excellent source of clear, odorless water. Simply bend the green bamboo stalk, tie it down, and cut off the top. Water will drip from the stalk during the night into a waiting receptacle.

Reaching into a rotted birch tree, pulling out the wet, spongy and punky wood and squeezing it in your hands can also produce water. Banana or plantain trees provide water too, if you have a tool to cut one down. Chop down the tree, leaving a stump about 12 inches (30 cm) high. Make a bowl-shaped depression by scooping out the center of the stump; water from the roots will immediately start to fill the hollow. The first few fillings will be bitter, but the rest should be palatable. The stump will supply water for a few days.

Vines can be a good source of water *if you can properly identify them.* (Poison ivy and moonseed are both poisonous vines, and they're found not just in tropical jungles but elsewhere.) The most water I've ever found in a plant came from a water vine I discovered when I was surviving for a week in the swamps of Georgia.

To extract water from a vine, cut a notch as high as you can reach. Make sure this is the first cut; if you cut the bottom first, the water will recede with capillary action. Next, cut the vine off close to the ground. Catch the liquid dropping from the cut vine in a container or in your mouth. When in the Georgian swamps I simply cut one end of the vine, let it drip for hours into a can, and ended up with fresh clear water (and a few swimming ants).

Some plants, such as the pitcher plant in northern Ontario, act as natural receptacles, catching water in their cup-shaped cavities. But again, you must have had on-site instruction in plant identification to be sure you are collecting water from non-poisonous plants.

The milk from unripe (green) coconuts will also provide your body with much-needed liquid, though it's not water. While you may survive for some time on milk from mature coconuts, note that these contain an oil that acts as a laxative. However, I've survived primarily on coconut water mixed with rainwater for a week in two separate tropical locations without any ill effects.

The following trees (most of which are found in tropical locations) can also provide water:

- Palms, such as buri, coconut, sugar, rattan, and nips, contain a sugary, drinkable liquid. If you bruise a lower frond and pull it down, the tree will excrete liquid at the site of the injury. Cut another slice every 12 hours to renew the flow.
- The Baobab tree, which is found in the sandy plains of northern Australia and Africa, collects water during the wet season in its bottle-like trunk. Water can occasionally be found in these trees even after weeks of dry weather.
- Some of the trees in the banana family can hold up to 2 quarts (2 L) of water at the base of the chevron of their leaf stalks (where the leaves attach to the trunk).

Water from a Well

Remember when you were a kid at the beach and you dug a hole so deep that water eventually started seeping through the walls of your creation? Well, you can use this method to procure fresh water in a survival situation. (If you're going to the effort of digging a hole, however, and have the necessary hardware on hand, you'd be better off making a solar still.)

I have dug for water in many places, often to no avail, but was successful when surviving in the plains and forested regions of northern South Africa. There, I found a mud-hole contaminated by wild boar feces and urine. I moved a short distance downstream of the mud-hole and dug a small hole in the soft sand. Within a short time I had a hole full of water—muddy, but free of animal feces and bacterial pollutants.

You will need to dig a hole deep enough to allow the water to seep in. How quickly it enters the hole will depend on how deep you dig and the concentration of water in the soil. Once seepage begins, use a rag to absorb the fluid, then wring it into your mouth or into a container. You may find water

- wherever green vegetation is found
- wherever damp surface sand is found
- in valleys and other low-lying areas
- at the foot of the concave banks of dry riverbeds
- at the foot of cliffs or rocky outcroppings
- in the first depression behind the first sand dune of dry desert lakes

Dig in a dry riverbed like this one and you may find water.

What a difference a storm makes! This riverbed was bone dry but suddenly started flowing as a result of faraway rains.

Water from Rocks

No, this is not a misprint! Believe it or not, rocks can be good (though inconsistent) sources of water, even in extraordinarily dry regions such as the desert. Depressions, holes, or fissures in rocks may collect water during rainfall. Any kind of flexible tubing can be used to suck the water from these difficult-to-reach spaces. Some types of porous rock may even act like sponges, soaking up water during a rainfall. You can get the water by inserting flexible tubing into a crack or hole in the rock. But bear in mind that every rodent in the area will also drink from—and likely urinate or defecate in or near—this same water. So if you can collect the water and boil it, you're better off. Wiping the dew off rocks in the morning with grass or cloth is another method of obtaining water from rocks.

Water from Animals

Fish usually contain a drinkable fluid, although you have to be careful. Large fish in particular will have a reservoir of water along the spine. You don't want to drink the juice from the flesh, however, as it is very rich in protein, and digesting it actually depletes (rather than replenishes) your body's water stores.

Gross though it may seem, animal eyeballs contain water. Extract it by cutting a small slice in the eyeball and sucking it.

Water from Urine

Few survival issues cause as much controversy as this one.

Some people are huge proponents of drinking urine—even in non-survival situations! Urine therapy has been used in various cultures for millennia. This therapy involves drinking urine or massaging it into one's skin for medicinal or cosmetic purposes. During the Renaissance, some people even used urine to clean their teeth.

My feelings on drinking urine? Don't do it! The primary dangers come from its salt and toxin content (the same dangers apply to drinking salty ocean water). The salt content (about 2 percent) tends to cause further dehydration, so it's a case of one step forward and two steps back. Urine also contains metabolic waste by-products, such as formaldehyde, ammonia, and dissolved heavy metals. The less diluted it is, the greater the concentration of the by-products you'll be ingesting. There are numerous documented cases of people dying from drinking their own urine.

If any case, if you're already dehydrated, you'll produce little urine. When I was surviving in the Kalahari Desert, the one time I did pee during the week, I produced very little and it was a disgusting yellow-brown color. A safer option than drinking your urine is using a solar still, as described previously, to distill your urine.

Purifying and Filtering Water

THERE IS ONE HARD AND FAST RULE regarding water purification and filtration: If you have the ability and energy to do it, do it.

STROUD'S TIP

Here is a neat trick developed by survival expert Allan "Bow" Beauchamp, assuming you're lucky enough to have two large plastic bottles (like a Pepsi bottle) or similar containers on hand:

"Fill one bottle one-quarter full with urine. Tape the mouth of this container to the mouth of the second container. Now lay them horizontal in the sun. Cover the clean container with some sand or soil and leave the contaminated container exposed to the sun. The contaminated container will heat up, causing evaporation. Moisture will migrate into the previously empty, clean container, leaving the residual waste behind."

As I mention above, rainwater collected in clean containers or from non-poisonous plants is safe for drinking. You should, however, *purify water from all other sources*. The quickest and easiest way to do so is with water purification tablets, iodine, or chlorine. If using iodine, which has been shown in medical experiments to be more effective than chlorine, mix no more than five drops per quart (liter) of water. Shake well and let the water stand for 30 minutes before drinking. Two drops of chlorine bleach is sufficient for a quart of water.

Note that these quantities are for relatively clean water. If you're using water that you suspect is contaminated, double the amounts suggested here. You should also increase the amount of time that the water sits before drinking, to give the agents time to kill any microorganisms.

Since it's unlikely that you'll have any of these items on hand, you'll probably have to revert to the old standby: boiling. You should boil water for five minutes to ensure you kill all possible harmful pathogens. Some people say you can get away with as little as one minute of boiling at sea level, adding one minute for each additional 1,000 feet (300 m) above sea level. Note that boiling *will not* neutralize chemical pollutants.

In both Africa and Alaska, I was able to bring water to a boil in plastic and glass bottles. The method is simple and is best accomplished if you have a rope and some long branches. Follow these steps:

Your plastic bottle will become black and misshapen but should not melt through, if you are careful.

1. Make a tripod by propping three similar-sized sticks together.
2. Tie the rope to the top of the bottle using a clove hitch.
3. Suspend the water-filled bottle above a fire so that the flames lick the bottle without completely engulfing it or going above the waterline. Boiling water over hot coals minimizes the risk that your bottle will melt, although this can still happen if the bottle gets too close to the coals. Heat until the water boils; you do not want to overheat the bottle so that it breaks or melts.

4. I suspect some fairly nasty chemicals are released when a common water bottle is heated this way, but I would rather take my chances with them than with the parasites.

Filtration without a high-quality, store-bought filter is not as ideal as purification because filtration likely won't remove harmful microorganisms from the water. What filtration will do is remove larger matter such as dirt and sediment, sticks, leaves, and any bugs or critters living in the water.

The simplest way of filtering or clearing stagnant, foul-smelling water is to place it in a container and let it stand for 12 hours or so. There are several, more active methods of filtering; most involve letting the water flow through layers of different types of material such as pebbles, sand, cloth, and charcoal. You can layer these materials over a receptacle with openings at either end, such as a piece of bamboo or hollow log.

Construct your filter so that the water passes through successively less porous layers of filtering material over a receptacle. A typical filter might begin with pebbles or stones, followed by sand, cloth, and then crushed charcoal (not ash), which is by far the best filtering medium available. As with most filtering systems, the water will become progressively clearer the more you filter it.

Region-Specific Water Considerations

Arid Regions, Deserts, and Canyons

Searching for a primary source of water should be your main goal, but in the world's drier places there's less chance of finding one. For this reason, you're likely limited to creating stills and ground wells to collect water.

A prevailing thought is that your best bet for finding water in arid regions is to look in valley basins or at the bases of sand dunes. But knowledge of your particular locale may tell you something different. When I was in the Kalahari Desert, I learned that the best place to find water was not at the bottom of the sand dunes but rather at the top. The hills there act like wicking agents and actually draw the water from the ground up. So it made more sense for me to look for plants (which had water in their roots) near the tops of the dunes rather than between dunes, where the only thing growing was brittle grass.

Given the sometimes radical temperature variations that can occur in these areas, you also might be lucky enough to find condensation on metal surfaces in the morning. Use a rag to absorb the water, then wring the water out into an appropriate receptacle.

Boreal and Other Temperate Forests

These areas have primary water sources in abundance. Follow game trails to valley bottoms or use topographic indicators to locate streams, rivers, or lakes. Watch out for stagnant and still water, or areas potentially contaminated with animal feces such as those close to beaver dams.

The Arctic and Polar Regions (cold weather season)

Winter is the toughest time to convince people to keep rehydrating. It's cold—who feels like drinking cold water as well? Yet I have always found that I am in much more need of drinking on winter treks than in tropical locations.

There are a number of reasons for this. Often your exertion level is higher: walking in snowshoes or deep snow takes lots of energy. And when it's cold, the very dry ambient air sucks the moisture out of you in much the same way that the desert wind does. I eat snow constantly while I work and travel outside in the winter. Clear and regular urination is the reward, indicating to me that I am properly hydrated. Dehydration in cold conditions also hastens chilling, substantially increasing your risk of hypothermia and frostbite.

Luckily, you are surrounded by all the water you need, thought it's in an altered physical state. Melting it is your goal, but if that is not an option, eat snow and ice, particularly in the morning or while you're working hard.

Slush is best for melting because it's mostly water anyway, followed by ice, which is denser than snow, and then snow. If you're melting snow, pack as much into your pot as possible. Always retain some water in the pot, as it will make your next melting session much easier.

If you're not lucky enough to have a pot on hand, there are other (though slower) methods. You can improvise a sack from an item of clothing or other fabric. Fill the sack with slush, ice, or snow and suspend it near your fire. Place a receptacle under the sack to catch the drippings.

Another technique is to place ice or packed snow on a rock over a fire. Hold the ice in place with small stones or other heavy objects and tilt the rock slightly to let the melted water run off. Collect the drippings in a receptacle.

It is also possible to spread snow out on a dark sheet (such as a tarp or garbage bag), and let it melt in the sun and then drip into a container or a depression made in the sheet. This requires the right air temperature, however—not too far below freezing—and a spot protected from chilling winds. You can also use a piece of coiled birch bark and small hot stones to melt snow into liquid, or even warm it for drinking.

If you need to collect sea ice, it's important to know the difference between *new sea ice*, which is essentially frozen, salty sea water, and *old sea ice*, which is a remnant of a glacier that has calved off and is therefore fresh water. New ice is milky or gray in color, does not break easily, has sharp edges, and tastes extremely salty. Old ice, on the other hand, is a distinctive blue or black, shatters easily, has rounded corners, and tastes relatively free of salt. You can lick the salty ice once a day, however, to satisfy your body's need for that nutrient.

On the Sea or Open Water

Having spent a week surviving in a life raft in the Caribbean Ocean, I understand how difficult it can be to obtain fresh water. Yet for all that I experienced during my week adrift, it was nothing compared to the 38 days that Dougal Robertson, his wife, Linda, and their children endured in 1972 when their boat sank after being rammed by a pod of killer whales 200 miles (322 km) from the Galápagos Islands.

The Robertsons used their ingenuity and intense will to live to survive for five and a half weeks on the open sea. They caught rainwater in the canopy of their dinghy. When the water became dirty and contaminated from the paint peeling off their raft canopy, Linda resorted to administering water enemas to her family with a plastic bottle, which allowed them to absorb it without actually ingesting the contaminants.

Rainwater is an important source of water when you're at sea. Maximize the area in which you're catching it, and ensure that your catchment system is clean. Wipe off all encrusted salt with sea water just before it rains. Rainwater is relatively clean and safe to drink (though not completely free of pollutants), so it would be a shame to contaminate it by catching it in a dirty receptacle. You can also use rags to collect dew and condensation from your boat.

When you're on the open sea, you can readily obtain drinking water from salt water by using a store-bought still or, provided you have the materials, to make an above-ground solar still. To do so, follow the instructions earlier in this chapter but use a large receptacle such as a bucket instead of a hole.

Jungles

Procuring water usually is not an issue in the jungle, as these tend to be extremely rainy places. Locating a primary water source should not be a problem, and harvesting rainwater is also an option.

In the Amazon rain forest, I found that the feeder streams to the rivers were better than the rivers themselves, which were subject to huge variations in height, volume, and turbidity. Rivers in these areas can rise by 10 to 15 feet (3 to 4.5 m) not long after heavy rainfalls, and turn the color of chocolate milk with all the mud and dirt they're carrying. Feeder streams are cleaner and less variable.

Plants, particularly water vines, and bamboo, banana, and plantain trees, can also be an excellent source of water.

Coastal Regions

If you're stuck on a beach and have no primary water source available, you can get a good supply from the ground itself by digging a beach well. Walk well back from the ocean's edge. When you reach the base of the back of the first dune, begin digging. The water you obtain here should be sufficiently filtered by the sand to desalinate it, especially the top few inches.

Should the water still be salty, you can desalinate it yourself, although the process takes a lot of energy. Build a fire and place rocks in it to heat them. Drop the hot rocks in the water still to create steam, and catch the steam in a cloth held over the hole. The desalinated water can then be wrung from the cloth.

Here's an easier way to find fresh water on the coast: when the tide is out, look for small rivulets making their way to the sea. These may indicate a freshwater stream just above the low-tide line.

Swamps

Though most people find it hard to believe, I don't have a problem drinking unpurified swamp water in North America. It's not as clean and refreshing as water from a mountain stream, but it will keep you alive, and that, after all, is the goal. Clearly, filtering and purifying is recommended, but if you don't have that capability, as I've said before, better to drink than dehydrate.

The obvious issue with swamps and bogs is that the water tends to be slow moving and full of muck. But this doesn't necessarily mean it contains parasites. On the contrary, I've drunk water from a clear river that wreaked havoc on my gastrointestinal system and I've drunk water from swamps with no ill effects.

Obviously, you want to filter swamp water as best you can, to minimize the sediment and dirt you're ingesting. At a minimum, you should let it sit for 12 hours, so that the heavier stuff settles.

If you follow a game trail to a swamp, it's especially important that you collect your water a good distance away from where the animals congregate and do their business.

As I mentioned in the Coastal Regions section, you can also use the earth to filter swamp water by digging a pit about 50 feet (15 m) from the edge of the swamp. The water that fills your pit may still require filtration, but it should be cleaner than swamp water.

Mountains

Mountains are good sources of water, especially in temperate climates. Depending on the season, snow and ice may be available for melting or eating. Snow lingers long into the summer at higher altitudes, particularly on north-facing slopes and in hollows.

Water courses are fairly obvious on mountains, so it shouldn't take more than a few moments of surveying the topography for you to determine places where there's a regular flow. Look for deep fissures and valleys in mountainsides where water accumulates after precipitation. And if all else fails, follow the mountain down to the nearest valley where you'll increase your chances of finding water.

On mountains, water often collects in deep fissures and valleys such as this one. Here, I'm drinking straight from the source.

Chapter Six

FIRE

I will never forget the first time I was surviving in a forest and made a fire using only what I could find. Before the trek, I had been practicing with the fire-bow method and some cedar in my basement, but when I needed cedar on the trip, I couldn't find any. So considering the characteristics of cedar, I chose another semi-soft wood for the baseboard and spindle of my fire bow: poplar.

As the first gentle column of smoke wafted up from the wood, I felt euphoric. It was a pivotal moment for me, and I realized that no matter how bad a situation I might find myself in, I could always make it better because I could make fire without traditional fire-starting devices such as matches or lighters. Over the years, the impact of that day hasn't diminished one bit. Once I learned how to make fire without matches, my confidence in my ability to survive in the wilderness jumped tenfold.

Fire does so much more than keep you warm. With fire you can signal for rescue, purify your water and cook your food, you can have light, make tools, and keep away the bogeyman. In short, the ability to make and maintain a fire is a huge advantage for your survival.

In some areas fire plays a bigger role as a psychological boost than as a physical one. In the jungle, you don't need a fire for heat, and possibly not even for food preparation, because you can eat fruit. But a fire will keep away the jaguar more effectively than just about anything else, and that goes a long way toward making you safe. The Waorani of the Amazon jungle *never* let their fires die. And for good reason: try making a fire after it has rained for six straight hours (and that's during the dry season!).

For me, fire is like a child that needs to be protected, respected, cared for, and ultimately, loved and appreciated. I can't count all the nights I have huddled in the dead of winter over a little fire in a claustrophobic shelter surrounded by snow, warming just enough of my face and hands to keep the chill away.

Many matters of wilderness survival are controversial, however, and fire is no exception. For example, two different survival experts I had the privilege of studying with in Africa held opposing views on the use of fire in lion territories. One felt that fire attracted lions; the other felt it served as a repellent.

Here is the perspective of my friend and survival crony Douw Kruger:

> During a survival course for air force pilots, I was leading three groups of eight people in the bush. They were instructed to build proper shelters to protect against lions and hyenas. During my inspection I found that the last group had put only small branches without thorns around their shelter. It was almost dark and too late to gather proper branches.
>
> That night a group of young lions was walking on the road about 100 yards (90 m) away and must have seen the fire. They approached and found seven humans sleeping on the ground and one (the night watch) sleeping against a tree, all within a shelter designed at best to keep out housecats.
>
> When the first lion pushed his head through the branches, the watch awoke and the excitement began! The pilots kept the lions at bay by hitting with sticks or throwing rocks. Fortunately, no one was hurt. Needless to say, the next night their shelter was so well constructed that not even an elephant could penetrate it!
>
> Fire is a part of nature, so animals are used to it. Big wildfires might scare them, but a small, stationary fire will not. In fact, it may make them curious and draw them to investigate. The reason fire makes you feel safe is that you can see what is going on around you and you have some burning wood to use as a weapon if necessary. But the downside of a fire is that it makes you visible from a long distance.

In the end, I *did* opt for a fire in the middle of lion territory, primarily because too many years of using fire for comfort won out. For me, it seemed to be the right choice. I needed the psychological boost, and I wanted to cook the freshwater crab I had caught. However, I stayed up all night listening to growls in the distance. I would learn later that lions had made a kill about 500 yards (457 m) from my shelter that night. Sometimes, ignorance is bliss!

Fire is very, very important. I will put up with many deprivations in a survival situation, but please don't ask me to go without fire.

Select Your Site Carefully

IN MY FAVORITE MOVIE OF ALL TIME, *Jeremiah Johnson,* the title character (played by Robert Redford) struggles to start a fire with a piece of flint, some charred cloth, and a steel striker. Huddled down in the snow with the wind whipping furiously, he finally gets his spark to take and then blows the ember into a small flame, only to have a big clump of snow fall from the branches above and put it out!

That's why the first step in the fire-making journey is to choose an appropriate location. We can all anticipate the risks associated with having a fire inside our shelter (although, you *can* do it, provided you're smart about it), but other risks are often ignored.

Your fire should be sheltered from the wind, rain, or snow. Make sure you have lots of firewood or flammable material close at hand (but not so close that it could lead to a forest fire or could fall on you and cause injury). Large boulders work well as protection against the elements: they not only act as a windbreak but also absorb the fire's heat and reflect it back at you.

Make sure you don't pick a low spot that will fill with water if it starts raining. Choose a place that seems dry relative to the surrounding area, since a fire draws moisture from the ground beneath it as it burns. If the ground is really wet, your fire won't even get going.

Always consider safety when it comes to fire, which can spread in ways you might not expect. A root can burn underground for many yards, allowing a fire to pop up elsewhere, developing into a full-blown forest fire, sometimes even a year later. Overhanging dry leaves can catch easily and start a forest fire.

STROUD'S TIP

If the ground is wet and covered with snow, one of my fire-saving tricks is to build the fire on a platform of wood, even if it's rotten. This protects my fire from the moisture below and provides additional fuel when the fire gets going.

Consider the flow of oxygen as well. Oxygen is a critical component of fire, and if you build your fire too deep in the ground or shelter it too much, it may not get the oxygen it needs. You'll waste a lot of time and energy if you have to keep it going by blowing on it.

What Type of Fire Should You Make?

THERE ARE TWO TYPES OF FIRE: the small one that protects you from the elements (and that you may even keep inside your shelter), and the big, conspicuous fire that also acts as a signal for possible rescue (provided you have enough fuel to keep it going). Keeping both alight simultaneously may be difficult, especially if you need to spend time seeing to other aspects of your survival.

In fact, keeping just one fire going at all times can be a challenge, and your ability to do so depends on the amount of firewood available. But if you have enough wood, then you should never let your fire die out. It's what all forest-dwelling and primitive peoples did, and I figure they must've known a thing or two about survival.

If you build a small fire inside your shelter, you must stay in there with it. So the trick is to maintain the big fire outside and then bring it inside when it rains or you are bedding down for the night. Most adventurers keep

If you can master the skill of making a small fire right outside your shelter, you'll keep the heat inside with you. It makes your survival experience not only more comfortable, but also comforting.

their fire right outside their shelter, then crawl into the shelter to sleep (only to wake up to a cold or rain-doused pile of ashes the next morning).

All of the same rules of site selection apply when making a fire inside your shelter, but there are additional considerations. Oxygen supply is one. You defeat the purpose of having a fire inside if you have to keep your shelter open to the chilly air in order to feed the fire the oxygen it needs.

Be careful not to make your fire in a shelter built against a rock with a big overhang. On one survival course, a young couple did just that. The fire heated the rock to the point that a Volkswagen-sized chunk cracked off. Had they been in the shelter at the time, they would have been crushed. I couldn't stop thinking about this story when I was surviving in the Utah Canyonlands inside a tiny cave, fire by my head and thousands of tons of canyon rock above me. If you find yourself in a similar situation, make sure that there is at least 4 feet (1.2 m) of distance between the top of your flames and the rock overhead.

Butch Cassidy and his “Wild Bunch” hid from the law in these same Utah caves.

Perhaps the most serious risk with an inside fire is that you might burn your shelter. I’ve made hundreds of inside fires, and for many years I’ve never had a problem. But once, on the coast of Alaska, I awoke one morning to find several-foot-high flames reaching up through my shelter’s driftwood roof. Had I not been only feet from the ocean, the whole shelter would’ve burned down.

Driftwood made a great shelter on the Alaskan coast, but nearly burned down when my inside fire grew too big.

Making a Chimney

1. Smoke inhalation is an issue with an inside fire, so make sure your smoke can escape through a chimney.

2. Constructing a chimney tunnel with a direct route to your flames will feed air to your fire without cooling you down.

3. This birch bark vent allows air to circulate from outside of the shelter right to your interior fire.

4. Your shelter will be warm from the fire and the chimney will allow oxygen to circulate to keep the fire going.

In any survival situation you should make the biggest, hottest fire possible, provided you build it safely and have plenty of fuel. I have spent many cold and unpleasant nights huddled by a tiny fire trying to keep warm—but only when I didn't have a choice. Don't waste your time thinking small when you can go big: a big fire will kick the chill right out of you.

An emergency is no time to wax environmental and worry that you're burning too many trees. And the advantage of making a massive fire is that once it gets going, you can burn almost anything, including big, punky logs that smolder forever, which means you can reserve small, dry wood for kindling.

During my plane crash survival experience in northern Ontario, I made a fire that was eventually about 6 feet (1.8 m) long and 4 feet (1.2 m) high. With a blaze that big and so much heat being generated, I was able to sit against a nearby tree and fall asleep in the middle of a cold and snowy winter—without a shelter! There's little risk of waking up to find a fire this size cold and dead, and in any case, the mounds of red-hot coals sitting there can easily be used to get it going again.

The other benefit of a big fire over a small one is that it takes much more rain or snow to put it out. I've had fires going that were so hot they continued to burn right through a downpour.

Believe it or not, a big fire requires less work and effort to maintain than a small one. You simply need to add a few large pieces of wood every once in a while to keep it roaring along. With a small fire, you'll burn all the small branches in the area to constantly feed its flames, and you'll spend a significant amount of your time and energy finding and collecting these branches. On top of this, if you need to leave the fire for a while, you run a real risk of it going out while you're gone.

A pilot friend of mine once found himself stranded on a beach covered with driftwood. He made a massive blaze that kept him warm until rescue. It was the right thing to do.

Preparation

THE GREATEST ENEMY OF A SUCCESSFUL FIRE is your impatience. It is vital that you are diligent in preparing your fire, though it may seem tedious.

An important aspect of fire preparation—especially if you're using one of the last-ditch efforts I describe later in this chapter—is making sure you have enough fuel before you produce a glowing ember or a small flame. You don't want to get to the point where you have a flame, only to discover that you don't have any tinder or kindling to add to it. This is one of the most frustrating things that can happen in the wilderness, and it happens all the time.

A strategy I use with my survival students is to have them gather as much wood as they think they need for the night. Once they're finished, and without looking at their pile, I tell them to get five times the amount they just collected. Even *after* they have done that, many of them run out of firewood before morning. It may sound like an exaggeration but it's true: most people misjudge their firewood needs by a ratio of five to one.

And don't take for granted the fact that you have a primary fire-starting method such as a lighter or matches, either. What if your lighter breaks or your matches get wet? Now the fire you've just started may be the only fire you will ever light. Do not let it die just because you don't have enough fuel available.

A big, *dry* tinder bundle is the key to success, followed by lots of *dry* kindling and lots of *dry* (and if possible, split) wood. You also need to make sure that your fire doesn't spread. Clear an area immediately surrounding your fire pit, particularly if you're in a wooded or brush-covered area. You can even build a wall from damp logs or rocks to both protect your fire from wind and reflect heat back to you. Remember, however, that wet and porous rocks (such as those pulled from a river or lake) have been known to explode violently when heated, so avoid using these very close to (or in) your fire.

Build Your Fire

When it comes to gathering fuel for your fire, you'll need tinder, kindling, and large fuel. Each component is critical, but none more so than tinder.

Tinder: Stages 1 to 3

If you don't have a lighter or matches and are making a friction fire by, say, rubbing two sticks together, the step that takes you from glowing ember to tinder ignition is critical, and one at which many people fail.

Though you shouldn't discount the tissue in your pants, the pages in this book, or even the lint in your belly button, your primary source of tinder in the wilderness will be fluffy, dead, and dry plant material. The greatest lesson you can learn here is this: Remembering the names of plants means nothing in a survival situation. What's important when it comes to fire-starting are plant *characteristics*.

When I first learned survival, I was taught that you can ignite milkweed fluff with a single spark. And it's true—it goes up like gasoline! But what I discovered later is that almost any plant with a light, fluffy part (usually the seed pods, and especially those that will blow easily in the wind) will do the same thing. Fireweed, various grasses, cattails, and numerous other plant species throughout the world work too. So rather than looking for milkweed, look for any plant with the *characteristics* of milkweed. Shoot a spark into it and you should have fire.

Don't get caught up searching for specific plants such as birch bark in Canada, white cedar bark in Kansas, or coconut husks in the tropics. Rather, keep your eyes open for plants that have the characteristics of good tinder. Think "Hey, that coconut husk is hairy and light and fluffy. I wonder if that works?" Not surprisingly, coconut husk is great tinder.

So, what characteristics should you be looking for in your tinder? Most important, it should be *dry*. Damp tinder leads to great frustration . . . and ultimately, no fire. Tinder also needs to be *thin, light*, and *fluffy*. If something has these characteristics, it will ignite into flame when a spark is introduced.

Note that dry leaves make surprisingly poor tinder. Most dead leaves need a fair bit of heat to ignite, making them a poor choice for fire-starting without matches or lighter.

I like to divide tinder into three stages. *Stage 1 tinder* is the lightest,

STROUD'S TIP

If you are traveling through an area that has loads of dry tinder, gather it now, and gather lots. You don't want to end up later in a survival location without tinder sources nearby, regretting that you didn't fill those big pockets in your hiking pants when you had the chance.

fluffiest stuff you can find—fine, very thin, even wispy material such as dead grass, birch bark, Spanish moss, or scraped cedar bark. These materials are best at capturing a spark or ember when formed into a bird's-nest-shaped bundle. Once the bundle catches, you can blow it until it glows and ignites.

Stage 2 tinder is slightly thicker and more substantial than stage 1 tinder, and includes toothpick-thick bits of wood, pine needles, or thinly peeled bark such as birch bark. These materials will take the flame you created with your stage 1 tinder, hold it a little longer, and burn brighter. You can jump right to this stage if you are lighting your fire with matches or a lighter.

Stage 3 tinder is another baby step up, to the smallest pieces of burnable material, such as pencil-thick dead and dry twigs. These will take the secondary flame and hold it even longer than stage 2 tinder. Remember, however, that although the flame may seem more substantial at this stage, you still don't have a fire. Sure, you have a flame, but it would take little to put it out.

The following are other possible sources of tinder:

- Bird down: I've never used bird down, but it certainly has the characteristics of good tinder.
- Cotton balls: These are fantastic as tinder, and you may have them in your first-aid kit (the end of a Q-tip works too). Cotton takes a spark well and converts it to flame. If you daub a bit of petroleum jelly or lip balm (which also may be in your first-aid kit) on the cotton, it will hold the flame longer than cotton alone.
- Lint: This is a favorite in many survival books, but lint is difficult to find in a survival situation.
- Sawdust: You can make a little by cutting wood with your folding saw. Produces a good stage 2 tinder.

Kindling

Once your stage 3 tinder has caught, you can progress to the kindling level. Kindling is not as readily combustible as tinder, so don't use it until you have a discernible flame.

Kindling generally comprises small twigs and sticks that are thin enough to burn easily but thick enough to last longer than a few seconds. You will slowly graduate from those that are about the thickness of a pencil to those that are the thickness of your thumb.

Fuel

Eventually you will get to the point where you can add large pieces of wood to your fire. As always, work your way up slowly in terms of thickness. Wrist- and forearm-thick wood is the most common type of fuel for survival fires, but don't hesitate to add larger pieces of split wood and even logs, as long as you've got a sufficient amount of fuel available and a solid flame.

When selecting wood for fuel (or for any stage of building a fire, for that matter), choose standing dead trees. They are far drier than anything else you'll find in the wild. Avoid wood that's lying on the ground, because it will have absorbed a fair bit of moisture from the ground.

Wood is your primary source of fuel, but there are other sources, including animal droppings, dried grasses, and animal fats.

Animal droppings: Dried dung patties from cows, deer, moose, elephants, rhinos, or other ungulates (grazing, grass-eating animal) can be very good for starting and maintaining fires. These are essentially concentrated plant waste—the natural version of the starter logs and briquettes that are popular these days. Animal dung doesn't flame very well, but makes for excellent coals.

Dried grasses: If you don't have much large fuel on hand but find yourself surrounded by grasslands, you can twist grass into tight bundles. By increasing the density of the grass, you make it more wood-like. It will burn quickly, though, so make sure you have lots on hand.

Animal fats: Chances are you won't have much animal fat available, and what extra you do have you will likely eat to stay alive. For years, however, pioneers rendered animal fat such as whale blubber into fuel for their oil lamps. Long before that, the Inuit people used rendered seal fat to fuel their *quuliit*, the soapstone lamps in their igloos.

Maintaining Your Fire

BUILDING YOUR FIRE IS JUST THE FIRST STEP. The second is making sure it doesn't go out; otherwise, you will have to start again from scratch. The

For millennia, the Inuit have been using *quuliit* (seal oil lamps) such as this one to heat their igloos.

bigger the fire you have (provided you have the fuel), the more likely it will keep going, even if you get hit with rain or snow, go to sleep, or need to leave it for a while to carry out other survival tasks.

Should you decide to leave your fire for a few hours, first, make sure it's not in an especially windy area, or else you'll burn through your fuel too quickly and also increase the risk of starting a forest fire. Try to find a location that affords at least a little protection for your fire, whether near rocks or in a place that offers natural protection from the elements. The exception, of course, is in the case of a signal fire, which should be out in the open and as visible as possible.

How long you leave your fire largely depends on how much fuel you have to add to it. If you've got plenty of fuel and you have made a big fire, you should be able to stay away for as long as eight hours and come back to hot coals, from which you can restart the fire. The smaller the fire, the less time you'll be able to stay away.

STROUD'S TIP

Once you get a fire going, make it a practice to never come back to your base camp without a piece of firewood, even if it's just one stick. This way you're always adding to your firewood stock. We've been doing this as a habit in my family for years. Even when my children were little, they always returned to the campsite with a twig or stick in their hands.

Resurrect a Fire

CHANCES ARE THAT IF YOU LEAVE your fire for any length of time, you'll return to something much smaller than what you left, usually just a pile of hot coals or a warm bed of ashes. In these cases, it is vital that you have all the stages of fire-starting materials already on hand, so that you can get the fire going again *immediately*.

Just how much your fire has burned down will determine which stage of tinder (or kindling) you need to get it started again. You should have gathered what you'll need before leaving and stored everything in a dry, protected area. You shouldn't have to scramble to get your tinder, kindling, and fuel.

I'm amazed sometimes at how far gone a fire can be and still be resurrected into flame. In the canyonlands of Utah, I awoke to a fire that had been reduced to nothing but white ash. Rather than sweep off the blanket of ash to search for hot coals at the bottom (which would have risked putting them out by cooling them down), I slid the empty cable I had ripped off my mountain bike into the ash. I then blew gently through the tube, which supplied oxygen directly to the warmest part of the pile of ash and coals without removing the protective blanket of ash. The coals began to glow, then slowly transferred their heat to the other dead coals around them. Only then did I brush away the ash and gradually begin adding tinder to the now red-hot coals.

How to Carry Fire

When your circumstances force you to move, taking your fire with you may save you a lot of trouble in the long run. This is why I recommend including a coffee tin with a lid in your survival kit. You can put some red coals and other tinder inside, where it will smolder while you travel. You can also make a fire bundle, light the end as if it were a large cigar, and carry the glowing bundle to your next destination.

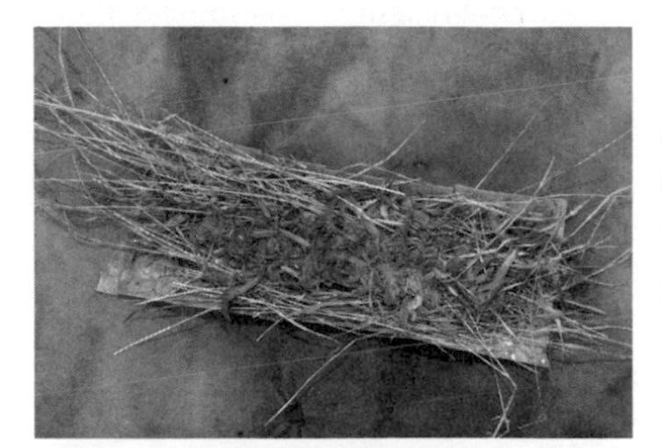

A fire bundle is a collection of tinder that begins with the finest material in the middle and graduates out to the shell or covering.

Tie the material tightly together into a cigar shape. Once lit, it should smolder for hours.

A properly lit fire bundle can last for days.

Ways to Make Fire

GIVEN THE MANY AND VARIED PURPOSES A FIRE SERVES in a survival situation, the ability to make one is an important skill. If you're a dedicated outdoors person, you should be able to get a fire going just about anywhere, even if it's been raining for two straight weeks and even in the pouring rain. If this sounds daunting, don't worry, with the right knowledge and training, you can do it too.

There are several well-known methods of making fire—some of them easier than others—so you're really limited only by your imagination. Should you find yourself stranded and with no available fire-making method, start thinking like the Professor from *Gilligan's Island,* and get creative.

I've seen some adventurers make fires by concentrating the rays of the sun through the concave depression of a teaspoon, and others, by concentrating the sun's rays through an ice cube. Ingenious methods, to be sure, though I wouldn't want to stake my life on them. That's why it's important to be practiced at several ways of making fire (see "Survival Kits," Chapter 2).

As with all survival tasks, there are *primary* and *last-ditch* tools for making fire. Primary methods are relatively simple, and will make your wilderness ordeal easier to survive. Last-ditch implements are well proven in the field, but they are difficult and finicky, subject to a host of variables that may not necessarily be in your control.

Here are the *primary tools* for making fire:

- lighter
- strike-anywhere matches
- magnesium flint striker
- fire piston

Here are some *last-ditch tools* for making fire:

- friction: fire bow, fire plow, and hand drill
- sparks: rock and steel, flint and steel, battery
- chemicals
- the sun's rays

I used one of the craziest last-ditch methods ever to make a fire in the Kalahari Desert. I polished the bottom of a pop can with chocolate (which has waxy properties) and sand to reflect the sun's rays onto the tinder I'd gathered.

Primary Fire-Starting Tools

Is it cool to know how to make fire using a hand drill or fire bow? Yes, and these are skills that dedicated outdoors people should know. But survival is not about proving that you're some kind of earth-skills guru; it's about dedicating your energies to getting home safely or getting rescued. That's why, for making fire, nothing compares with a lighter, some solid strike-anywhere matches, a flint striker, or a fire piston. Even with those items, building a fire can be a challenge; without those, all bets are off.

Butane Lighter

Nothing compares with a good 'ol butane lighter for starting a fire. As simple as it may be to make a fire this way, however, there are still a few considerations.

First of all, make sure that whatever lighter you have is in good working order, and either waterproof or in a waterproof container. If you fall in the lake or river with a traditional lighter in your pocket, it won't function when you come out. I prefer a fluorescent orange one. Ugly, I know, but a lot easier to find in a pile of dried leaves than that cool camouflage one from the outdoors store.

My favorite kinds are the butane lighters that act like little torches and can't be extinguished by a gust of wind or a few drops of rain, as can traditional lighters with other types of fuel. These butane lighters shoot out a hot jet of blue flame that stands up to the toughest conditions. Note that over time, lighter fluid will evaporate, and all lighters have a finite life span: make sure yours has plenty of fuel and use it only when you absolutely have to. You never know how long you're going to need it!

Matches

Matches have been starting fires successfully for a long time, so they should be at least one component of your fire-making strategy. My preference is the solid, strike-anywhere type found in any local hardware store; make sure you store them in a watertight container. Even though these matches do, essentially, *strike anywhere*, provide yourself with a backup by tearing the striker edge off the side of the box and including it in the container with your matches.

In outdoors stores you may come across boxes of matches that claim to be waterproof. Don't buy these; they're the biggest rip-off going! These matches are tiny and flimsy and come in a little cardboard box with a striker on the outside edge. If the box gets wet, the striker edge also gets wet, and now you've got nowhere to strike your dainty little waterproof matches.

Magnesium Flint Strikers

Wonderful devices, magnesium flint strikers can be struck anywhere, come with their own emergency fuel source (the magnesium shavings themselves), and—best of all—you can get them soaking wet and they still work like a charm.

But the real beauty of the magnesium flint striker is that it produces a powerful spray of sparks. If you don't have any other tinder material available, you can scrape magnesium shavings off the flint stick itself and light these with a spark.

Fire Piston

A relatively new addition to my collection of fire-starting devices, the fire piston gives me the ability to start a fire quickly and easily. In a nutshell, the fire piston works because heat is generated when air is compressed.

The fire piston is made up of three components: an outer barrel, a plunger with a hollow tip, and a gasket. Insert a small piece of tinder (usually a dry, punky wood bit) into the hollow tip of the plunger, which fits into the barrel. Then thrust the plunger down one (or more) times and the tinder should ignite. The compression of the air inside creates the heat that ignites the tinder.

Fire pistons are not without their drawbacks: they are a little bigger and bulkier than other primary fire-starting methods, and their success relies heavily on a gasket, which can get worn out or lost. And although all fire-starting methods require the right selection of tinder, the fire piston seems dependent on it. You need the right type, and it has to be *very* dry. But if your other option is a last-ditch fire-starting method, opt for the fire piston.

Lighting a Fire with a Magnesium Flint Striker

1. Use a knife or similar hard object to shave a pile of magnesium off the striker. The pile should be about the size of a nickel, and 1/4 of an inch (0.5 cm) high.

2. Strike a spark into the filings for a fast, hot flame.

Last-Ditch Fire-Starting Tools

Once you've exhausted the primary tools of starting a fire, you now have to turn to what I call the last-ditch efforts. Other books and survival instructors call these *primitive* tools: they were used by our ancestors thousands of years ago. If you have no choice but to make a fire by one of these methods, rest assured that they do work, although you may pay for your flame in blood, sweat, and tears.

Charred Cloth

One of my favorite ways to make fire is to char cloth. Making charred cloth is a bit of a chicken-and-egg exercise, because you actually need fire first. But once you have created charred cloth, it will go a long way toward saving your matches or lighter fluid, as you need only a single spark to reignite it.

As the name indicates, you need cloth to make charred cloth. Linen is the traditional fabric of choice, but I use 100-percent cotton and it works well. Punky wood or bark can be used instead of cloth. Either way, your fabric must be natural; synthetics won't work. Your piece should be a few inches square.

Take a can with a tight-fitting lid and punch a small hole in each end. Put the cloth inside the can and place the can in the coals of a fire. Make sure the cloth inside does not ignite, or you'll be left with nothing in the can but a small pile of ashes. As the cloth begins to heat up, it emits gases that fill the interior of the can, driving out the air. These gases are vented through the holes, appearing as small jets of flame. This will be followed, eventually, by smoke.

When the smoke subsides, turn the can over to ensure even charring of the cloth (this momentarily increases the amount of smoke coming out of the holes in the can). When the smoke again dies down, the process is finished and the can should be removed from the fire. At this point, plug the holes with twigs to create a tight-fitting seal. If air gets into the can while it is still hot, your cloth will ignite and burn.

After the can has cooled (wait at least 10 minutes), open it and remove the charred cloth. If properly charred, it should be uniformly black.

Making a Charred Cloth

1. You will need a can, a punctured lid, and a fire.

2. Place the closed can on the fire. Once you see flame coming out of the can's holes, you're nearing the end of the process. Smoke will soon follow, signaling that you should remove the can from the coals.

3. Allow the can to cool, then open it up. It doesn't look like much, but this charred cloth is ready to take a new spark . . . and re-ignite easily the next time you want to start a fire.

The magic of charred cloth is that when a spark hits it, a tiny red ember on the cloth slowly grows larger. The ember is virtually impossible to blow out and will increase in intensity if oxygen is introduced. It's relatively easy to start a fire with charred cloth, and it allows you to save your primary fire-starting tools for circumstances when you need them most.

While surviving beside a downed plane in northern Ontario, I made a small container from some thin metal I had found inside the plane. I then ripped canvas from the body of the plane, placed it in the metal container, and charred the cloth by putting the container in a fire. Later, when I needed to make a new fire, I struck a rock I had found in a creek bed against the back of my axe to throw a spark into the charred cloth. It gave me the ember I needed to build a new fire.

If you don't have a metal container, you can also char cloth by partially burning small strips of cotton and quickly smothering them in dry sand or soil.

Flint and Steel

There are many ways of generating sparks. One way is to strike a flint rock (such as I found in the creek bed) or other hard, sharp-edged rock with a piece of high-carbon steel.

Friction

Of the last-ditch efforts, the most common are the three methods of making a friction fire, or "rubbing two sticks together." These are the fire bow, the hand drill, and the fire plow. The hand drill and fire plow are advanced skills, so I do not cover them here. The fire bow is a method you can employ effectively, though not easily, if caught in a survival ordeal.

STROUD'S TIP

What type of fire warms twice? The friction fire. It not only keeps you warm once you get it going, but also warms you while you're trying to make it, even in the winter. But try to sweat as little as possible while building your fire. Anticipate the fact that you'll be working hard for the next little while, and remove layers of clothing as necessary *before* you start sweating.

Fire Bow

The fire bow is an effective last-ditch fire-starting method, but it depends very much on the availability of the necessary materials.

Components: The fire bow is made up of four components: the baseboard, the spindle, the bearing block, and the bow.

The *baseboard* is the part of your fire bow that eventually produces the smoldering mound of wood dust that will (hopefully) start your fire. You can use various types of wood depending on your geographic location, but in my home location in north-central Canada, I prefer semi-soft woods such as cedar, poplar, aspen, or basswood.

Choosing the proper wood for the baseboard is critical because the spindle, a long stick that rubs against the baseboard, will grind the baseboard away as you spin. Some instructors prefer a hardwood spindle because they feel it's more effective at grinding the baseboard. Personally, I prefer semi-soft wood for both pieces, because then you're grinding not only the baseboard but also the spindle, possibly producing double the wood dust for your effort. Choosing a wood for a friction fire mostly comes down to what works for you. To test if a wood is semi-soft, jam your thumbnail into the wood. If it makes an impression, it's semi-soft or soft.

After practice, the most important aspect of making a proper friction fire is finding the right kind of wood. This is where a little local knowledge goes a long way. How else would you know that the dry saguaro cactus makes a great friction-fire fuel, or that if you're in the boreal forest of northern Ontario you're better off using poplar, cedar, aspen, or birch than pine, which is so full of resin that it polishes instead of burns?

Your *spindle* should be as straight as possible. The spindle will turn rapidly as you move your bow, creating friction on the baseboard. The size of the spindle is up to you, but I typically shoot for one 8 inches (20 cm) in length and as thick as my thumb. Make sure the wood you use is dead and dry.

Most people use branches because these are naturally the right size and shape. In fact, the molecules inside a tree branch are tighter together than those throughout the rest of the tree, making the wood a bit harder. By comparison, the heartwood of the tree—the wood right in the middle of the trunk—is softer. Therefore, you're better off finding a downed tree, breaking off a piece, and carving it into a spindle. Basswood branches (dead and dry ones) are superb spindles.

The *bearing block* is the part of your fire bow that you use to apply weight and pressure to the top of your spindle. Many things can be used for this purpose, but I like a piece of rock with a small indentation knocked into it, where the spindle can sit.

You might also consider using a piece of bone; the knee-knuckle bones of a deer or other ungulate work well. Travelers often use a piece of wood as the bearing block, but if you do so, lubricate the point where the spindle contacts the bearing block so that it doesn't grab. Beeswax, ear wax, pine pitch, or oil from your skin or hair can all serve as lubricants in a pinch.

My friend and fellow survival instructor Doug Getgood was once using a piece of wood as his bearing block and accidentally got the ember forming in the bearing block instead of the baseboard, likely because the bearing block was softer than the baseboard. Accepting the circumstances, he turned the whole set upside down and got his fire going that way.

The *bow* ties your entire fire bow drill together. It can be any kind of wood, as long as it's strong and has a slight bend to it. Hopefully you've got some kind of parachute cord or other strong rope, shoelace, or string on hand. If you don't, you may have to resort to making your own, which is an extremely slow and laborious process (see "Essential Survival Skills," Chapter 14).

The Fire Bow

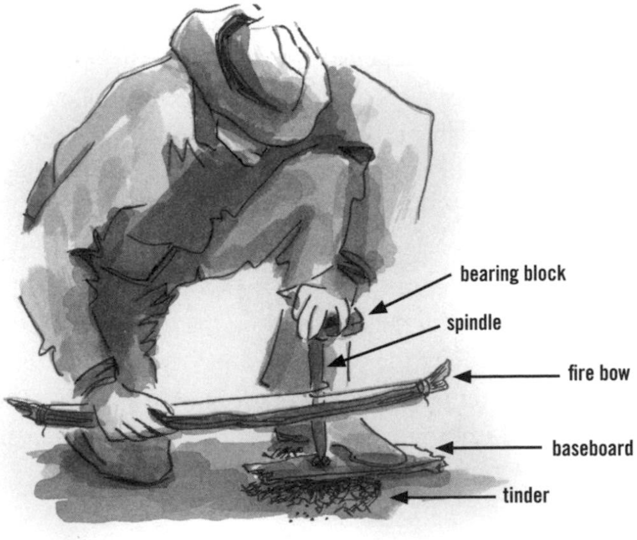

Fire Bow Components

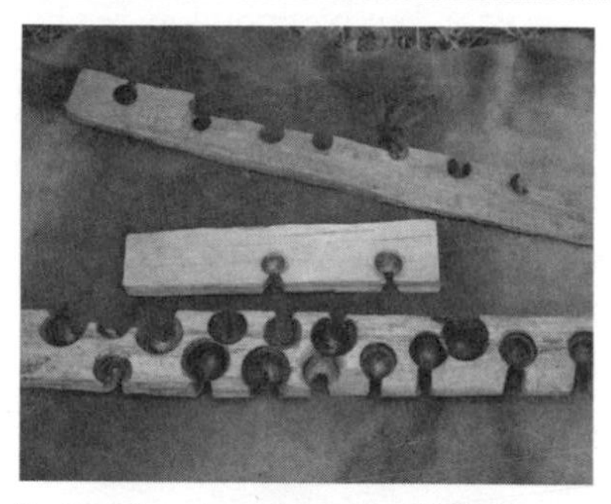

Various baseboards, each of which successfully resulted in fire with the fire bow.

An alternative two-stick method for the baseboard (courtesy of Allan "Bow" Beauchamp): instead of making a notch in the base, simply place the spindle in the groove of the two branches, and the dust will fall through.

A bearing block can be made from almost anything, as long as the material is heavy and allows you to bear down on the spindle.

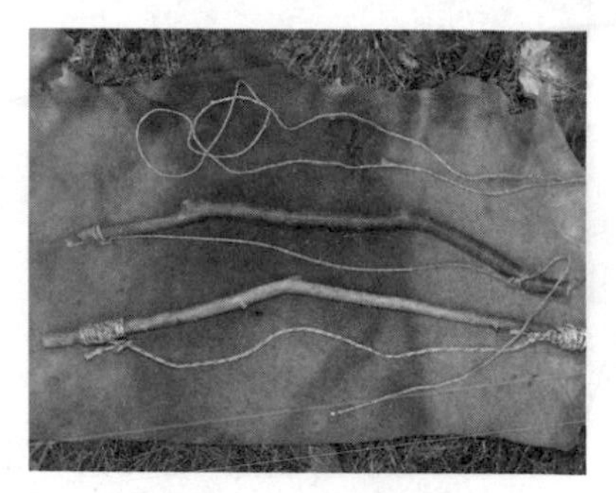

Fire bows, with some handmade cord made from basswood bark.

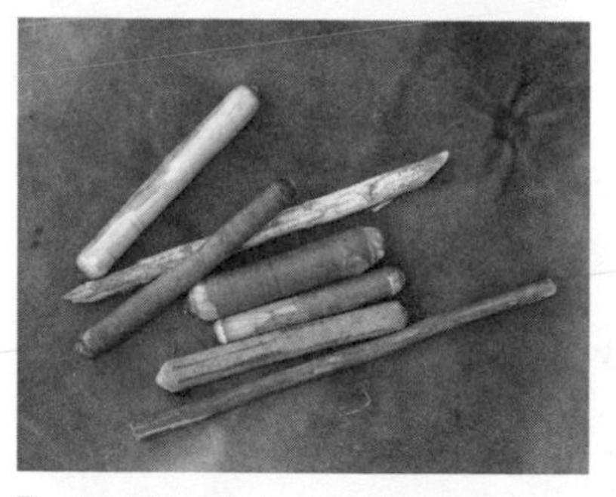

They're different shapes, sizes, and types of wood, but these spindles all worked.

The Process: As with any fire-making method, preparation is the key to success in making a fire bow. Once you have your four components ready, make sure your tinder bundle is as big as possible, at least the size of a five-pin bowling ball. Fibrous materials like scraped cedar bark tend to work best.

Then get comfortable and settle in for what may be a long process: it can take from minutes to hours. You don't want to get halfway through—just to the point where you're getting wisps of smoke—and realize you're kneeling on a rock and can't take the pain any longer. Also, ensure that nothing will inhibit the motion of the bow.

STROUD'S TIP

There are two schools of thought on where to put your tinder pile with the fire bow. One says that you should have a small piece of leaf or bark under the baseboard to catch your ember, which you then transfer to your tinder pile. I feel this just adds an extra step to the process, as well as the risk that you'll drop the ember, or that it will go out, or be blown by the wind.

I prefer to put my tinder directly under the notched-out hole in the baseboard, so that the ember falls right where it's intended to go. Put the finest tinder in the center, just below the notch. Make sure that you pat down the tinder bundle enough that it doesn't sneak up and get caught in the spindle during the spinning process.

Rest the baseboard on the tinder bundle to flatten it out (make sure the ground isn't damp!). Your body should be positioned such that if you drove a steel rod straight down through the top of your shoulder blade, it would go through the back of your hand, through the spindle, and right down to the baseboard.

Place one foot—the one opposite the bowing arm—on the baseboard and start slowly with a fluid back-and-forth motion, applying gentle pressure to the bearing block. Don't forget to breathe! Focus on your breathing and establish an even rhythm.

I find that placing a bare foot on the baseboard gives me a better feel and more control than a pair of boots. By wearing boots you also run the risk of accidentally kicking the baseboard when you decide it's time to transfer your ember to your tinder pile. But comfort is important here, so wear what feels right.

Once you have achieved a slow, fluid motion (it's all about the *feel*), and as you get comfortable with the process, gradually build up your speed, pushing down a little harder on the bearing block. Eventually, you will find that you're spinning as fast and pushing as hard as you can, without the spindle binding or popping out on you.

At this point, three of your senses play a critical role: touch, hearing, and sight. You want to feel a grinding going on between the spindle and the baseboard. You should also be listening carefully to the sound you're producing. You don't want to hear chirping, squawking, or squeaking, which indicate that you're polishing the wood, not grinding it. If that occurs, stop and roughen (or chip) the hole and the end of the spindle to increase the friction between them. If the noise continues, this may mean that you have chosen the wrong type of wood for one of your components.

After this, your sight comes into play. You'll see fine wisps of smoke appearing in the baseboard. This is your cue not to *stop* but rather to keep going using maximum speed and pressure. At some point, the smoke you see will not be from the grinding of the spindle into the baseboard but from the ember that has formed in the clump of wood dust in the baseboard. The curl of smoke you see then will be thicker and whiter than the wisps you first noticed while spinning the spindle.

What if you're not alone? It takes time to establish the rhythm, but doing the fire bow with two people can be more effective that with one person alone. One person assumes the standard solo position and holds the bearing block, with the other in a comfortable position facing his or her partner. Each person holds an end of the bow, pushing or pulling as required. If you can master the rhythm, the two-person method allows you to spin much faster and longer than if you are by yourself.

STROUD'S TIP

Don't let your forehead sweat drip onto the ember you're creating. This can put it out!

The Grand Finale: One of the most common (and significant) mistakes people make with the fire bow is at the end of the process. They'll get the smoke and the ember, then blow it by trying to make the fire as fast as they can because they think the ember is going to burn out. You don't have to jump up like a jackrabbit; the ember is not going to burn out in a matter of seconds. You've put a lot of kinetic energy into that glowing mass, and if you treat it right, it will smolder for a while.

So once you're pretty confident that you have an ember down there, pull away slowly and cautiously, all the while holding the baseboard down with your hands to make sure you don't upset it when you take your foot away. You'll need to transfer the ember to the tinder pile very carefully.

Slide your hands underneath the tinder bundle, and gently close it around the ember, being careful not to suffocate it. (You will likely be shaking from exhaustion at this point, which is normal.) Essentially, you're creating a mini-furnace in the middle of the tinder pile. Blow softly onto the pile until the heat from the ember transfers onto the tinder and catches the tinder itself.

Blow slowly at first. Once you've got a glowing red ping-pong-ball-sized mass inside the tinder pile, you won't likely blow it out, so you can begin blowing more vigorously.

At this point you should be ready to transfer your tinder pile to your fire pit, where you can begin to add stage 2 and 3 tinder, followed by small, dry kindling.

The Fire Bow Method

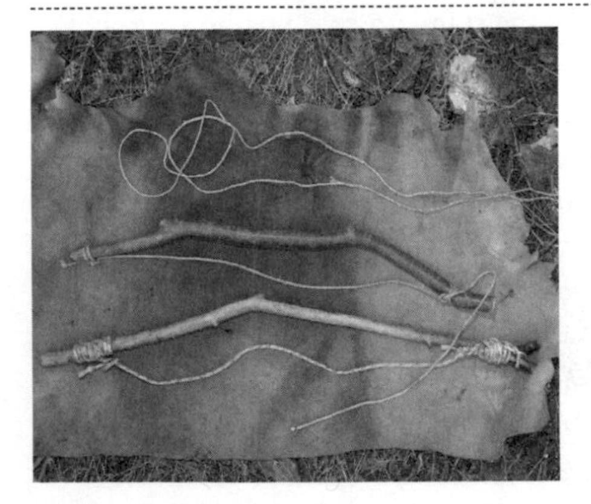

1. Make a fire bow using a piece of wood with a slight bend in it and any piece of cord (shoelace, string, rope, etc.).

2. Next, prepare the baseboard by making a small indentation for the spindle to grind into.

3. Cut the spindle on each end like a pointed crayon.

4. Loop the spindle in the fire bow string. The string should be tense, but not too tight or too loose.

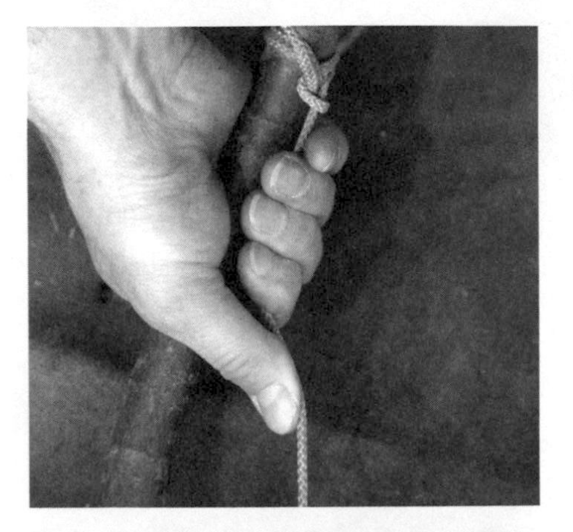

5. Grip the string and bow as shown so that you can adjust the tension. As I push and pull the bow, I like to feel the string with my fingers, which allows me to tighten the pressure on it as needed. Be sure to spin the spindle only enough to make a small indentation.

6. Your body position, the string tension, and the smoothness of your motion are critical to success with the fire bow. You should be able to drive an imaginary straight line down through the shoulder of the arm holding the fire bow, your hand, and the spindle. Get the feel of the motion while "seating" the spindle in the indentation.

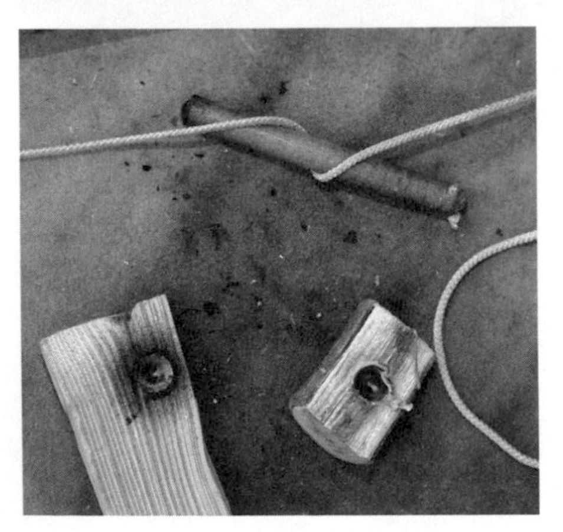

7. Note how the black wood dust that was created by the spinning has spread around the hole, with no place to go to form an ember.

8. Cut a notch into the baseboard, next to the indentation, to give the hot dust a place to fall and catch a spark. Note how the notch nearly reaches the center of the indentation.

9. Put the finest tinder under the indentation, just below the notch. Surround the rest of your baseboard with stage 1 tinder.

10. Return to the action position described in Step 6, and begin to spin again while slowly increasing the downward pressure on the spindle through the bearing block.

11. When smoke begins to form, this is your signal to give it all you've got. Once the actual ember forms, the curl of smoke you see will be thicker and whiter than the wisps you first noticed when spinning the spindle.

12. Lift the baseboard slowly and carefully, and transfer the ember from the notch in the baseboard to the middle of the stage 1 tinder pile.

13. You might find that the ember sticks to the baseboard. The best way to dislodge it is to give the board a couple of light taps or a nudge with a twig, so that the ember breaks away and falls into the tinder bundle.

14. Gently lift the tinder bundle.

15. Blow into the tinder pile from underneath (as if you are praying to the fire gods), so you don't burn your hands. If you're lucky, the tinder will ignite into flame.

16. But remember: it's only a flame! You don't have a full-fledged fire yet. Carefully transfer the flame to your stage 2 tinder.

Other Last-Ditch Fire-Starting Methods

There are a variety of other last-ditch techniques for starting fires. All of these require supplies that you may not normally carry, but as long as you've got sufficient tinder, you can get a roaring blaze going with any of these methods.

Provided you have a lens or some type of highly reflective object, you can use the rays of the sun to make a fire. You can find lenses in binoculars, cameras, telescopic sights, and magnifying glasses, but don't limit yourself. As I mention earlier, I've seen people get fires started by concentrating the rays of the sun off the inside of a teaspoon, or through an ice cube.

Clearly, the success of these methods requires a bright, sunny day and usually intense sun. Your tinder pile is also critical: you'll have no luck igniting a pile of twigs or objects of similar size, so make sure you've got light, dry tinder material. Angle the lens to concentrate the sun's rays on a single spot on the tinder until it begins to smolder.

Another way to get a fire going is with steel wool and batteries. To get a hot, glowing ember quickly, simply run two batteries end to end in series so that the positive end of one is contacting the negative end of the other. You can use any type of battery that has a positive point on one end and a negative point on the other, but D cells work the best.

Stretch out the steel wool so that it contacts each of the battery terminals. Almost instantly, the steel will puff up and ignite. Make sure you have your tinder pile at the ready, because this all happens very quickly!

Finally, there are ways to make fire from various chemical combinations, although you have to be sure that your combination won't produce a noxious gas that will leave you gasping for air—or worse. In the past, I've had great success using potassium permanganate combined with sugar.

To become adept at any of these methods, whether primary or last-ditch, it makes sense to take time to practice them. I acquired these skills over the course of several summers. Each year, I chose a different fire-starting method and that would be the only way I would make fire during my camping trips that season. One summer I allowed myself to use only a flint striker; the next, I used only a piece of rock and steel; and the next, only the fire bow. By practicing this on safe, easy camping trips (I was an outdoors adventure guide for many years) and through repeated efforts, I finely honed these skills.

In Africa I used a small vial of potassium permanganate and glycerin to make a fire. The tinder is rhino dung.

Dried animal dung makes a great fire starter because it has all the characteristics of good tinder.

Believe it or not, dry dung doesn't smell when burned.

Making Fire in the Rain and Snow

Making fire when you're struggling to survive can be difficult enough when the weather is dry. Add a constant rain, and most people just give up. Don't! With a little forethought and diligence, you can get a fire going—and keep it going—even under these conditions.

The first trick is finding dry material in the rain, particularly tinder and kindling. This *is* possible, if you know what to look for and where to look. First, you need to search for materials that are protected by natural shelter. This means looking under overhangs, in animal holes and dens, in caves, and in rotted logs. Holes or crevices are where you have your best chance of finding dry tinder and kindling.

If you're not able to find tinder and kindling, though, you should be able to make it. Here's where having a folding saw and belt knife really comes in handy.

First, look for forearm-thick branches. Cut off a section about a foot (30 cm) long. You might be surprised to find that other than the outer 1/8 inch (3.5 mm) the rest of the wood is dry. Now you need to split it.

You can then take some of those twigs and make fine wood shavings from them. Soon you'll have a pile of a dry tinder and kindling, all of which you've made from one forearm-thick branch in the pouring rain (see next page).

Fire Ingenuity

While surviving beside a downed plane in northern Ontario, I was able to make fire with gasoline from the busted gas tank, two long strips of metal from the frame of the plane, the plane's battery, and some tinder.

I touched each metal strip to a battery terminal, then brought the other ends together to create a spark. At first I was trying to spark the liquid, which didn't work. But when I remembered about the fumes, I put a cloth on top of the cup of gas (which allowed the fumes to concentrate), then sparked the air space above the liquid. Without matches, and with barely 2 ounces (59 ml) of gasoline, a battery, and some metal, I successfully made fire.

Splitting Wood with a Knife

1. Stand the branch on its end and place the blade of your belt knife (or a sharp object such as a stone) on the top center of the log.

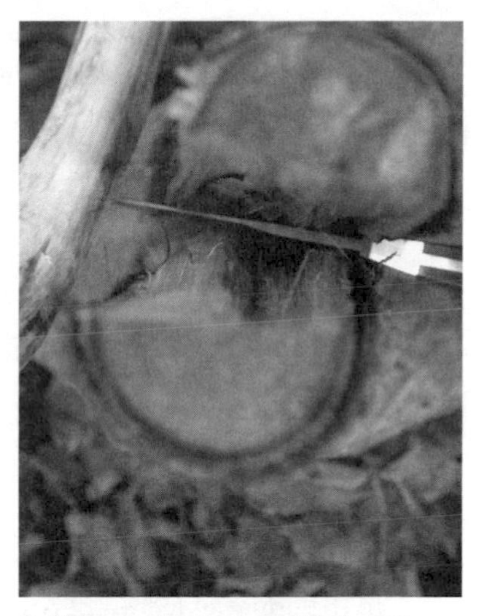

2. Strike the back of your blade with a heavy object, preferably wood or bone, knocking it farther down until the wood eventually splits.

3. Hit the tip of the knife once it becomes embedded in the wood.

4. Using this method, you can continue to split the wood into successively thinner pieces, all of which will be completely dry.

A variation on this method also worked in the middle of the Kalahari Desert. I had no gas this time, but took some local tinder and formed it into a tight bundle, soaked it in oil from the vehicle's oil filter, and placed it on top of the battery, where I again crossed the terminals with a piece of metal for a spark . . . and got fire.

Duct tape holds a flame like a candle and is a great way to get and keep your fire going. Road flares too can be used. And lip balm or petroleum jelly daubed on cotton also takes and holds a flame well.

Region-Specific Fire Considerations

FIRE IS SUBJECT TO THE VAGARIES OF GEOGRAPHICAL LOCATION. What works as fuel in one place may not work at all in another. Here again, local knowledge and expertise help tremendously.

In the Sonoran Desert of Arizona, I used some bits of mesquite wood in one of my fires. I was surprised to find that a small fire there lasted a very long time, much longer than a similar-sized fire would have lasted in the boreal forest. There were a number of variables at play.

Arid Regions, Deserts, and Canyons

Although making and maintaining fire in these regions is compromised by the fact that often there is a significant lack of fuel (particularly wood), the good news is that whatever fuel you can find is usually already dead and very dry, so it burns well. Dried cactuses, for example, are an excellent source of fuel. The irony is that in the desert you usually find the best wood to make the easiest fire during the heat of the day, when the need for fire is almost non-existent.

Boreal and Other Temperate Forests

Perhaps the greatest advantage offered by these regions is the readily available supply of fuel. The trick is to be aware that sooner or later it's going to rain, so gather your material when you have the chance and try to shelter and protect it as best you can.

Low-lying, gnarly pine shrubs and trees are renowned for the incredible amount of sap they build up. These are very flammable and make great stage 2 tinder when shaved down with a belt knife.

The bark of the cedar tree is a good source of tinder. Squirrels, chipmunks, and other rodents will scrape the bark of these trees into a light fluff and use it for their nests. You can create this same type of fluff by scraping cedar bark with the back of your knife blade or a rock.

Tinder fungi grow on birch trees in temperate forests. Tinder fungi are large, black, and lumpy on the outside, orange-brown on the inside. They catch a spark very well and are a great fire-starting material.

The Arctic and Polar Regions

Believe it to not, you *can* get a fire going in these regions, although it's likely not going to be a big one (unless you're on the coast and have ample driftwood on hand, see below). One of the reasons why the Inuit are so accustomed to eating raw food is that they can't build big fires.

But even on the tundra, it's surprising how many twigs and small scrub bushes you can find if you look hard enough.

In addition, mosses in the Arctic burn reasonably well, provided they're sufficiently dry. Inuit have used seal oil lamps for thousands of years, so that's an option as well.

Jungles

Rain is your biggest threat to fire in the jungle, where it can easily fall for 10 or 12 hours a day. The challenge, then, is to shelter your fire.

Even so, any fire you get in the jungle isn't likely to be a roaring one. The general dampness of the area and the restricted availability of dry fuel will limit you to a small fire. But fire will still provide you with a psychological boost, warmth if needed, and the ability to cook your food—and it may help keep the animals away.

Coastal Regions

Driftwood is a godsend in coastal regions, and often there is lots of it. Although some of it will be very dry, don't assume it will all be so. In my experience, at least half of all driftwood is waterlogged and unusable as firewood.

Chapter Seven

The controversy over what is the most pressing initial survival task will continue as long as there are survival stories to be told. After you have calmed down and assessed your situation, your priorities will shift among several needs, depending on the variables involved. Water is crucial—without it you won't live long—but you can survive for quite some time without food. And in some circumstances, I have lasted many days without bothering to make a fire. But if the deck is stacked against you in terms of the elements, *nothing* will kill you quicker than lack of shelter. Remember, however, that searchers have a much more difficult time finding victims who have made a shelter, which is, after all, the perfect camouflage.

You don't need a log cabin to call home in these situations (though it would be nice). Your shelter can be extremely simple. But there's no question that you will need something—*anything*—to shelter you, beginning on your first night. Though the primary purpose of shelter is to protect you from the elements, it offers other advantages. It gives you a place to store and protect your supplies. A shelter also provides psychological comfort when you're facing the possibility of a predator attack. In reality, it would take a matter of seconds for an aggressive 600-hundred-pound bear to tear apart a tent, but there's something about that thin piece of nylon between us and the wilderness that makes us feel safe.

Although shelters are not barriers against wildlife, they can be deterrents. Even a flimsy nylon tent or roof of pine boughs may serve to confuse the animal long enough to buy you time to decide your next move . . . at least that's the hope. In Africa, for example, I used thorn bushes to build a 5-foot-high (1.5 m) thorn corral that effectively deterred curious lions from getting too close. If the lions really had wanted to get me, the corral would not have stopped them, despite the fact that thorns in Africa can grow to be 4 to 6 inches (10 to 15 cm) long!

A survival partner-in-crime with me for many an adventure, Doug Getgood, relates this next story: "During a survival course I was on in Utah, a group of students went to sleep in a substantial brush shelter, big enough to fit a number of people. In the middle of the night, a large black bear crept into the shelter, reached over two students and grabbed the one that was 'just right.' Nobody even awoke until they heard her screams and she was already halfway out the door, with the bear's mouth clamped around her ankle. They eventually scared off the bear, but clearly it had no fear and understood the purpose of the door!"

Humans are creatures of habit, so one of the most comforting qualities we can hope for in a survival situation is familiarity. As soon as you realize you're lost, your entire world becomes unfamiliar, intimidating, and scary. A shelter gives you "home." And the sooner you start undertaking familiar tasks and routines, the sooner you begin to build confidence and overcome your fear. Creating a shelter, big or small, is a significant accomplishment that will boost both your mental and physical well-being. You can also use a shelter as a place in which to plan operations, or as a workshop for making survival aids.

Exactly what type of shelter you should build depends on your surroundings, the time of year, the climate, and the expected length of your ordeal. You're not going to make an A-frame, small-log shelter in the sand dunes of a desert, and you can't build an igloo in the jungle. The ability to make a successful shelter is not about memorizing methods thrown at you in a book. It's about understanding the basic characteristics of a good survival shelter, and then using your abilities to improvise and invent.

One of my first survival teachers, Dave Arama, says, "Most lost persons become lost very late in the day . . . therefore, the ability to improvise and build quickly, and have shelter items in a survival kit, are critical."

The first order of business is to look around at your supplies and what the surroundings provide and decide what you can use, break, cut, make, or put together that will give you shelter. Sometimes you just get lucky. In Africa, I landed on the ground in a hot-air balloon in a mixed forest and plains area. The parachute material from the balloon provided plenty of waterproof roofing for a shelter that I made with the balloon's basket. I was even able to design a hammock from the fabric to keep me off the ground at night, and a blanket to keep me warm.

Take stock of all the man-made materials you have on hand, and don't be squeamish about destroying what you have if you can use it to make something that will keep you alive.

The Importance of Site Selection

THE FIRST DECISION YOU'LL MAKE with regard to a shelter—no matter how long you think you'll need it—is where to put it. Even if you have all the right materials, building your shelter in the wrong place could be a fatal mistake.

The first time I made a survival film, I flew to a beautiful area in Ontario known as Wabakimi. I built my shelter in a spot I figured would work both for filming and survival: close to a smooth rock outcropping on a small remote lake. It worked great . . . for a few nights. Then the wind turned on me and my shelter became a wind tunnel. I spent one entire night pacing on the outcropping and doing push-ups to try to avoid hypothermia. My poor choice of shelter location was the reason I had to endure that horrible night. Well, that and the fact that I hadn't been diligent in ensuring that my shelter was sealed off and had a tight-fitting door!

What do you need to consider in selecting a site? First, choose a spot that is relatively flat and free of loose rocks. And as my buddy and premier desert survival expert David Holladay says, always remember the five W's: widowmakers, water, wigglies, wind, and wood.

I spent one long and miserable night in the "wind tunnel" shelter in the Wabakimi area of northern Ontario.

Widowmakers: Widowmakers are the standing dead trees just waiting to come down in the next big wind storm. It can be dangerous to build your shelter in the midst of widowmakers—though you may not have a choice.

Water: Your shelter needs to be as close as possible to a source of drinking water; the farther you have to travel for water, the more energy and precious calories you burn in doing so. That said, you shouldn't choose an otherwise poor location—for example, the coldest or buggiest spot in the valley—just for the water source. Try to balance the proximity to water with other factors.

And while you want to be close to a source of drinking water, make sure you don't build your shelter where the water will get to you, such as in a dry streambed that may fill the next time it rains, or in any depression that may turn into a puddle. Remember, flash floods kill more people each year than most other natural occurrences.

Wigglies: Build your shelter in a place that keeps you as far as possible from the wigglies: biting, stinging, slithering, and crawling creatures such as snakes, spiders, and ants. In the Amazon, the bullet ant—which the Waorani call the *Maunyi*—grows to be nearly 2 inches (5 cm) long and sports a massive pair of mandibles. Jim Yost, my guide and Waorani interpreter, describes the painful bite/sting combination of the bullet ant this way: "Imagine jamming a scorching-hot pair of pliers into your skin, squeezing and twisting them as hard as possible, and keeping them there for at least five hours." The Waorani fear this more than a snakebite; they know that three to six stings from the

Bullet ants live in colonies of about 60 occupants. They will attack humans if their nests are disturbed.

Maunyi can knock a full-grown man to the ground, if not kill him. So avoid building close to anthills because ants and snakes use these as shelters.

Weather/Wind: Protection from the wind is a critical consideration in site selection, for of all the elements, wind is the most likely to cause hypothermia. It will slice through your temporary home no matter how well-built it is. Build your shelter in a location that is as protected as possible. If you're in hilly terrain, make sure your site is on the leeward (downwind) side of a rise.

Wood: Assuming you are surviving in a part of the world that offers wood, choose a spot that is close to it, both for building and for burning.

Beyond the five *W*s, temperature is an important consideration when selecting a site. If you're in hilly terrain and seeking warmth, it's typically better to pick a spot about three-quarters of the way up a hill. Cold air settles in the valleys at night, and the hilltops are often windy; both will chill you in the middle of the night.

Another place to avoid putting up a shelter (in Africa especially) is under or next to a fruit tree. Fruit attracts insects and animals, and ripe fruit will fall on your shelter interfering with much-needed sleep. Bird droppings will mess up your survival area. Avoid building on or near animal trails because passing creatures might destroy your shelter and possibly hurt you.

Remember that time of year and geographic location will play a large part in determining the ideal location for your shelter. You will want to choose a location that is close to a source of drinking water, and in warm regions or in summer, as free from insects as possible. In cold regions or in

STROUD'S TIP

Don't get hung up on what kind of shelter to build. Anything that keeps you warm, dry, and protected is a good shelter, regardless of the design. Remember, though, that shelters made from forest materials are camouflaged and difficult to see from above—not a good thing when there's a chance that passing planes are looking for you.

the winter, seek a site that offers protection from the cold prevailing winds, is close to wood for fuel, and has direct sun exposure.

Shelter Construction Basics

Step 1: The Bed

When you are ready to build your shelter, don't make the mistake of starting with the frame. You're better off creating your bed and then building your shelter around it. Why? First, with this approach you'll have lots of room to build the bed, rather than constructing in the cramped confines of your shelter. Second, you'll be able to correctly size your bed and, as a result, your shelter. One of the most common mistakes travelers make in building their first shelter is making it too small. More times than I can remember, people I've known have made the bed too small, built a terrific shelter around it, then crawled inside, only to look down and see their feet sticking out the door!

It's also important to create distance between you and the ground, either by elevating your bed or by putting as much material as you can underneath you. *This step is vital!* Aside from the wind, nothing will suck the heat out of your body more quickly than sleeping on the ground.

If you have wood available, you can get yourself off the ground by starting with a layer of logs.

Your next step is to cover those logs with your insulation/bedding layer. This can be made of almost anything, as long as it's somewhat soft and provides loft. Boughs, grass, or leaves work well in many environments. Snow and boughs work well in the winter.

You can use almost any type of material available for your insulation/ bedding, but be careful not to choose a poisonous plant such as poison ivy, or anything that's infested with insects that are likely to feast on you during the night. Be careful even when gathering materials (such as grass), as you could be disturbing a poisonous snake or spider. Poke long grass with a stick *before* reaching in with your bare hands.

Whatever you use for your insulation/bedding layer, you should use much, much more than you think necessary. You might put down 6 inches (15 cm) of spruce boughs or leaves and grass, but once you roll around on them all night, they'll flatten down to almost nothing and you'll be lying on the hard ground again before daylight.

Most people don't change their bedding during a survival ordeal, although changing it may not be a bad idea (provided you've got the materials) if you're stuck somewhere for a very long time. Regularly replacing your bedding gives you a sense of pride in your surroundings, a continued level of comfort, and keeps your mind occupied, satisfying the all-important psychological aspect of survival.

The Cree of northern Quebec have a weaving method for evergreen boughs that renders their floor and bedding soft. They replace it often for freshness.

Step 2: The Shelter Frame

Once your bed is built, it's time to turn your attention to the frame of your shelter. No matter what type of shelter you decide to build, keep in mind these key points:

Don't underestimate the importance of the roof's pitch. A flat roof is very difficult to keep from leaking. The steeper the pitch the better.

- The pitch of the roof should be steep enough to shed rain and snow easily. This is especially important if you don't have a piece of plastic, such as a tarp, as part of your roof.
- The roof should be strong enough that it will hold the weight of whatever insulation materials you're going to use along with any snow that may fall on it. A sign of a great shelter is that it can support your weight (although that's not always necessary).
- Insulation is important as it will keep the heat where it belongs—inside the shelter. After your roof and walls are built, insulate them with anything and everything you can get your hands on, the thicker and fluffier (i.e., the "loftier") the better.
- Pay attention to your body while constructing your shelter. Building is one of the most strenuous tasks in a survival situation, so don't wear yourself out. Stop often to rest, drink water on a regular basis, if your supply allows, and if it's cold outside, pace yourself so that you don't sweat too much.

The boughs of evergreen trees work well as roof insulation, as do plant fluff, grass, leaves, bark, moss, fur, or even snow.

Step 3: Windproofing and Waterproofing

Windproofing and waterproofing a survival shelter is difficult, particularly if you don't have some sort of plastic sheeting. Increasing the pitch of the roof helps substantially, as does using whatever material you have available as shingles.

Shingling a Shelter: There are many ways to shingle a shelter, depending on the materials you have at hand.

To shingle a shelter, start at the bottom and apply each subsequent layer of roofing material (bark works best) by slightly overlapping the previous layer.

Large strips of birch bark can be very useful as roofing.

Always enclose your shelter to make it as windproof as possible.

Fire in Your Shelter

Your shelter's primary purposes are to keep you warm and to increase your sense of well-being, and there is no better way to achieve these goals than to build a fire inside. This isn't possible in all shelters, however, and you'll need to be very careful even where it is possible. But should conditions permit, it's worth the effort to use this technique in a survival situation. An inside fire takes you one step up from feeling like an animal in a hole.

If you're planning to have a fire inside your shelter, you'll have to create the space for it before you do anything else, even before making a bed. Clear an area for your fire pit against a boulder, sand embankment, or a few bowling-ball-sized rocks you've moved together, as any of these will help to reflect heat into the shelter. Create a barrier between the fire and your bed area with rocks (best option), dirt, or wet and punky logs. When building the frame for the shelter, make a smoke hole in the roof, allow for the height of the flames, and ensure that no combustible material is directly above it or close enough to catch fire. Oxygen should be able enter the shelter to get *to* the fire without blowing across your body. Finally, create a space to pile and protect your collected firewood. See "Fire," Chapter 6, for more on building fires within your shelter.

The benefit of a fire in your shelter is that it will keep you warm and comforted at night or when trapped inside due to storms. Although the fire will not be big (a long, narrow fire along a rock face will keep the length of your body warm), it requires serious effort. Shelter fires need to be fed constantly with small pieces of dry wood, so you'll sleep very little. You sleep 20 minutes; the fire dies, you get cold; you wake up and feed the fire . . . and so on until the first rays of sun bring you the relief you have been praying for all night.

STROUD'S TIP

Build your shelter big enough that you fit comfortably in it without feeling claustrophobic, but to maximize your shelter's heat retention, don't make it so large that you have extra air space to keep warm. Also, build your door as small as possible and lower in elevation than your bed (particularly important in the cold).

Heated Ground Shelter

An aggressive and calorie-burning (yet effective) way to keep your shelter warm without a fire inside is to build a fire in the place where your shelter *will be* (on a large, flat rock is perfect). While your *large* fire burns throughout the day, prepare the materials you will need to construct your bed, walls, and roof.

As day turns to night, let your fire die down and cover the hot coals with an inch (2.5 cm) of soil or sand. Construct your shelter and mattress *directly over this spot.* Heat will emanate from the coals throughout the night, keeping you toasty and warm. If you have built your shelter on a large, flat rock, push the hot coals off to the side (they will become the small fire that you keep inside your shelter all night). Then put your forest-debris mattress on the heated rock. I have often done this so efficiently that I can't even crawl into the shelter for two or three hours because my bed is too hot!

Emergency Short-Term and Long-Term Shelters

THERE ARE A FEW BASIC SHELTER TYPES, all of which can be modified and adapted according to location, the materials offered by your surroundings, and whatever you brought with you.

An important distinction must be made between emergency short-term shelters and long-term shelters. Emergency short-term shelters are the ones you need *right now*, usually on your first night or two, to protect you from the elements and from any immediate dangers. These shelters tend to be crude, cramped, uncomfortable to varying degrees, leaky, drafty, and largely unable to stand up to the rigors of human occupation for any length of time. They will, however, keep you alive for a short time, and that's why it's critical to know how to build one.

Once you've spent a night or two in an emergency short-term shelter, it's important to think about a longer-term solution to your predicament. In building a long-term shelter, you'll pay more attention to comfort and practicality. For this reason, building a long-term shelter is generally harder, takes longer, requires more materials, and will use more of your energy. But if you have the other aspects of your survival covered, a long-term shelter will act as a tremendous psychological benefit. You'll be warmer, more comfortable, better protected, and better rested . . . and more likely to survive.

Emergency Short-Term Shelters

Sleeping sitting up against a tree trunk or rock is *miserable*, and during a survival ordeal you must do everything you can to find shelter that will keep you warm and dry, and allow you to get some rest. To succeed at finding and successfully using an emergency short-term shelter, remember that you are, in essence, an animal. So make like an animal and toss aside your aversion to filthy clothes and grimy fingernails.

Children often do much better in these situations than adults, because they have no qualms about getting dirty and, for example, crawling into a rotted log for shelter. As adults, on the other hand, we are burdened by our phobias. *Crawling into that rotted log might protect me from the snow and wind, but it just looks so filthy, slimy, and full of insects.* Insects, by the way, are a fair concern, but that rotted log may be the one thing that will keep you warm and dry that night, and save your life.

The simplest form of emergency short-term shelter is something many of us played with during the autumns of our childhoods: fallen leaves. If you find yourself lost in a deciduous forest in the autumn, it doesn't take too much time or effort to create a big pile of leaves, into which you can slither like a worm. You'd be surprised how much warmth leaves will hold.

Natural hollows in the ground or fallen trees are another form of emergency short-term shelter, and work especially well if you can fill them (and cover yourself!) with leaves. Caves or animal dens also work, but make very sure they are no longer inhabited.

Crawling like an animal into a pile of forest debris (making a "nest") can get you through a night or two.

The Lean-To: A Short-Term/Long-Term Hybrid

Straddling the line between emergency short-term shelter and long-term shelter is the lean-to. This structure requires some constructive effort, making it more effort than a true emergency short-term shelter, but not really suitable as a long-term shelter because it has many drawbacks.

The lean-to offers wind protection from only one side. This may be fine if the wind always comes at you from only one direction. But if the wind changes, the lean-to offers little, if any, protection against the elements, and you will find yourself getting slammed with wind and rain on your bed and your fire. In addition, absolutely no heat is retained in a lean-to.

When weather isn't an issue or scarcity of building materials makes constructing a full shelter challenging, use the lean-to. To build a lean-to, place a cross beam between two trees that are far enough apart to fit your sleeping body. The cross beam should also be high enough to allow you

I wouldn't want to spend a very long time in a lean-to, though it's okay for a night or two. If you're going to the effort of making one, why not make another wall and build yourself a proper A-frame, which is a terrific long-term shelter.

to sit up comfortably. If you can't find two trees a suitable distance apart, you can make do with two Y-shaped branches or tripods. Place these far enough apart to fit your sleeping body, and drive them into the ground. Lay the cross beam between the two Y supports.

Line the cross beam with branches (use as many as you can), which will act as the ribbing for your roof. The steeper the ribbing, the more effectively the roof will shed rain. If you have plastic sheeting, drape the sheeting across the ribbing as a waterproofing layer. Be careful not to puncture the sheeting.

If you don't have a tarp, crisscross a layer of windbreak/roofing materials over the ribbing. Keep adding layers until you feel the shelter will provide the protection you need.

To reinforce your lean-to, you can build a short wall underneath the high end of the structure. Drive two sets of stakes into the ground, far enough apart to hold the logs you will use for the wall.

Stack logs inside these stakes. You can make the wall more airtight by filling the cracks between the logs with dirt, grass, moss, or any other suitable material you can find. Once complete, this kind of wall works well as a fire reflector, particularly if built with green logs, which don't ignite as quickly as older logs.

Lean-tos are not my favorite shelter in any location where wind is an issue—which is almost everywhere. In a place like the Amazon jungle, however, where the near-constant rain comes down in torrents, these shelters can be quite effective, especially if the roof hangs far enough over the front.

Consider the lean-to as your first step toward a more secure A-frame structure. Close in the open side of a lean-to and you have an A-frame that is strong and protected on all sides.

STROUD'S TIP

Lack of sleep is extremely dangerous and will lead to frustration, clouded thinking, clumsiness, depression, and despair. But sleeping during the day in the warmth of the sun reduces your chances of rescue. So ensure that you get as much sleep at night as possible by making a good shelter.

In the Amazon, Kinta, one of my Waorani guides, taught me to use banana leaves to rain-proof my lean-to.

Long-Term Shelters

Making the transition from emergency short-term shelter to long-term shelter is necessary if you realize that rescue is not coming soon. Crawling into a pile of leaves might work for a night or two, but it's not going to keep you alive for three weeks and proves particularly uncomfortable in the rain.

As you consider your long-term shelter, think comfort. Try to build a temporary home that will at least allow you to sit up. Being able to stand in your shelter is a luxury that few wilderness shelters can accommodate, so don't make this your goal. The following shelters can be created in many geographic regions, depending on the natural features and materials available.

Finding a Long-Term Shelter: The ideal long-term shelter is one that you don't have to make at all, saving you an incredible amount of energy . . . and potential grief. If you're on the move, the key is to determine, calmly, whether you should spend the night in the dry cave you just stumbled across or keep moving, in which case you'll have to make a shelter in a few hours anyway.

In fact, in some parts of the world—especially North America—local authorities construct survival cabins in strategic locations throughout the wilderness. These structures not only provide much-needed shelter in emergencies, they are usually stocked with a small supply of survival gear and food.

As part of your trip planning and preparation, you should look into the availability of such shelters and note their locations on your topographical maps. I once came upon such a shelter in the northern Canadian region of Labrador, after a long day of running a dog team and with bad weather closing in. Though the relatively new, 100-square-foot (9-m^2) cabin had no food or supplies, it came with a wood stove and some split wood, turning my concerns about staying dry and comfortable that night into non-issues.

Beyond man-made structures, your next best option is finding a natural shelter that will serve your long-term needs, although these are rare in some areas. The best natural shelter is one that you don't have to build, that is big enough, and that allows you to have a fire inside. One of the few structures that fits these criteria is a cave. In Utah, I found shelter in a small cave that had been used by Butch Cassidy and the "Wild Bunch" during their desperado days.

Because I had consulted with local expert David Holladay before the trip, I knew that the type of rock in this cave didn't "calve off," so it was safe to make a fire inside.

A rock "calf" big enough to crush you.

The danger you'll face in a cave is making a fire inside it. As you can imagine, the rocks that form caves are not used to heat, so a fire may lead to a fracture and cause a piece of rock to break off from the cave roof.

If you're lucky enough to find a large cave, don't get lost while exploring it. Mark the walls or the floor, or even tie a piece of cord to the cave mouth. Bear in mind that caves sometimes have occupants already or may attract other animals seeking shelter while you're there. If you do make a fire, build it near the cave mouth to prevent other animals from entering (then again, some of those animals seeking shelter could be a source of food!).

Complete natural and man-made shelters are rare. Don't expend energy going out of your way to search for one; just consider yourself extremely fortunate if you find one.

When discussing natural winter shelters, many survival manuals mention "tree wells," snowless rings found at the base of coniferous trees and surrounded by walls of snow, which (they say) require no additional construction (not true; they always do). I have spent many winter nights snowshoeing around the forests of North America, and I *rarely* find one of these magical, ready-to-sleep-in, tree-well snow shelters. They are predominant, however, in the mountains of the North American West Coast, but finding one takes a lot of searching and wastes your time and energy. You'll likely have to make a tree-pit shelter, which I discuss later in this chapter.

If you can't find a cave, the next best natural shelter is an overhang.

Making Your Own Long-Term Shelters: The thing to remember about these shelters is that they can be built in many geographic regions, depending on the natural features and materials you have on hand. Your ability to construct a viable long-term shelter, as with so many survival tasks, depends on your adaptability and ingenuity.

The A-Frame: Unlike the lean-to, the A-frame is a long-term shelter that, if properly constructed and maintained, can serve you well for an extended period. A-frames can be made to be strong, to adequately (if not completely) repel the rain, and, when well enough insulated, to keep heat in and wind out. One of the best things about the A-frame is that you can continually improve it by adding more roofing, insulation, and waterproofing materials every time you return to your camp.

To make an A-frame (one-person version), first clear the area (and create a fire pit, if necessary) and make your bed. Then, find a fallen tree that will act as a ridge pole (around 12 feet [3.6 m] long) as well as a standing tree with a thick, sturdy branch about 4 feet (1.2 m) off the ground. Rest one end of the ridge pole against the inner edge of the branch, where it meets the trunk of the tree. If you can't find a tree to lean the ridge pole against, use a boulder, two forked branches, a root bed, or any other similar structure. Now line the pole on either side with a series of branches that will serve as ribbing; these should extend away from the ridge pole at approximately 45 degrees and be spaced a few inches apart. The steeper the ribbing, the more effectively the roof will shed rain.

Try to keep the top end of the ribbing poles no more than an inch or two (2.5 to 5 cm) higher than the ridge pole they are resting against, or you will not be able to cap the peak with shingles. If the ribbing poles are thin or you feel the need, criss-cross another layer of insulating/roofing material over these branches. Then cover the roof with anything and everything that may provide insulation. Get down on your hands and knees like an animal and even scrape up debris from the forest floor to use for insulation.

Don't forget to pile some insulating material at the entrance to your A-frame, which you can pull toward you once you are inside. (Did you remember to build the door lower than the shelter itself, or at least at the low end of the shelter?) You can construct a door by lashing together some sticks and small branches in a grid pattern. A door will provide more insulation if you make two stick grids this way, place a layer of insulation between them, and then lash them together.

Doug Getgood, who spent a winter sleeping in an A-frame, had this to add: "The problem I had when I spent my winter in the debris hut was that I leaned the ridge pole against a tree. When the rains fell, the water would run down the tree, then channel down the ridge pole and drip all over me. I would have much preferred to use two forked sticks, thus eliminating the problem. When I did use the tree, I extended the ridge pole about 6 feet (1.8 m) past the tree. This gave me a working and changing area in the front, and a smaller sleeping area in the back."

The Bent-Pole Frame Shelter: The bent-pole frame shelter is a fantastic solution if you are in an area with a lot of 6-foot (1.8-m) shrubs or underbrush with trunks approximately the thickness of a pool cue. Collect at least 20 of these "poles," then strip them of their branches and leaves.

1. After you've collected at least 20 poles, strip them of their branches and leaves. Jab the branches into the ground while making the general shape of the shelter.

2. Tie off the branches at the top to hold them in place.

3. Then, using whatever materials you have on hand, layer your insulation and windproof materials over top.

The Hanging Shelter: Hanging shelters—hammocks or platform beds—are useful in two ways. First, they get you off the ground, thereby keeping you warm. Second, they put some distance between you and any creepy crawlies, such as scorpions, snakes, spiders, and other biting or stinging critters.

A platform bed, such as this one I built in the Amazon, is a good alternative to a hammock.

The Wiki-Up (or Tipi): A close relative of the tipi so ingeniously used by many North American native groups, the wiki-up comprises three center poles that are tied or fitted together at the top to form the basis of a tripod frame. For additional support, place more poles against the tripod. Cover these poles with any material you can find in the surrounding area. By comparison, a tipi uses the same rough frame, but its walls are covered with whatever man-made materials you have available, whether a tarp, plastic sheeting, parachute materials, or even canvas.

The beauty of both these shelters is that they are very strong, shed the rain well due to their steep wall pitch, let you sit up (sometimes even stand up!), and allow you to have a fire inside because the smoke exits the shelter through the top. Building an air trench to provide oxygen to the fire helps to force the smoke out.

Tarp Shelters: If you have a survival kit, you should have at least two garbage bags, and maybe even a solar, or "space," blanket. Items such as these (or a tarp if you're lucky enough to have one) are invaluable in making shelters because they can be used almost on their own as a tent, provided you also have some kind of rope or cord.

When using a plastic sheet as your only roof material, however, remember that rainwater and other precipitation may collect in pockets. This can cause leaks and even bring your entire shelter down on you!

Any time you incorporate a plastic sheet into the construction of a shelter, be careful not to puncture, rip, or otherwise damage the sheet. Not only will the sheet no longer be waterproof, it will continue to tear once the process has started.

In the desert and other arid environments, a plastic sheet can be used in conjunction with rocky outcroppings or sand mounds to provide much-needed protection from the sun.

Anywhere there are trees, you can stretch your rope between two, then drape the plastic sheeting over them to make a rudimentary A-frame. Use rocks or other heavy objects to hold down the edges of the plastic. Similarly, you can use your plastic sheeting to make a lean-to.

STROUD'S TIP

I advise against digging shelters unless you have no other option. Not only is digging labor-intensive, but (other than in snow) there are very few places you can dig effectively without running into some kind of natural obstacle such as roots or rocks. Even desert sand is extremely hard to dig into.

If, on the other hand, you are lucky enough to find a hole or depression in the ground, by all means use it as the basis of your shelter (assuming it's not in an area that collects water). After clearing out any debris you may find inside, build a roof by adding branches and other deadwood. Cover the roof frame with plastic sheeting (if you have it), leaves, and earth.

I used a solar blanket as part of my shelter's roof during a rainy week in the mountains of British Columbia, Canada. I dug into the sandy ground to create shelter. It was the warmest shelter I've ever made.

Region-Specific Shelter Considerations

The type of shelter you make is going to be largely—if not entirely—dependent on the region in which you find yourself. Your location will determine what materials you have to use, the type of shelter you require, how much protection you need from the elements and animals, and whether you need a fire inside.

I had enough parachute material during my week in Africa to make this hammock and another shelter.

Arid Regions, Deserts, and Canyons

These are environments where you should have the benefit of rock overhangs and caves, usually lots of them. Early American bandits and gunslingers used the cave systems of the West as their hideaways for decades.

Staying out of the rain is not of particular concern in the desert, so shelter becomes less important in that respect. Where shelter plays a vital role, however, is in keeping you out of the sun and the wind. Rocky

STROUD'S TIP

Sleeping in a shelter during a weekend survival course with a group of well-fed friends often doesn't give a fair indication of just how miserable it can be to sleep in a true survival shelter, when all you really want to do is go home. Sleeping in a survival shelter is *always* uncomfortable, usually barely warm enough, often claustrophobic, and always smoky (if you've got a fire going). But don't be discouraged. All the shelter has to do is keep you warm and dry, and allow you to get some sleep.

outcroppings and overhangs afford at least some protection from the elements. Caves offer still more protection. Study local topography and try to identify features that might house a cave.

If you need to build a shelter in the desert, plastic sheeting such as garbage bags, solar blankets, and tarps are vital. You can construct a sun-break by suspending plastic sheeting from a rocky overhang or stretching it between mounds of sand.

No matter what type of shelter you end up using in the desert, your bed should be up off the ground and away from poisonous critters, such as scorpions and spiders, which are attracted to your body's warmth. Also keep footwear off the ground while you sleep, and in the morning before you put them back on, hold them upside down and bang them together to check for scorpions. Scorpions get more people by invading their shoes than any other way.

Boreal and Other Temperate Forests

If you have to make a shelter in a survival situation, this is the place to do it. The abundance of trees not only gives you ample fuel for making fire, it also provides lots of natural materials.

The best suppliers of shelter-building materials in the forest are coniferous trees such as spruces and pines, and rotting birch trees. The boughs of the evergreen trees are terrific wall and roof materials and are particularly good at repelling rain if angled with the butt end of the broken branch toward the sky (they're not quite so good at repelling the wind, however), and can double as insulation/bedding materials.

Large sheets of old bark can provide you with ample roofing material. Bark is often filled with small holes, but these can usually be covered by laying the bark in shingles.

As with any natural material, boughs may not always be where you need them to be. Once, while teaching survival skills to a husband and wife, I was touting the benefits of boughs as shelter materials. It was a perfect teaching opportunity, because we were walking right through a "Christmas tree" forest. Two hundred yards later, however, we had left the spruce forest and entered a deciduous forest, where there wasn't a bough to be seen! Our discussion naturally turned to making an emergency short-term shelter out of leaves.

A couple hundred yards can make all the difference in the world when it comes to survival. When you travel, make a note of the natural materials you see.

You might be lucky enough to come across a tree that's been blown down by the wind, root bed and all. These root beds are walls of earth as large as 10 feet (3 m) in diameter that often stand up perpendicular to the ground and can be used to form the walls of a shelter.

You may also come across a boulder in the forest. If it's large enough, use this as one wall of your shelter, as described above for root beds.

A root bed is also great to use in an emergency short-term situation because it provides a ready-made windbreak and wall.

The added benefit of incorporating a boulder into your shelter's construction is that if you build a fire up against it, it will reflect the heat back at you.

The Arctic and Polar Regions (or anywhere in the snow)

The best shelter to use in the Arctic (in the winter) is the igloo. The problem with igloo building, however, is that it takes skill and practice. Few people can make an igloo on their first try if they haven't been trained. You have to know what kind of snow to look for—it feels like you're cutting into Styrofoam—and understand the process. A few photos in a book will not give you the instruction you need to build one successfully. That's why it's imperative that everybody planning to travel in the Arctic in the winter take a survival course, and one that includes igloo building.

Another option in areas of ample snow is the snow cave. Although most books make the snow cave seem like an easy shelter to build, it's not (at least not the first time). I've been in survival mode in the middle of winter where there was snow all around me, and still I could not find a suitable spot for a snow cave. In the right location, however, a snow cave can provide protection that could save your life in winter conditions.

Related to the snow cave is the *quinzee*. The difference between a quinzee and a snow cave is that a snow cave requires that you find a snowdrift and dig into it. With a quinzee, you take matters into your own hands and make the pile of snow yourself, then dig out a cave. This can work, but I hesitate to call it a survival shelter because a) you have to be in a place where you can maneuver enough snow into a large pile, b) you need a shovel (or at least a snowshoe) for digging, c) building it exhausts you, and d) you get soaking wet while making it.

If you decide to make a quinzee, dig your entry hole on the side away from the wind. And with any snow-cave shelter, make sure you poke a hole in the ceiling for ventilation. Finally, make a small fire inside for a few minutes to glaze the ceiling. The ice-glazed ceiling will reflect your body heat back inside and any moisture will drain down the sides rather than drip on you.

Whether you decide to build a snow cave or quinzee, the effort you exert making one (as well as the snow that accumulates all over your body) will make you wet. So brush off snow constantly and remove layers as necessary to minimize sweating.

Summer in the Arctic changes your perspective greatly, and your first priority will be getting away from the bugs. Choose as windy an area as possible; that's where the bugs *won't* be.

Making a Snow Cave

1. Start by digging a snow trench. A snow trench is the emergency short-term version of the snow cave. As you dig, use the excess snow to make the walls higher.

2. Make a bed on the floor of the trench using available materials and cover the top with branches to make the roof frame.

3. Close the roof off to the weather with a tarp or emergency blanket. If you don't have this type of man-made material on hand, you can also use boughs, bark, or leaves.

Making a Quinzee

1. Find a spot that has a large enough deposit of snow for a quinzee, or the right pitch and angle to allow you to dig a snow cave. This is a task unto itself.

2. Place a few sticks at strategic locations throughout your snow shelter. Then, if you come upon one when you're digging out from the inside of the quinzee, you'll know how far you've come and how thick the wall is.

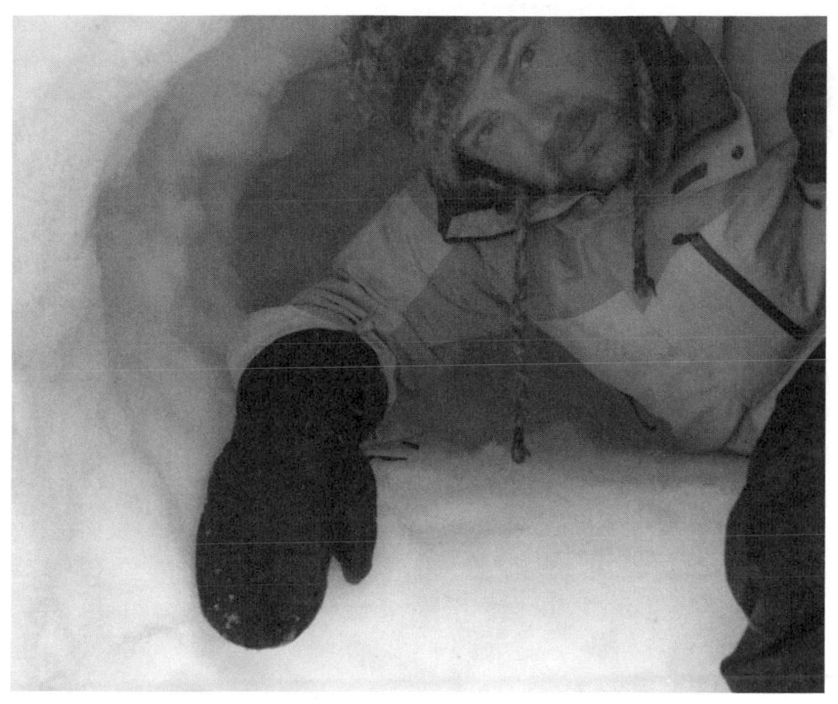

3. Hollow out the snow pile to create a cave. The inside platform must be higher than the entrance so that the cold air flows out and the warm air stays in.

4. Keep a pole inside with you while you dig your cave. It can save your life if the roof collapses. Should this happen, twist the pole slowly until it bores an opening in the snow above you.

STROUD'S TIP

It's important to keep the inside of winter shelters free from snow. Native peoples, particularly the Inuit, are fastidious about shaking off every last fleck of snow before they crawl inside a shelter. You need to be the same way. If you aren't, the snow will melt, leaving you damp and miserable.

Jungles

The best type of shelter in the jungle is a lean-to combined with a hammock or platform bed to keep you protected from the critters that live on the jungle floor.

Wind is not usually a consideration because of the denseness of the vegetation, and a lean-to should allow you to make a fire. Just make sure your bed is well up off the ground! A Waorani friend of mine once woke up to find a snake sleeping curled around his legs. He lay still for the next seven hours until the snake finally moved on, apparently fully rested.

Your jungle survival kit should contain bug netting, which will make all the difference in the quality of your sleep. Drape it over your bed or cover yourself with it to keep most flying and stinging insects from getting to you.

Coastal Regions

Most coastal regions provide ample materials for shelter, as they are usually not too far from temperate forests. Driftwood is another possible shelter-building material found along the coast.

One often-ignored material in these regions that may help you when constructing a shelter is the flotsam (beach junk) that washes up on shore. You may find items such as fishing nets, pieces of plastic, and barrels, all of which you—the adaptive and ingenious survivor—can use to your benefit.

In some coastal areas you may find enough large rocks to construct a rock shelter. Build the shelter in the shape of a U, and cover the roof with any suitable material, including driftwood. Be warned, though: these shelters are labor intensive and difficult to build, especially if you are lacking food and energy.

I built this shelter from flotsam collected from the beach.

Mountains

Mountainous areas are often surrounded by forests, so any of the shelters that use trees or are mentioned in the boreal/temperate forest section apply here as well.

A possibility in coniferous mountain forests where the snow is deep is to dig a tree well, also known as a tree-pit shelter. Locate a tree with low-hanging boughs and dig out the snow around the trunk until you reach your desired depth and diameter, or until you reach the ground. Clear away any dead bottom branches that are in the way (use them for firewood). You can place evergreen boughs or other material in the bottom of the pit for comfort and insulation.

No matter where you build your shelter in the mountains, take into account the risk of avalanche, rockslide, or rockfall.

Swamps

The ground near swamps is generally damp, so your primary concern is to make sure your bed is well off the ground. One option is to make a swamp bed. Find three or four trees clustered together. Use sturdy poles to connect the trees at the same height; this is the frame of your bed. You can either rest the poles against the trees' branches or attach them using rope or cord. Now fill the space within your frame with a series of cross pieces. Cover the top of the bed with any soft insulation/bedding materials you can find.

While a swamp bed can get you out of the water, it can't get you away from alligators.

Chapter Eight

FOOD

Almost everybody who travels, it seems, worries about starving in a survival situation. In reality such concerns are largely overblown: you can survive for a month (or longer) without putting any food in your body. This is hard for some people to wrap their heads around, since most who live in developed nations are comfortably used to eating three or more meals a day. The thought of going days—or even hours—without a substantial meal is a scary proposition. But though it's not necessarily comfortable to go for a stretch without food, it *is* possible.

Your quest for food will be easier if before you leave you research what you can eat, how to catch or pick it, and how to make it edible. There may be food in abundance all around you in the wild, but you have to know it's there, and if necessary, how to prepare it. And there's danger in consuming something without knowing if it's edible.

The first time I saw star fruit was in Costa Rica. As I stared, wondering if they were poisonous, my survival buddy and military survival expert Mike Kiraly was stuffing his face with them. Had it not been for him, I might never have tried them, thereby missing out on an important and abundant food source.

Many early explorers died from scurvy while sleeping on beds of spruce boughs, which when boiled into tea would have provided all the vitamin C they needed.

Manage Your Energy

THE MAIN EFFECT YOU'LL NOTICE FROM LACK OF FOOD is a significant decrease in your energy level. In many survival situations, I'm fine without eating for a week, but I really notice the loss of energy. As my energy fades and I tire quickly, I can work for only an hour or so at a time, and then I have to sit down and rest for 20 or 30 minutes. Then I work a little more, only to have to sit or lie down again. I repeat that pattern throughout the day.

So forget about needing massive quantities of food on which to feast, accept the stomach growling as part of your ordeal, and focus on getting something, anything, into your system that will increase your energy.

Closely manage your activity level so that you require less food than usual. This means sitting down if you don't need to stand, lying down if you don't need to sit, and sleeping if you don't need to be awake. Anything you can do to slow your heart rate and relax will preserve your energy for the things you need to do to stay alive. The major risk you run from lack of energy is that it can lead to listlessness, apathy, and ultimately, depression.

STROUD'S TIP

The more food you eat, the more water your body needs for digestion. So if you are short on water, then eat less food, or you'll speed up the dehydration process. On the other hand, if you're near a large source of fresh drinking water, force yourself to drink every half hour. This not only keeps your system flushed and clean but also makes your stomach feel like something's in there. This is a trick I use all the time while filming survival ordeals.

The Myth of Wild Edibles

PERHAPS NOTHING IS AS OVER-ROMANTICIZED IN THE world of survival as the notion of gathering and eating wild edibles such as plants and mushrooms. Many people envision the wilderness as providing a bounty of plants to feast upon. Don't be fooled; the search for plants to eat can be fraught with danger. These are the some of the challenges you'll encounter.

Identification

Plant identification in various parts of the world is difficult at the best of times, even if you have a book telling you their Latin names and accompanied by photos. The same plant may look different depending on your location or the time of year, and this is not easily gleaned from most guidebooks. Some plants are safe to eat, abundant, and easily identified, but for the most part reading a book is not the way to learn about most wild edibles. You really need an expert on the local vegetation to offer you first-hand education *on location*: you should smell it, touch it, taste it. Then, when the time comes, you'll know it.

Availability

Contrary to popular notion, wild edibles often are not plentiful. There are some regional exceptions, such as coconut trees on tropical islands or prickly pear cacti in the Sonoran Desert. But even with coconuts, once you've eaten what's fallen on the ground and knocked down what you can reach with a stick, you've got to climb 30 to 60 feet (9 to 18 m) up the tree to get at the rest, and that's not easy to do.

The truth is, you might have to walk for miles before you find a single wild edible. When I was in the Amazon, the only significant source of fruit I found was in an overgrown jungle area that had previously been a farm. Otherwise there was nothing but big green leaves everywhere, which my Waorani teachers didn't eat.

Even while spending a year in the wilderness in northern Ontario, my wife, Sue, and I found only one or two places where the blueberries and raspberries grew so thick that we couldn't eat all of them in one sitting.

Season

Most wild edibles, especially fruits, grow only at certain times of the year.

Latitude

The availability of wild edibles is region-specific. As a rule, the farther you are from the equator, the less abundant wild edibles become. So if you're in the Rocky Mountains, the best time to find wild edibles is really limited to spring and berry season. Everything but berries is unpalatable and difficult to digest.

The farther you get from the equator, the more you have to rely on meat or critters for food. That said, it seemed peculiar to me that the Waorani of the Amazon could not teach me about very many wild green edibles. It turned out they believe that because greenery is eaten by the small animals it will make them weak, so they stick primarily to meat, manioc (a potato-like root), and a few fruits.

Personal Sensitivities

You may have a severe allergic reaction to a plant you've never before eaten. Given this risk and the many other variables in identifying and eating wild edibles, your best bet is to know two or three that are plentiful and easily identified for each of the world's regions. These are listed later in this chapter as my Top Three Wild Edibles and Top Three Critters.

The Edibility Test

IF YOU HAVE NO CHOICE BUT TO EAT WILD PLANTS that you cannot identify, you should employ a last-ditch effort called the edibility test, which exposes your body to the plant in slow increments.

Since the edibility test requires a lot of time and effort (and potential risk), make sure there is enough of the plant available to make the test worthwhile. Note that it does not work with all poisonous plants! Here are the steps to follow:

1. Test only a single plant type at a time; don't eat anything else during the test period.
2. Rub the plant on a sensitive part of your body such as your wrist; wait 45 minutes to an hour for signs of any adverse effects like nausea, hives, dizziness, or shortness of breath.
3. If there's no negative effect, take a small part of the plant and prepare it the way you plan on eating it.
4. Before eating, touch a small part of the prepared plant to your outer lip to test for burning, tingling, or itching.
5. If there is no reaction after five minutes, place the plant on your tongue. Hold it there for 15 minutes.

6. If there is no reaction after 15 minutes, chew a very small amount for 15 minutes; observe for any adverse effect. Do not swallow.
7. If you still feel fine after chewing for 15 minutes, swallow it.
8. Wait eight hours. If you begin to notice any adverse effects, induce vomiting and drink as much water as possible. If there are no adverse effects, eat a small handful of the plant.
9. Wait another eight hours. If there are still no negative effects, you are likely safe.

STROUD'S TIP

In almost all parts of the world most grasses are chewable. Don't swallow the grass itself, just chew it and swallow the juice. It's a good way to get some nutrients into your system.

Critters and Creepy Crawlies

THE GOOD NEWS ABOUT CRITTERS is that they are plentiful in many parts of the world. From worms to ants to frogs, there are usually lots of items on the menu. The problem, obviously, is that most of us find the prospect of eating bugs and slugs and snails downright disgusting, a phenomenon known as plate fright. Believe me, after a few days without food, you get over plate fright pretty quickly.

Almost every culture on the planet has either an active or recent history of eating critters as part of its diet, whether it be tarantulas in the Amazon, chocolate ants in India, or grubs in northern Ontario. We're not alone, either: most predators and big-game animals will eat bugs too. If you're at risk of starving, the fact that these creatures are almost universally high in protein and fat may make them more appealing. Don't forget that insect larvae are also edible.

To successfully eat critters, follow a few basic rules:

- Get over plate fright. Remember, your ancestors feasted on slimy, wriggly creatures. Why can't you?

- Recognize these warning signs of potentially poisonous creatures. Avoid those that
  - are very hairy
  - are brightly colored
  - give off a strong odor
  - sting or bite
  - may carry diseases from parasites such as flies, mosquitoes, and ticks
  - move very slowly and out in the open. Poisonous creatures are not afraid because they *know* they are poisonous!

Though generally you should stay away from poisonous creatures, there are some that you can eat, provided you remove their dangerous bits. In the desert, I survived almost exclusively on scorpions. Once I cut away the stinger, they tasted like shrimp. Of course you'll have to consult a local expert beforehand, as attempting to eat something known to be poisonous should *only* be a last resort.

If you lack the knowledge, perform an edibility test on anything you suspect might make you sick.

Gathering and Catching Critters

Many edible creatures, such as frogs and snakes, prefer damp, dark places like rotting logs and rock crevices. Just make sure you don't shove your hand into one of these places without first inspecting it.

If you're close to a body of water such as a lake, you have only to sit by the shore to see how many critters there are. For example, you may see a dozen or more leeches swim by in a matter of minutes; reach down and scoop them out. They do taste better cooked, by the way—kind of like little anchovies.

When I was in the Kalahari Desert, I trapped dozens of scorpions with something akin to a bottle trap. All I did was dig a little hole about an inch (2.5 cm) from the scorpion hole and drop a jar into it. When a scorpion came out of its hole, it would fall into the jar and get stuck.

Cooking and Preparing Critters

The safest way to eat critters is to cook them first, since this kills the parasites carried by many, particularly those with a hard outer shell.

First you should get rid of as much waste as possible. This means eliminating the entrails or squeezing out the waste, provided you know where the critter's anus is. Worms will clean themselves out naturally if you submerge them in water for a few minutes. Grasshoppers can be cleaned by holding on to the head with one hand, the body with the other, and pulling.

All edible critters should be verified by a local expert. Taking a chance on some harmless-looking frog in Costa Rica, for example, could result in death.

This bottle trap will work wherever scorpions are found. It even works with just a hole, if you make the sides steep enough. Scorpions can't climb vertically very well. The trap needs to be placed right at the opening of the small scorpion hole, as shown.

Fish

FISH ARE A FANTASTIC SOURCE OF SURVIVAL FOOD. You can leave your hook in the water 24 hours a day and let it work for you while you rest or do other things. But don't think that catching fish is easy, no matter how remote your location and how abundant they may be. Luck is definitely part of the equation.

When I was in Alaska, I fished from my sea kayak with a long line, a well-made fish hook, and a big chunk of bait. Though the salmon were jumping all around my kayak, nothing would take my bait. During that same time I had a fishnet in the water for 48 hours and saw schools of salmon running by, and still couldn't catch a fish dinner.

Although there are no poisonous freshwater fish, the skin of some saltwater fish is poisonous when eaten raw. Several species of tropical fish are also very poisonous; the only way to identify these is to have consulted a local expert. Without that knowledge, you have to decide if eating a fish is worth the risk. Try the edibility test on fish you suspect of being poisonous.

As with any creature you catch in the wild, try to eat all parts of the fish. The skin (provided it's not poisonous) has lots of nutritional value, so eat that too. Many experts advise against eating fish that appears spoiled (sunken eyes, strong smell, strange color), but I believe that as a last-ditch effort, it's okay to eat. If you become ill after eating what you suspect to be a rotten fish, however, either consume some charcoal (described on page 207) or induce vomiting.

Catching Fish

Of the various fishing methods available, the most common is the hook and line. You need only some type of basic cord or rope, the thinner and more transparent the better (and, of course, some kind of hook). If you don't have any thin line, you can unravel a piece of clothing, such as a sweater, or unwind a piece of cord or rope to use the component threads.

To greatly improve your chances with hook and line, use bait. If your food supply is limited, using it for bait is a trade-off: you may have to sacrifice some of what you have for the prospect of acquiring something larger. Insects, raw meat, and worms are all good bait. In all cases, fish are much more likely to take bait that is native to their waters.

If you don't have bait, you can try your hand at making lures. An effective lure can be anything that moves and therefore catches the fish's attention: a piece of credit card, the zipper off your pants, a piece of thread, a coin, or a key. Obviously, the more hooks you have in the water, the greater your chances of catching something. If you're near a moving body of water, consider stringing a line across (tying it to a couple of trees or rocks) and attaching to it several other lines and baited hooks.

More elaborate than hook and line are fish traps. These take time to build, but can also reap greater rewards under the right circumstances. The most common type of fish trap is essentially a stick fence that helps to corral the fish or move them in the direction you want them to go.

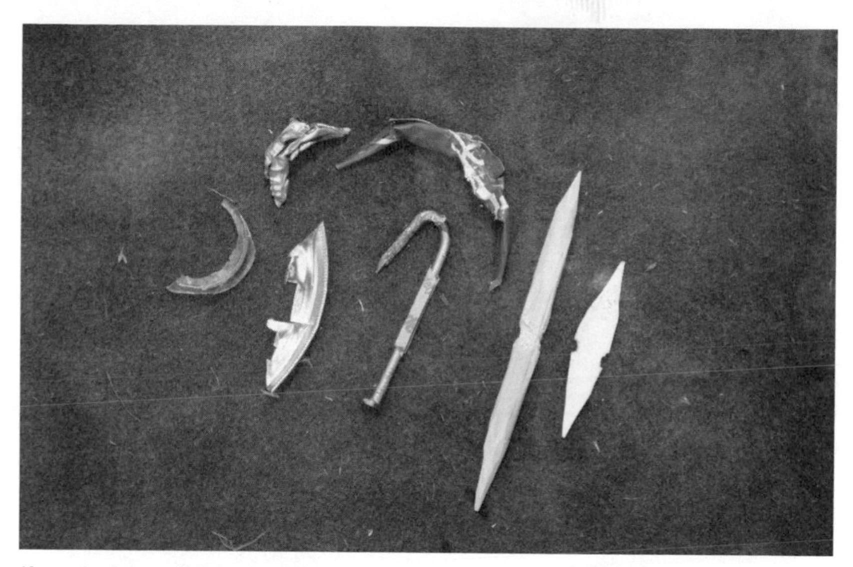

If you don't have fish hooks with you, they're easy to make from bones and thorns; metal objects such as safety pins and nails work well too. Ironically, fish bones are great to make into fish hooks because they are easily carved.

To make a simple fish trap, tie a series of sticks together with rope or cord (you want the water to flow through, not the fish). You can make one or more sections, depending on your needs. Push the sections into the soil bottom of the waterway. Ideally, the fish will be channeled into an area where you can then spear or net them.

In coastal regions, you can use the tide to help you trap fish. Build a circle of rocks on an area of beach that is covered by water only at high tide. The tide brings small fish in with it. As the tide recedes, fish may get caught in the trap.

Although fish trapping is possible, I have yet to be in a survival situation where I've had the time or energy to do it. Fish-trapping methods are closer to being traditional living skills than survival skills. They are not as easy as they look, take a long time to accomplish, require a lot of energy, and you must have all the necessary supplies (or be able to adapt what you do have). You also have to be in the ideal place to attempt these methods during the right season. There are a lot of ifs in this scenario!

Ranking pretty high in the realm of romanticizing wilderness survival is the idea of drugging fish. Though it is possible to introduce concoctions

Fishing Techniques

Build walls in narrow channels to trap fish in one area. Then, you can spear them (but beware—it's not easy!).

Build a rustic "fishing pole" that has several lines instead of just one. This way, you increase your chances of catching a fish.

Use sticks and logs to create a fish trap. Once you corral the fish, they are easier to catch.

of certain plants to water sources to stun or kill fish, this is an exercise better left to experts in plant identification. Even if you have a local teach you which plants to use, your chances of catching fish this way are slim.

And although Tom Hanks made it look easy in *Cast Away*, there is nothing easy about spearing fish. If by some lucky coincidence you find yourself in an area where many fish congregate in a small pool, however, consider making a barbed fishing spear. Take a long piece of wood, no more than an inch or two (2.5 to 5 cm) in diameter. To be effective, you first have to whittle the tip to a very sharp point. Carve a few barbs (curved upward) into the top of the stick to prevent a fish from sliding off after you spear it.

The barbed fishing spear is made from a long piece of wood, no more than an inch or two (2.5 to 5 cm) in diameter. For the spear to be effective, you first have to whittle each tip to a sharp point.

Carving a few upward-curving barbs into the top of your spear will prevent the fish from sliding off after you spear it.

If you have a net or can make one, you can either set it in or drag it through the water to catch fish and other creatures such as freshwater shrimp. Another effective fishing method with a net—particularly in smaller bodies of water such as streams and creeks—is to build a border around the perimeter of the net, usually with sticks. Attach a series of ropes or cords around the edge of the net, all of which come together at a central point about a foot or two (30 to 60 cm) above the net. Attach another (lead) rope to these and drape it over a nearby branch. Hold the far end of the lead rope in your hands. Dangle the flat net in the water. When fish swim over the center portion, quickly raise the net.

Finally, fish are attracted to light at night. If you have a light source, try pointing it at the water while using your primary fishing method.

Waorani women are masters of net fishing, as seen here in the feeder streams of the Amazon.

Torch fishing in the South Pacific increased my chances of catching fish, because fish are often attracted to bright light. It also allowed me to see sleeping fish. The task was not without danger, however. Accidentally stepping on a stonefish could have proved fatal.

Game

THE NOTION OF CATCHING GAME IN A SURVIVAL SITUATION is an attractive one, mostly because you can end up eating something substantial that tastes like the meat many of us eat on a daily basis. The reality, however, is that catching game is difficult, especially if you're talking about anything larger than a rabbit.

Without a gun, ammunition, and hunting experience, the idea that you might kill big game is wishful thinking at best. So what does that leave us with? Small game.

Trapping and Snaring Small Game

Once you accept the reality that nabbing big game is an exercise limited to only a handful of survival situations, the world of small game opens before you. The advantage of trapping and snaring small game is the same as that of fishing: you can set a series of traps that work while you don't. Done properly—and in the right location—these simple devices can add enough sustenance to your diet to keep you going for a while.

In addition to (hopefully) providing you with food, the other benefit of creating traps and snares is that it is proactive and enables you to feel like you're doing something to better your situation. When you build these tools, you're concentrating for hours on a specific survival task. This helps to occupy your mind—and to defeat boredom, apathy, and depression—thus helping to keep you alive.

Another benefit of traps and snares is that they're effective anywhere in the world. A figure-four deadfall, for instance, will work just as well in the African savannah as in the northern boreal forest.

There's strength in numbers when it comes to traps. The more you set, the more luck you'll have. If you can set 45 rabbit snares, do it. You'll have to invest more energy at the front end, but you're also setting yourself up for greater rewards at the back end.

Although many people tout the benefits of complex traps and snares, my philosophy is to follow the KISS method: Keep It Simple, Stupid! The elaborate ones require tremendous effort and expertise and often don't yield any more than the basic ones.

You'll increase your chances of success if you use bait in your traps and snares. Begin by scattering some of it around your trap. This will encourage the animal to develop a taste for the bait. When the outer supply is exhausted, the animal likely will venture into the trap, its desire for more of the bait overcoming its natural sense of caution. Keep in mind that most types of traps and snares do not always kill the animal, and a trapped animal that's still alive (and probably injured), no matter how small, can be a formidable opponent, clawing, biting, and scratching. In these cases, you must hit the animal on the head with a club or some other heavy object to kill it. It won't be pretty. Survival never is.

If you are lucky enough to snare or trap an animal, remember that you're not looking for a few choice pieces, the way you might when you shop at the butcher. In a survival situation, you eat *everything* on the animal, with the exception of the bowels and excrement, and (of course) any known poisonous bits.

Snares

A basic snare is a simple device: a looped cord or rope that tightens around an animal as it walks through. Getting a snare to work exactly as designed often requires a bit of fine-tuning, though. The loop must be big enough for the animal's head, not so big that the animal walks through unscathed, and at the right height off the ground for the animal's head.

A variation on the simple snare is the drag noose. Place forked sticks on either side of the animal trail and lay a crosspiece from one to the other across the trail (well above the height of the animal's head). Dangle the noose from the crosspiece. If the animal becomes ensnared in the noose, the crosspiece becomes dislodged and caught in surrounding vegetation. The animal tires quickly as it struggles to get free.

Where to Set Snares and Traps

Never set traps and snares too far from your shelter. You don't want to have to travel a great distance to reach them, for two reasons. First, you waste energy going back and forth to check the traps. More important, if the distance is prohibitive, you may not travel to the location every day. And if you are lucky enough to trap something but wait too long to retrieve it, you may find that some other animal has come along and eaten your catch.

Always position any trap or snare in a location where there is evidence of animal activity: runs and trails, tracks, droppings, chewed or rubbed vegetation. Try to disturb the area as little as possible when setting the trap, otherwise you will tip animals off as to your presence.

The best areas to set traps and snares for small game are where different types of forest meet, such as where an old-growth forest turns into a swamp. The big animals come there for the small animals, which are there for the smaller animals, and they are all there for a drink.

A simple snare is nothing more than a noose positioned along an animal's path and attached to a stake. The idea is that the noose tightens around the animal's throat as it passes through the snare. As the animal struggles to get out, the noose tightens.

STROUD'S TIP

A simple noose is all you need to make an effective snare. To make one, tie a small loop at the end of the rope. Pass the working end of the rope through the loop to form the noose.

Rabbit snare: Use a rope or cord to make a noose; drape it loosely over some foliage growing close to the ground. Attach the lead rope of the snare to a bowed branch overhead, then continue the lead rope to a trigger mechanism that will release at the slightest movement. If you're lucky, the rabbit will walk through the noose but catch the rope with a leg or paw. This releases the trigger, sending the bowed branch skyward and catching the rabbit in the noose.

The catch mechanism is a critical part of the rabbit snare. It must be tight enough that it doesn't release accidentally but sensitive enough to release when the rabbit passes through it.

The cord shown here is attached to a bowed branch. The branch needs to be strong enough to support the weight of a rabbit.

Squirrel snare: Since squirrels are relatively plentiful in many parts of the world, squirrel snares can be a huge boost to your survival efforts. A squirrel snare is a long pole or branch that you lean against a tree at approximately a 45-degree angle.

The idea behind the squirrel snare is that the squirrel will use the pole to climb the tree. Should it feel the noose on its neck, it will try to leap to safety and hang itself.

To build a squirrel snare, loosely wrap three or four wire nooses (a few inches in diameter) on the top and sides of the pole. You want the squirrel to pass through at least one of them when going up or down the pole. Placing bait between the snares is effective.

Traps

Even without snare wire or some kind of string or rope, you can catch game by building traps. These run the gamut from very simple and basic to extremely intricate and may include the use of rope. As with so many things in survival, the simpler the better . . . and often the more successful.

Figure-four deadfall: A figure-four deadfall works by crushing its prey. To be effective, the weight must be heavy enough to kill, or at least immobilize your intended prey.

To make the trap, gather three sticks of approximately the same size—anything from a few inches to a couple of feet (7.5 to 60 cm) if you are going after big game—and notch them as shown in the picture.

Note that making an effective figure-four deadfall takes practice; the skill with which you cut the angles in the sticks will determine how effectively it releases.

Figure-four deadfall sticks (top to bottom): the upright stick, the release stick, and the bait stick.

Bait is set on the bait stick first. The sticks are then placed together in the shape of the number four, with the weight leaning against the (release) top stick. When the animal begins to nibble on the bait, the trap releases, crushing the animal.

Doug's deadfall: This is similar to the figure-four deadfall. To build this trap you need three sticks of varying length (two short ones and one longer one) and a heavy crushing object such as a flat stone.

Doug's deadfall uses components similar to those of the figure-four deadfall: two upright sticks and a bait stick.

For Doug's deadfall, bait is placed on the end of the longer stick. When an animal disturbs the upright sticks, the rock or trap should fall, crushing the prey beneath.

Paiute deadfall: Similar to the figure-four deadfall (but easier to set), the Paiute deadfall incorporates a piece of rope into its design. You need three long sticks of approximately equal length, and one short stick. See photo captions on the next page for detailed instructions.

Bottle trap: Similar to the scorpion trap I used in the Kalahari, a bottle trap is effective in catching small rodents such as mice and voles.

Dig a hole about a foot (30 cm) deep, making sure it's wider at the bottom than the top and that the hole in the top is as small as possible, but big enough to fit your prey. Place a long piece of bark or wood an inch or two (2.5 to 5 cm) off the ground and over the hole; you can use rocks or bark to elevate the wood.

Small rodents will seek shelter from danger under your bark or wood and fall into the hole. They will not be able to climb out because of the angle of the walls. Use caution when checking this trap, however: snakes like holes too!

Making a Paiute Deadfall

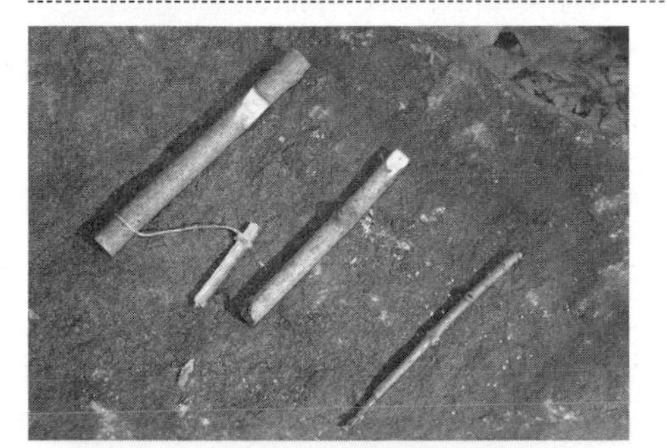

1. Gather and whittle Paiute deadfall sticks: (from top to bottom) the diagonal stick, the catch stick, the upright stick, and the bait stick.

2. To set up a Paiute deadfall, bait the stick, then set up the trap as shown. The diagonal stick holds the weight of the rock.

3. Here is the Paiute deadfall from another angle. If an animal disturbs the bait stick, the catch stick will release. The diagonal stick will fly up, the rock will fall, and dinner will be served.

Birds

ALL SPECIES OF BIRDS ARE EDIBLE, but I do not consider them an important part of my small-game diet, for two reasons: birds are very difficult to catch, and bird traps tend to be complex and hard to build.

If you hope to have any chance of catching birds, you must make tracking them a significant part of your trip preparation and planning, *and* have extremely good luck. When I was in the Cook Islands, for example, I happened to be there during the one or two weeks when Brown Booby hatchlings were trying to take flight. They were practically falling out of their nests right at my feet! Had I been there a couple of weeks earlier or later, however, I would not have seen them.

Believe it or not, the easiest birds to catch are songbirds, because you might find several dozen of them together in a tree or bush. The throwing stick (see page 203) is the best primitive hunting tool for nabbing songbirds.

If you have a net (or can make one), one method of hunting birds is to string a net between trees near their nests. Birds tend to use the same flyways, and you may snare one this way. If you find some nests, bird eggs are also a good food source.

Tracks and Other Signs of Animal Activity

IS IT NECESSARY TO KNOW THE DIFFERENCE between squirrel and mouse tracks? No. You couldn't care less whether the animal you're after is a shrew or a vole or a pika; all you want to do is eat it. All you need to know about tracks is *where* they are, which indicates where the animals are, and consequently, where you should set your traps and snares.

In addition to watching for tracks, you can determine where animals spend their time by keeping an eye out for trails or runs, droppings, nests or burrows, holes, and scratchings.

Hunting

UNLESS YOU'RE AN EXPERIENCED HUNTER and have a weapon with you, you won't have much success hunting for your food. I have yet to meet someone who can run down and catch a deer with their bare hands. In North America more than half of all people who get lost in the wilderness *are* hunters. But remember that hunting is labor-intensive, and as your energy level dwindles, so will your ability to hunt effectively.

Making Hunting Tools

The best hunting tools, like the best traps and snares, are the ones you can create simply and easily. For this reason you won't find me explaining how to make bows and arrows. Not only are they extremely difficult to make but learning how to use them effectively takes practice. A person can't, without years of experience, take a bent branch, attach a rope to it, and bring down a deer.

The simplest yet most versatile hunting tool in a survival situation is the throwing stick. A throwing stick is a wrist-thick piece of hardwood in a

A throwing stick is used intuitively: you throw it at an animal or bird in the hope of dazing or killing it. In essence, the throwing stick is opportunistic hunting. You should always have one with you, so that if you spook a bird or small animal while walking, you have the stick ready.

curved J shape that looks like a miniature hockey stick, about 1.5 to 2.5 feet (0.5 to .75 m) in length. Some people sharpen one end of the stick, though that's not necessary. The throwing stick can be used for protection from wild animals and can also double as a digging stick.

A throwing stick does you little good, however, if it's not at hand when you need it. In the African plains, I was hiking with my throwing stick strapped to my backpack. A few minutes into the walk, I stirred up some ground birds about 5 feet (1.5) away from me. Of course, I missed the chance to kill them because by the time I got my throwing stick out, they were gone. That's a mistake I won't make again.

You *do not* want to travel long distances with the throwing stick looking for game; this requires too much energy and the stick is not accurate. Use it only when an opportunity presents itself.

Skinning and Dressing

If you are concerned about predators, make sure you clean game some distance from your camp, preferably near a water source. To skin large game, lay the animal on its back and split the hide from throat to tail, avoiding the sex organs. Turn your knife blade up to ensure that you cut only the hide and stomach muscles, not the internal organs, as cutting internal organs such as the stomach or kidneys can sometimes introduce foul-tasting liquids, effectively spoiling your catch.

Smaller game is easier to skin. Cut the hide along the bottom or back legs and across the anus. Insert your fingers under the hide on both sides of the cut and pull it apart, using the knife to cut away places where the skin is holding on. The skin should slide back quite easily.

Carefully cut through the stomach muscles. The exposed internal organs can now be cut or pulled out; they are attached only at the throat and anus. Don't throw them away, though: most are edible. At the very least, they can be used for bait. You can eat the lungs, heart, kidneys, and liver (but be wary of liver that appears discolored or diseased). Avoid stomach and intestines, and although the stomach contents may be edible (such as crawfish inside fish) they should be considered a last-ditch food source.

Cooking

As far as I'm concerned, there is only one way to cook food in a survival situation: boil it. Boiling food is most effective because many of the nutrients remain in the cooking liquid, and there is also something comforting about drinking warm broth.

It's true that boiled food can taste pretty bland, but I'd rather put up with bland flavor in an emergency than eat something that was grilled or cooked on an open fire, with many of the nutrients and fat dripped away.

If you don't have the option of boiling because you lack a pot, then you must use an alternative method. Spit cooking can be accomplished by skewering your meal on a green sapling and suspending it over a small fire. The hot coals of a fire work best here; high flames will only singe your meal without cooking the inside. Turn the spit regularly to cook the meat through.

Another effective method is rock frying. Heat a couple of flat rocks in your fire, then place your food directly on the rocks to fry it.

Preserving Food

If you are fortunate enough to have more food than you can eat at any given time, the greatest tragedy is to see it go bad. For this reason, it's important to know the various methods of preserving food in the wild.

First, cut away all the fat. Fat can be rendered on its own and used as a food source, as bait, as grease in a *qulliq* (candle), as waterproofing, and more.

If weather allows, the easiest technique is to hang your food to dry. Find a sunny, windy place, and set up a few sticks and logs to create hanging racks. Cut the meat into thin strips and hang it over the racks. After a couple of days it will be dry. You may find the meat turns black and crusty, and this is not necessarily a bad thing. In fact, it prevents flies from laying their eggs in the meat and becoming maggots. (But if they do, keep the maggots—they're edible too!)

A better way to dry meat is to smoke it. Hang thinly sliced meat from your racks, but also build a small, smoky (punky wood works best)

When meat has been properly smoked, it will look dry, shrunken, and brittle. It doesn't need to be cooked to be eaten. Here the meat is drying in the sun while the smoke keeps the flies away.

fire underneath. Smoking not only gives the meat great flavor, it prevents the flies from getting at it. If you have cloth among your supplies, you can wrap some of it around the racks to make an enclosure, which speeds up the process by keeping the smoke and heat in. For generations, Native North Americans have used tipis as smokehouses.

Finally, you can preserve meat by soaking it in salt water. Salt water must cover the meat *completely*. If you happen to have lots of salt, you can layer the meat, covering each layer in salt. In both cases, be sure to wash the salt off the meat before cooking it.

Eating Carrion

CARRION—THE CARCASS OF A DEAD ANIMAL—is something many of us would never consider eating. Until we're trying to stay alive in the wild, that is.

Most readers of this book live in a society where the only interaction they have with rotten food is when they throw it in the garbage. And in an age when food has spent time on a truck, train, or ship, has traveled between continents, and has been handled by dozens of people before it hits the grocery store shelves, that's probably smart.

But in the wild, it's amazing what kinds of rotten (or seemingly rotten) foods our stomachs can handle. That's why I ate a rotting fish when I was in Alaska. Even though it had been out in the sun all day, I figured it wouldn't hurt me, and I was right. Most cultures in the not-too-distant past included raw or rotting meat as a staple of their diet. For example, the Montagnais of northern Quebec fill the stomach of a woodland caribou with its internal organs and let it hang in the heat of summer in a tree for a couple of weeks. Then, when it has turned into what can graciously be described as stinky mush, they eat it as a delicacy.

If you resort to eating carrion, you should cook it whenever possible. But if I were presented with the choice between uncooked carrion and starvation, I'd eat the carrion.

Eating Charcoal

IF YOU FIND YOUR STOMACH BECOMING UPSET because of your new diet, eating charcoal (pieces of burnt wood from your fire) may help cure what ails you. Charcoal will absorb many drugs and toxins from the gastrointestinal tract.

African survival expert Douw Kruger uses charcoal extensively for stomach problems. He grinds charcoal into a teaspoonful of fine powder, mixes it with water, and consumes this a few times a day as necessary. Don't take too much, though, as it can cause constipation. And don't ever eat charcoal made from poisonous wood.

Region-Specific Food Considerations

THE KEY TO SUCCESS IN GATHERING AND CATCHING FOOD in a wilderness environment is knowing a few plants and creatures native to each region. The wild plants and creatures listed below are safe to eat, easy to identify, and found in relative abundance.

Arid Regions, Deserts, and Canyons

Top Three Wild Edibles:

- pads of the prickly pear cactus
- fruit of the prickly pear cactus
- mesquite beans

Top Three Critters:

- mice and rats
- grasshoppers and scorpions
- rattlesnakes: Be sure to cut off and bury the head and its potentially lethal fangs.

Boreal and Other Temperate Forests

Top Three Wild Edibles:

- cattails
- berries (in season)
- wild teas (from needles, leaves, and fruit): spruce, blueberry, blackberry, raspberry, Labrador

Top Three Critters:

- creepy crawlies (earthworms, grubs, grasshoppers)
- rodents (including squirrels)
- rabbits

The Arctic and Polar Regions

Top Three Wild Edibles:

- caribou lichen (reindeer moss)
- berries (in season)
- willow shoots

Top Three Critters:

- rodents
- bird eggs (in season): The Arctic is one of the few places where you can find entire colonies of bird eggs.
- fish: Fishing in a place like the boreal forest is an uncertain undertaking. You could walk through miles of thick bush without finding a lake. In the Arctic in the summer, however, there are all kinds of running streams. (There aren't always fish in them, but checking streams is worth a shot.)

On the Sea or Open Water

Top Three Wild Edibles:

- bull kelp
- seaweed
- any other type of greenery

Top Three Critters:

- barnacles and other crustaceans that attach themselves to the bottom of your vessel
- small fish that follow in the shade of your vessel
- plankton: You can catch plankton by trailing an open sock behind your vessel. The plankton collect in the sock, giving you a teaspoonful of salty mush.

(Of course, you should also try your hand at catching big fish from your vessel, but this isn't easy to do. Some have sustained themselves by killing birds that occasionally landed on their vessels.)

Jungles

Top Three Wild Edibles:

- fruit
- palm nuts
- palm hearts

Top Three Critters:

- fish from feeder streams (small, shallow, muddy little runoffs from rainfall): If you have a net, you can often scoop small fish and crustaceans from these streams.
- fish from rivers
- insects and grubs (as long as you can distinguish the benign ones from the poisonous ones)

Coastal Regions

Top Three Wild Edibles:

- bull kelp
- bladderwrack seaweed
- sea lettuce

Top Three Critters:

- creepy crawlies (earthworms, grubs, grasshoppers)
- rodents (including squirrels)
- rabbits

Mountains

Top Three Wild Edibles:

- berries (in season)
- wild teas
- mushrooms (only if an experienced mushroom hunter has taught you which ones are safe)

Top Three Critters:

- rodents (including squirrels)
- rabbits
- creepy crawlies (earthworms, grubs, grasshoppers)

Swamps

Top Three Wild Edibles:

- cattails
- pond lily tubers
- wild teas

Top Three Critters:

- frogs and leeches
- snakes and turtles
- rodents

Africa

Top Three Wild Edibles:

- wild cucumbers
- wild melons
- gemsbuck (marama) bean roots and bulbs

Top Three Critters:

- snakes, lizards, and tortoises
- ground birds and sociable weaver birds (found in big nests in trees)
- rodents and mongoose

Group Versus Solo Survival

Being part of a group that's struggling for survival can be both a blessing and a curse when food is an issue. There is the obvious advantage of having more people to collect food and identify food sources. But when it comes to rationing food, you may find that the other members of your group have vastly different opinions about the proper proportions.

Another benefit of being in a group is that you may find it easier to eat things you might otherwise consider disgusting. If you're hungry and see your buddy eating maggots, for example, you just might do it too.

And with more people in your group, there's a greater chance that at least one of them is a proficient hunter or angler, which could radically change the food landscape for everyone.

On the downside, there can be endless discussions about favorite foods and what you miss the most (as you feast on a slug or two). These conversations can lead to a couple of hours of euphoria but are inevitably followed by depression as the reality of your situation becomes clearer.

Chapter Nine

SURVIVAL TRAVEL AND NAVIGATION

When you're struggling to survive, most of your decisions revolve around prioritizing your immediate needs: should you search for water, food, or shelter? Should you make a signal or a fire? All are vital to your well-being; the only decision to make is which one should come *first*, and the answer usually becomes obvious when you take into account your circumstances, the region, and the weather in which you find yourself. But perhaps the single most important (and difficult) decision you will face in the wilderness is whether you should move or stay put.

There may be instances, for example, in which you have to move at least a short distance to escape an immediate hazard, such as a rockfall or an avalanche. Barring that, however, the choice to stay or go is never an easy one. There are pros and cons to each.

Should You Stay or Should You Go?

Many people—particularly those who have attended survival classes—have had it drummed into their heads by their instructors that they should stay put no matter what the circumstances. Unfortunately, this is not always the best advice.

You may find yourself in a spot that offers you ample food and water, protection from the elements, and even wood for a fire. But at the same time, you're in a remote location and nobody is going to come looking for you, so there's only one hope of seeing home again: you've got to make it out on your own.

Here are some crucial questions to ask yourself before moving on:

- Do you know which way safety lies and how to get there?
- If not, do you run the risk of getting even more lost?
- How far will you have to travel to reach safety?
- Are you or any of your travel partners injured, and do you have the physical strength to walk out?
- Do you have enough supplies to make it to your destination?
- Does anybody know where you are, and is there a chance they'll come looking for you?
- If so, how long before they even start looking?
- Are you on a well-used trail that might have other travelers and potential rescuers heading your way?
- Which is more dangerous: where you are now, or where you have to travel?
- Does the current location offer necessity-of-life benefits such as water, shelter, fire/fuel, and food?
- Are you now with a vehicle or other large object that may be seen easily from the air?

In many situations, staying in one place is the *best* thing you can do. After all, there's no guarantee that there's anywhere better just around the bend. As a general rule, if you don't have any idea where to go or how you will provide for yourself along the way, then staying put makes sense. Most studies show that people walk in circles when they are lost, due to the unfamiliar terrain and land features in their way. As a result, they become even more lost and make it harder for searchers to find them.

Here are some reasons to stay:

- You're injured and run the risk of getting more hurt while on the move.
- Moving may take you into more dangerous territory.

- You're with a large vehicle, which not only offers shelter but is a lot easier to spot (especially from the sky) than you would be walking alone through the bush.
- You can build a better camp, create a signal fire, and maybe even start hunting and scavenging for food.
- Some individuals (friends, family, or official personnel) were informed of your route and destination. Chances are they'll begin searching for you shortly after you don't show up at your destination or return home. If you head off down a different path, you may miss them—and rescue—completely.

Your chances of being rescued are better if you left behind a trip or flight plan. Within the first 24 to 72 hours, there's a high probability of rescuers finding you alive. After five or six days, they are more likely to find bodies.

Yet as good an idea as staying put may seem, there *are* times when moving is the best option. On one occasion I was searching for a place to teach a survival course in a swampy part of Algonquin Provincial Park, a well-known Ontario park. I was at the peak of my teaching days and starting to get overconfident. I headed out into the bush, off the established trails, without telling anyone where I was going. Even my wife was not expecting to hear back from me for at least three days.

After finding the perfect spot to teach—in a swamp a few miles into the bush—I started my hike back to my hidden and waiting canoe. Not more than 30 feet (9 m) away, a beautiful cow moose was grazing in the setting sun. I decided to try out my moose call and see how she would respond. I cupped my hands in front of my mouth and made the sound of a female moose.

It was the rutting season, and during this "season of love," the bull moose may be the most dangerous animal on the continent. These creatures have been known to attack and destroy tractor-trailer trucks. So I didn't make a bull sound for fear of bringing an angry male around.

This gentle cow moose just looked up once and then went back to eating. So I made the call again. This time, no response at all. I shrugged and turned to continue on my merry way. That's when more than half a ton of angry male moose, his truck-destroying antlers pointed at me, came charging out of the bush beside the female. Clearly, he was not amused.

I ran for all I was worth through the thick boreal forest. Several hundred yards later I spotted a partially fallen tree and scrambled up, out of reach of the bull. He stayed below the tree grunting, snorting, and stomping, all the while trampling down the small trees in the area.

I suddenly remembered (and this is the point of the story) that *nobody knew where I was*, and nobody was expecting me anytime soon. If I didn't do something quickly in the failing fall sunlight, I would be there for the night . . . or longer. I realized I had to move.

After several minutes, I climbed down and hit the ground running, and with the bull moose still giving chase, eventually wound my way back to the lakeshore, where I slipped quietly into the water (fully clothed) and swam as stealthily as possible back to my canoe. To this day, that experience remains the most frightening and dangerous situation I have ever faced in the wilderness.

Planning and Preparing for Survival Travel

Survival travel is very, very different from any other kind of wilderness travel. For that reason, it is imperative that you take the time to prepare for the journey that lies before you. Leave only when you're completely ready to do so.

Before you head out, set up some kind of sign that tells anyone who's looking for you or comes upon your camp that a) you were there, b) how long ago you left, and c) which direction you went. You can leave a note, leave a marker pointing in your direction of travel, or conspicuously mark your trail. Orange surveyor's tape is the best for marking, if you have it. If you're writing a note, the more details you can include, the better, such as the status of your supplies and your health.

If possible, before you go, build up a stock of food and water, and pack any protective clothing you think you'll need. Make at least a couple of tinder-balls to take with you and store them in a dry, protected place for the journey. If possible, also bring signaling gear.

Real-World Survivors

Life-or-Death Decisions

When it comes to getting out of a survival situation alive, the toughest choice facing any of us is the one between staying put in the hopes of being rescued or venturing out for help. Often, it's a life-or-death decision.

This was the dire predicament facing Thomas and Tamitha Garner, a suburban couple from Salt Lake City, when they found themselves stranded in a snowstorm in a secluded part of southwestern Utah. A sudden winter storm paralyzed their vehicle, cutting them off from civilization and virtually all hope of immediate rescue. Stuck in the snow-blanketed mountains for 12 agonizing days, the Garners struggled to survive in their pickup truck, with two boxes of granola bars, some frozen bottled water, a can of spray deodorant, some carburetor cleaner, a lighter, and Medusa, the family dog.

Dressed only in jeans and light coats, they kept warm by starting the truck from time to time. For nine frigid days and nights, Thomas and Tamitha carefully rationed the granola bars and water, but eventually, when they were reduced to eating Medusa's remaining kibble, they knew they had to make a choice: stay where they were and hope rescue teams would find them in time or leave the cold comfort of the truck to set out in search of help.

Thomas, a former Eagle Scout, got to work. Recalling an episode of "I Shouldn't Be Alive: The Science of Survival," in which I fashioned a set of makeshift snowshoes from seatbelts and foam car-seat padding, he created boots using the truck's seat cushions and a few bungee cords. With his wife in sneakers behind him and Medusa in tow, he blazed a trail through snow well over two feet deep. When night fell, all three huddled around a fire, which they made by lighting carburetor cleaner. When the fire waned, they kept it going with spray deodorant.

The couple and their dog continued hiking—despite dehydration, exhaustion, and frostbite—for an astonishing three » days and nights, covering 15 miles (24 km) in deep snow. When in doubt, Tamitha repeated her mantra, "One more day and I'll be home." On the 12th day of their ordeal, the couple spotted a bright yellow snowplow in the distance and flagged it down.

Because of their resourcefulness and sound decision-making, the Garners—and Medusa—made it out alive. At that critical moment when they were forced to choose, they weighed their options carefully and chose well.

Travel Considerations

ONCE YOU MAKE THE DECISION TO HIT THE TRAIL, there are many factors you need to consider.

Weather and Climate

How will short-term weather conditions affect you? This is a vital consideration. If a violent storm is brewing in the distance, stay put, at least for the time being. Most big weather—especially violent weather—comes and goes fairly quickly. Traveling all day in the rain with poor rain gear is a sure recipe for hypothermia.

Carrying Gear

When you're on the move, you'll likely need a way to carry the things that will help keep you alive on the journey (hopefully your survival kit is one of them). The less equipment you have to carry in your hands, the better off you'll be. You're going to need your hands to protect you from falling, to move obstacles from your path, and to mark your trail. If you're fortunate enough to have a backpack, great. But what if you don't?

With a few raw materials and a little time and effort, you can construct a makeshift carry bag. All you need is a blanket or similar item and some rope. Make your carrier sturdy so that you can travel as fast and as far as possible. It would be tragic to arrive at your destination after a grueling day of wilderness travel to find that you'd lost your lighter because it fell out of your makeshift bag.

Making a Makeshift Carry Bag

1. To construct a makeshift carry bag, lay all your equipment out on a blanket or similar ground cover.

2. Roll up and tie as shown.

3. Using this roll-up method, you can carry your supplies on your shoulder and have your hands relatively free.

Carrying People

You may find yourself in an emergency where you need to carry an injured person. Injured travelers pose a real challenge, one that is nearly impossible for a single able-bodied person to handle. Transporting another person is much more manageable when two or more are doing the carrying.

If you need to carry small children, you can put them in a backpack frame or makeshift carry bag. For larger children or adults, you can make a chair or stretcher out of poles. A rough stretcher can be carried by two people, although it is an exhausting task. If you are the sole able-bodied person, your only option for transporting your injured partner is to make a sledge that can be dragged. This type of device is a stretcher with crossed front handles that point (or curve) upward, allowing the carrier to pull without having to crouch too low. See "Survival First Aid," Chapter 13, for more advice on coping with injuries.

Rate of Travel

THE STAKES OF SURVIVAL TRAVEL ARE HIGH, so you can't afford to make any mistakes. Know that your rate of travel will be considerably slower than normal. Move deliberately, carefully, and at a medium pace; it is not a race. Most important, know where you are headed!

Set realistic travel goals for yourself. Pick a destination that you're pretty sure you can reach without exhausting yourself. It can be demoralizing to set a goal and then not attain it. The faster you go, the greater the risk that you'll hurt yourself and the more likely you'll bypass a route or trail that may lead you to safety. You may even miss the cave that could provide shelter for the night, or the cabin tucked in the woods. Go at a reasonable pace and the world will open up in front of your eyes; you'll begin to see the possibilities before you, possibilities that may make all the difference to your survival.

STROUD'S TIP

While you're traveling, look backward often to see where you've come from so that you can recognize that view if you have to return. Few people do this, but it's well worth the mere seconds it takes.

If you're traveling in pairs and one of you becomes injured, fashioning a stretcher with crossed handles will allow you to walk upright as you pull the stretcher.

Traveling at Night

Traveling at night is a risky undertaking and one I don't generally recommend. The greatest—and most obvious—danger here is that you can't see where you are putting your feet, so you risk stepping on a poisonous snake, or falling and injuring yourself. Furthermore, unless you know the area like the back of your hand, your ability to see in the dark—a fork in the trail or a possible shelter—is almost nil. And most predators are more active at night than during the day, so you may be exposing yourself to the possibility of attack. Finally, traveling at night may force you to sleep during the day, which is the time when rescuers (if there are any) will be looking for you.

On the rare occasion when you absolutely must keep moving at night, it can be safe to travel on certain flat-water rivers or lakes. However, I would recommend this only if you are proficient at canoeing.

The main exception to the "don't travel at night" rule is when you are in the desert, where daytime temperatures may be too high to allow a safe journey. Nighttime travel in the desert can be glorious; when the temperature drops, the heavens open up above you, and you can use the stars or a full moon for navigation.

I have traveled at night in the Amazon jungle. As I stepped outside of an old, abandoned native hut in the failing light, I looked up to see a large jaguar staring back at me. I knew it would take me a while to follow the dense jungle trail back to my destination, a tiny Waorani village, but I weighed the risks and took my chances. Using the light from my video camera to guide me and with the jaguar on my heels the entire way, I finally made it back to the village (which, incidentally, was surrounded by a chain-link fence . . . to keep out jaguars!). I learned the next morning that my stalker had been a male jaguar weighing more than 200 pounds.

STROUD'S TIP

When traveling, take particularly good care of your feet. If you have extra socks, change them regularly, and avoid walking in wet footgear.

Traveling by Water

Whether it be a swamp, river, lake, or stream, traveling by water may be the best route to safety if your only other alternative is to hack through dense and tangled bush. As you may suspect, however, water travel comes with its own set of risks. That body of water may seem calm and peaceful now, but what will you do if you encounter rapids or if a wind storm kicks up while you're in the middle of the lake? You also need to consider the possibility that the water may be home to dangerous creatures such as (depending on where you are) alligators, crocodiles, hippopotamuses, polar bears, walrus, sea lions, sharks, or elephants. And then there's the additional responsibility of waterproofing your gear.

When it comes to exactly *how* you travel by water, there are few options. Clearly, it's best if you have your own vessel, like a boat or canoe. Barring that, you're limited to making something, which usually means a raft. And as romantic as Huck Finn may have made it seem, making a raft—and traveling with it—is not easy to do. If this is your only option for safe travel, or you are convinced that making your way down a certain watercourse will lead you more quickly to safety, then it will be worth the effort. Just be sure to test your creation before loading it and setting out; never trust your survival to a flimsy raft.

If you can't swim or have little boating experience, stay as close to the shore as possible. When approaching bends in a river, keep to the inside edge where the current is less forceful. Swift-moving rivers can pose a variety of hazards, including snags (submerged trees and other foliage that can grab your vessel), sweepers (overhanging limbs and trees), rapids (portage around them; don't attempt to run them), and waterfalls.

If you're following a river on foot and come to an impasse that forces you to take to the water with no vessel, there are a couple of last-ditch ways to float downstream, but these are extremely dangerous. You could try to hang onto some sort of inflatable waterproof container (such as your trusty orange garbage bags), or if you have something buoyant like a food container, try to build something atop it. Cattails are also quite buoyant, and travelers have been known to construct floats from them.

Making Rafts

Rafts can be hard to make in survival situations. Depending on your circumstances, you may be able to tie up a raft that can transport you some distance.

Make a simple raft platform by collecting logs of a uniform size and tying them together in any of the three ways shown.

Construct a rudder pole on your raft, if possible. This way, you'll be able to steer yourself away from obstacles.

Crossing Water

NEVER UNDERESTIMATE THE POWER OF MOVING WATER. If you can get to your destination without crossing water, you're better off.

You must find the right spot to cross, and it may not be where you first reach the water. Look for the shallowest or slowest-flowing section (sometimes the most frothy, white-water section is actually the easiest place to cross as that is where the water is shallow enough to expose rocks you can step on). Make sure that you know you can get up the opposite bank *before* you enter the water.

When crossing moving water such as a river or stream, you should always face the current and lean your body upstream against it. Never turn your back to the current and never lean downstream, or you run the risk of being swept away. Use a stick, branch, or other aid to help you maintain your balance. It only takes 6 inches (15 cm) of moving water to knock down a full-grown man.

If you have to swim in rapids, keep your hind end as high as possible to avoid injuring your spine. Use your feet to repel any rocks you hit, and keep your feet high so they don't snag in a rock crevice, flip you over, and turn you face down. Paddle backward with your arms to reach a safe exit point.

Slide your feet along the bottom rather than taking large strides, which would leave you on one leg for much of the crossing time. If you're wearing a backpack, undo the hip strap and loosen the shoulder straps so that you can slip it off if you get knocked over. Don't let go of it if you can help it; but you also don't want it to take you under. Never attempt water crossings in bare feet. It's a rough compromise to make, especially if your boots or shoes are dry, but wet shoes are less debilitating than a twisted or broken ankle or severely gashed foot.

If you're crossing in a group, the strongest person should face the current with the rest in line behind, each holding the person in front by the waist. The stronger members of the group break the force of the river for the weaker ones. You can also cross as a group with each member in line locking arms. The strongest person is always in front, with the weakest in the middle. Yet another option is to secure a rope to objects on either bank; people can work their way across while holding the rope from the downstream side.

If you do slip and fall and find yourself being swept away, make sure you're floating on your back with your feet facing downstream. Your toes should be pointing out of the water (or as close to the surface as possible), and your rear end should be lifted as high out of the water as you can manage, to prevent your cracking your tailbone.

There are thousands of horror stories of travelers who fell out of their boats and subsequently drowned because they let their feet dangle under the surface and catch on trees or rocks or other debris in the water. Once this happens, the force of the flow throws you face first, and holds you under until you drown. Keeping your feet in front of you prevents this from happening and allows you to push yourself away from rocks and other obstacles as you float downstream.

There may be times when you need to cross frozen water. Although this can be an easy way to shorten your journey, it's not without risk. Falling into water in the middle of winter can be deadly. A pair of ice picks bought at any sports store and a flotation survival suit could save your life.

Expect weak ice in the following places:

- where objects protrude through the ice
- in straight sections in rivers
- where snow banks extend over the ice
- at a confluence of water courses
- wherever you see sinkholes
- where you see darker sections under the snow

Basic Survival Navigation

If you venture into the wild without basic navigation skills such as how to use a compass, you put yourself at unnecessary risk. The essentials of navigation are fairly straightforward and easy to master, and can be learned by anybody. As you learn how to paddle a canoe, build a campfire, or set up a tent, also learn to read a map and use a compass. I highly recommend that you get some *hands-on* experience well before venturing out on your own. Many colleges offer night courses on the subject.

The Map

A topographical map improves your chances of survival many times over, but only if you know how to use it and always protect it from damage.

Before setting off, check the date of your map. Depending on its age, you may find that some features have changed, which could drastically throw off your perception of where you are. I have seen entire lakes disappear (and new ones appear) on old maps.

Make sure that you can interpret the map's symbols and identify major terrain features.

To correctly use any map, you first need to orient it. In simplest terms, a map is oriented when it is placed flat on a horizontal surface, and its north and south markings correspond with north and south on your compass (or at least with your understanding of where north, south, east, and west lie).

If you're not sure where north is, you can still orient the map using terrain association. To do this, you must know your approximate location on the map. Seek out the major terrain features in your vicinity (such as hilltops, valleys, and ridges), and identify them on the map. This is more difficult in "close" places such as the jungle and the forest, so you may need to wait until you reach something more easily identified. Some topographic maps also mark different types of vegetation, which may help you to determine your location.

Knowing your map-based route is noted as a major priority in "Trip Planning and Preparation," the first chapter of this book. If you are on a charter trip, sit down with your guide on the first day to familiarize yourself with the map.

The Compass

The compass course I took at my local college always ended with an orienteering race. It became tradition that those of us who also took survival courses were under big-time peer pressure to win. Fortunately for me, I avoided much teasing by winning the year I took the course. My time, however, was not as good as my survival buddy Doug Getgood's had been a few years earlier, so I felt it appropriate that he join me in writing this, and the next, section.

In a world where the techno-savvy are all too used to having electronic gadgets flash and beep at them, the simple compass sometimes seems almost boring. After all, it just sits there, pointing north. Yet, simple though it may be, the compass is the one instrument above all others that will help you find your way out of the wilderness. Basic compass understanding is vital to your survival.

If you can comfortably and effectively use a compass, you can stand in the middle of nowhere, pick a destination off in the distance and be confident that no matter how many obstacles lie in your path, you will get there.

Parts of a Compass

To use a compass, you first have to understand its various parts. The compass shown below is an orienteering compass, a very practical one when used with a topographic map.

The compass has three basic parts:

Base plate: Shows the direction-of-travel arrow, parallel orienteering lines that are used in conjunction with a map, and the index mark.

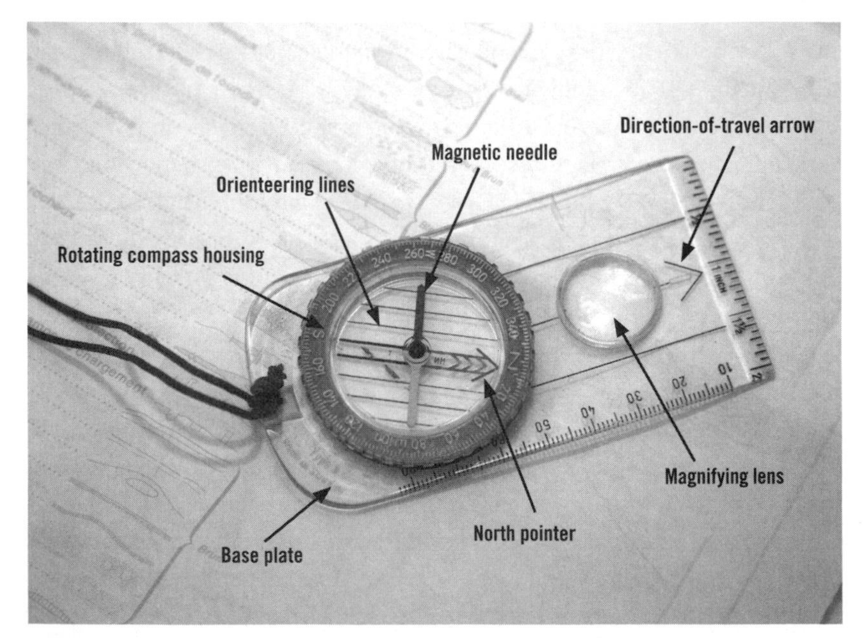

Parts of a compass.

Rotating compass housing: Rotates in either direction. Its border is inscribed with numbers and markings. It begins with *N* for north and ends where it began, 360 degrees later. On the bottom of the compass housing is the red orienteering arrow, as well as parallel orienteering lines.

Magnetic needle: Balanced inside the compass housing, the magnetic needle is usually red and always points to magnetic north (as long as the compass is held flat and is not placed near certain types of metal).

Taking a Bearing Without a Map

In simple terms, a bearing (one of the 360 points on a compass) is the direction you want to travel in relation to magnetic north. The idea behind taking a bearing is that it allows you to travel in a chosen direction using landmarks as navigational aids. Hillsides, big rocks, unique-looking trees, ponds, and lakes can all be used for this purpose. See the picture captions and other steps that follow for instructions on taking a bearing.

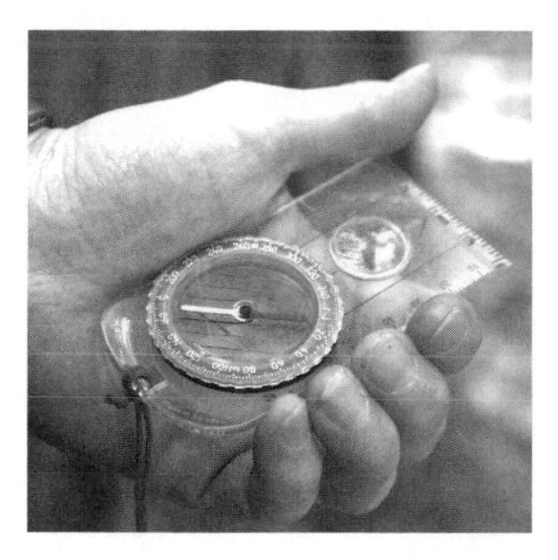

1. Face the direction you want to go. Level the compass to allow the magnetic needle to swing freely, and point the direction-of-travel arrow in the direction that you have chosen.

2. Now spin the compass housing until the orienteering arrow is directly underneath the magnetic needle. The bearing is shown at the index mark (e.g., 148°). Choose a topographical landmark in that direction that you can easily differentiate from others around it.

3. Keeping your compass at the chosen setting, take your eyes away from the compass and make your way toward the object. Once you reach the object, find another landmark in your path in the same direction. This is done by doing the "compass shuffle." As before, put the compass flat in your hand. Make sure the bearing still reads 148° (or whichever bearing you've chosen) and shuffle your body until the red end of the magnetic needle is directly over top of the red portion of the orienteering arrow. The direction-of-travel arrow will point to where you want to go.

4. Always place the back end of the compass near or against your stomach with the direction-of-travel arrow pointing ahead. This way both you and the compass will always be facing the same direction. Don't simply stare at your compass and walk, as you could easily sway to one side and not actually head in a straight line. If you choose a landmark in the right direction, you can put the compass down and make your way to that landmark, walking around obstacles en route. Adventure racers use this method very effectively, noting a landmark in the distance and running between landmarks at top speed.

To reverse your steps you can do one of two things:

1. Align the white (south) end of the magnetic needle with the red portion of the orienteering arrow and follow the direction-of-travel arrow back, OR

2. Add 180 degrees (half of the 360 degrees of a circle) to your original 148-degree setting (180 + 148 = 328) and travel back to where you started. Ensure in this case that all red arrows are aligned.

The Map and Compass

THE BEST MAP TO USE in conjunction with an orienteering compass is a topographic map. The following is a basic introduction to working with a map and compass. As I explain above, it's wise to further your studies in the field of orienteering with a local educator.

The Topographic Map

A topographic map is a scaled replica of an outdoor location. The average topographic map has a scale of 1:50,000, where 1 inch equals 50,000 inches. It shows contour lines, grid lines, man-made objects, and natural features such as lakes, swamps, and rivers.

The contour lines are to help you to decipher various terrain features such as peaks and valleys, cliffs and slopes. Grid lines run both north and south (up and down, called grid north) as well as east and west (left and right). On a 1:50,000 scaled map, the grid lines represent one square mile. The north/south lines run almost the same direction as true north, but not necessarily the same direction as magnetic north. The difference between the map's grid north and magnetic north is called the angle of declination.

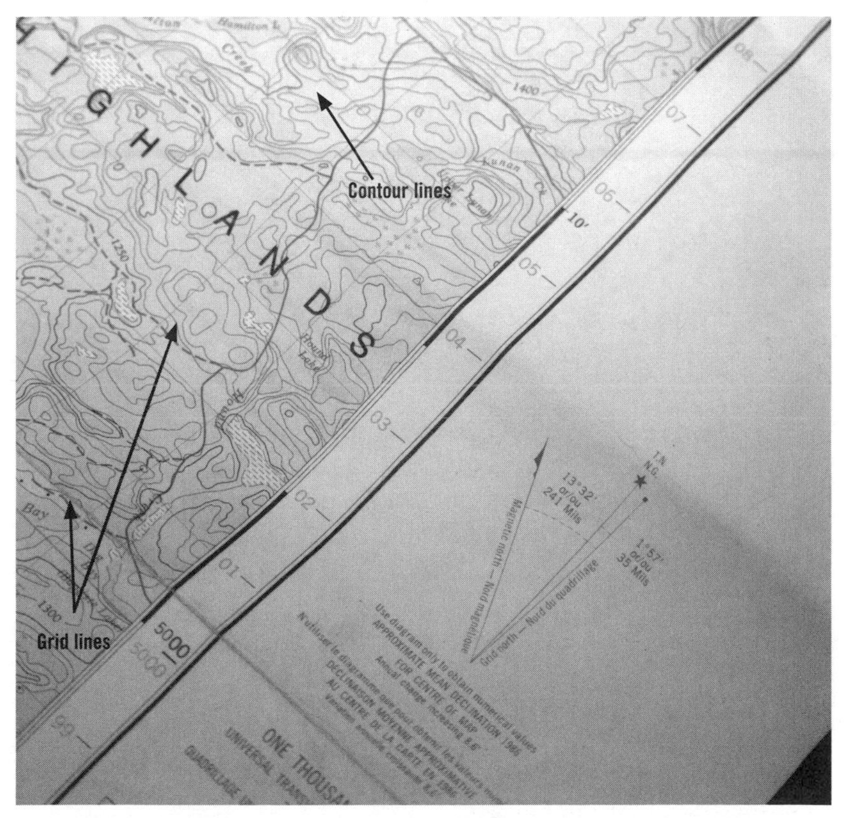

A topographic map gives you geographic detail about the landscape you'll encounter.

Taking a Bearing with a Map

Using a pencil, mark on your map (a) the location from which you want to take a bearing and (b) your chosen destination Then draw a straight line connecting the two. Place the side of the compass along this line with the direction-of-travel arrow pointing in the direction that you want to proceed. Rotate the compass housing so that one of the orienteering lines runs exactly parallel to or completely covers one of the north/south grid lines on the map.

To achieve the correct reading, it is imperative that the orienteering arrow end up pointing toward the top of the map. The correct bearing is shown at the index mark.

Adjusting for Declination

Now that you have taken the bearing, an adjustment must be made to correct for declination. Using the diagram on the side of the map, find the degrees of difference between the map's grid north and the compass's magnetic north. Notice that the map below shows magnetic north, true north (T.N.), and grid north. (For the purpose of map-and-compass work, T.N. should be ignored.) The degree of declination is also shown. Because the bearing was established using the map's grid line, the grid north marking on the diagram dictates which direction the compass housing should be rotated. If the diagram shows magnetic north toward the left of grid north, turn the compass housing to the left (counter-clockwise). If the diagram shows magnetic north toward the right of grid north, turn the compass housing to the right (clockwise). In either case you will rotate the compass housing the number of degrees indicated on the map.

Keep in mind that magnetic north changes slightly each year. The map will indicate how far it moves each year and how you can adjust for the difference. The compass should now be adjusted for declination, and will give you a true indication of what direction to travel.

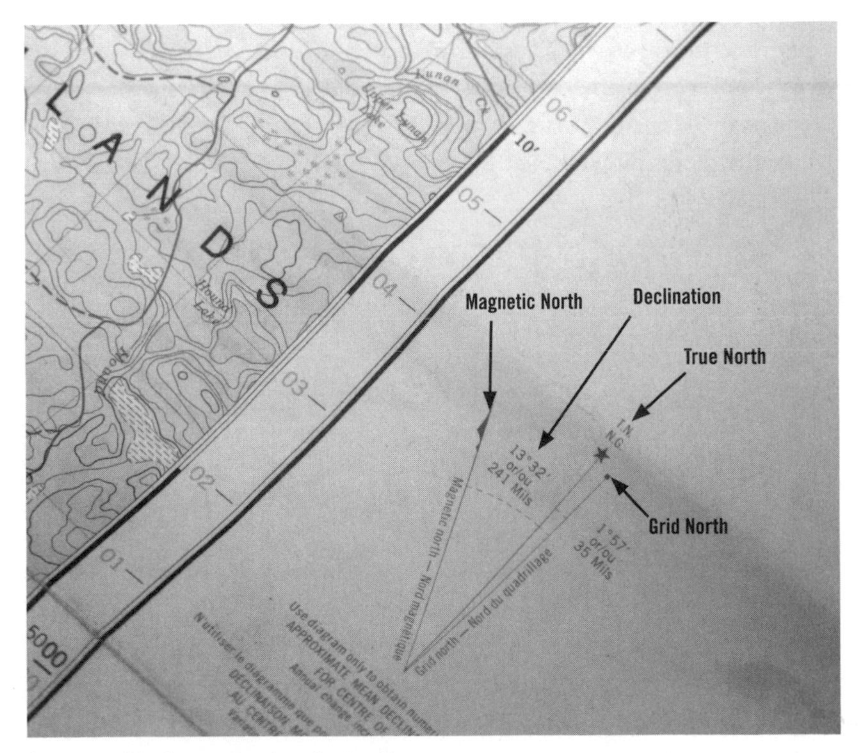

A topographical map showing declination.

Adjusting for Declination from Field to Map

If you want to convert a bearing taken in the field to a map, use the magnetic needle as your starting point. Using the topographical map's diagram for declination as a reference, rotate the compass housing toward grid north.

STROUD'S TIP

When transferring from map to field, rotate the compass housing toward magnetic north. When transferring from field to map, rotate the compass housing toward grid north.

Making Improvised Compasses

Although it may be daunting to see your compass float down the river or plummet to the bottom of a crevasse, don't panic. There are ways to determine north, south, east, and west from ordinary materials that you may be carrying or that you can find in your immediate surroundings. None of these methods is very accurate, but each will give you an idea of where the major directions lie.

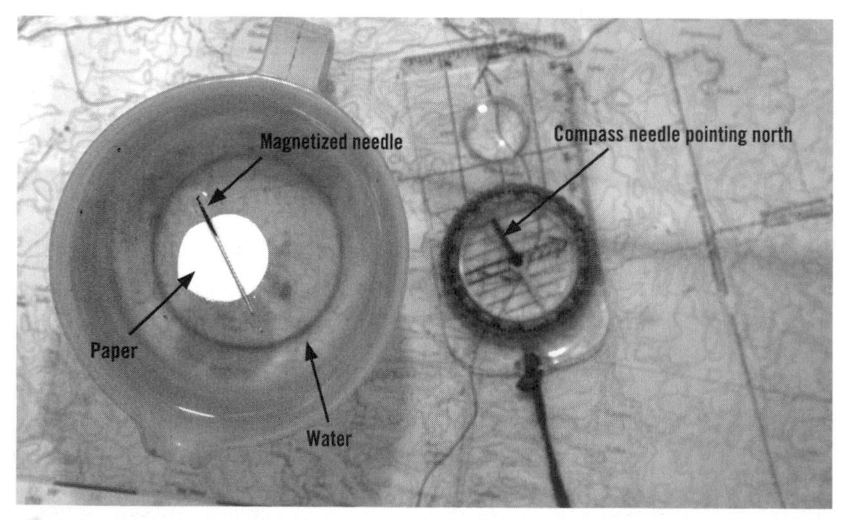

Magnetized needle and paper in water method. A magnetized needle will always point north/south. See tip on page 27 to learn how to magnetize a needle.

Shadow stick: The shadow stick method uses the sun to determine direction. Stand with the west mark to your left. North is in front of you, east to the right, and south behind. This method cannot be used effectively in regions above 60 degrees latitude.

Using a Shadow Stick to Determine Direction

1. Start by poking a stick or branch into the ground. Choose a level spot where you know a distinctive shadow will be cast. Mark the tip of the shadow; this mark will always be west.

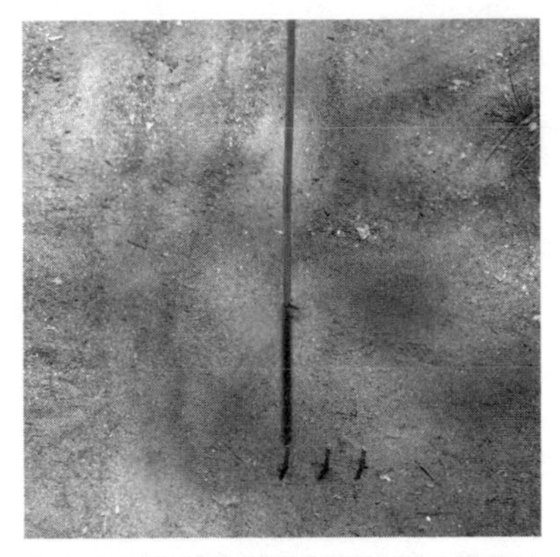

2. Wait about 15 minutes, during which time the shadow tip will move. Mark the new position of the tip. Repeat.

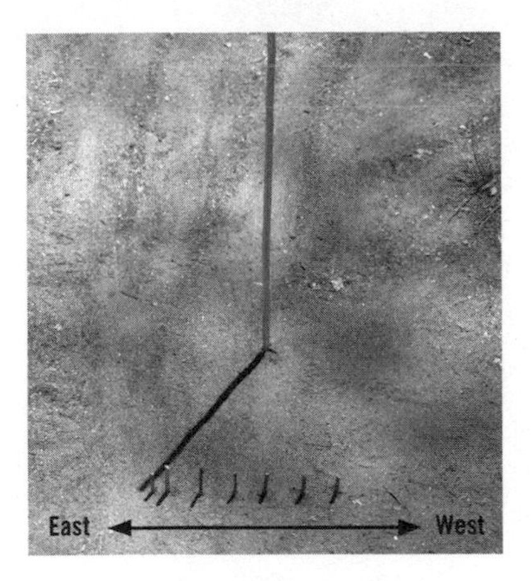

3. Draw a straight line through the marks; this is an approximate east/west line.

Watch method: Although it can be off by as much as 24 degrees and doesn't work everywhere on the planet, a watch can sometimes be used as a makeshift compass. If your watch is digital, draw a watch (with hands) on a circle of paper with the correct time on it and use the following method to determine your direction.

This method should be used during standard time; in daylight saving time, the north/south line is found between the hour hand and 1 o'clock. If it is before noon, use halfway to the right side of the hour hand; if it is after noon, use halfway to the left of the hour hand.

In the south temperate zone (the area between the Tropic of Capricorn and the Antarctic Circle), point 12 o'clock toward the sun. Halfway between the 12 o'clock position and the hour hand will be a north line. During daylight saving time, the north line lies midway between the hour hand and 1 o'clock. Note that this method becomes less accurate the nearer you are to the equator.

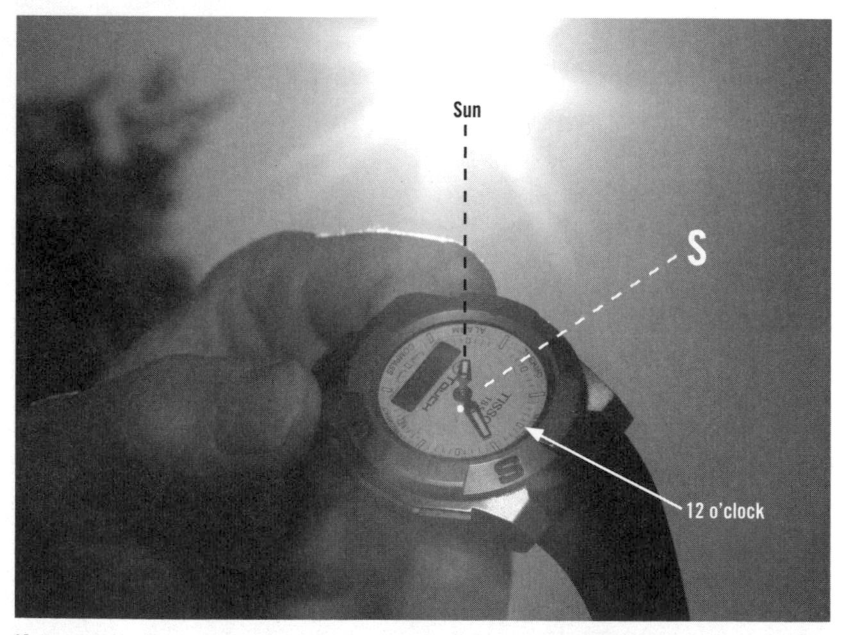

If you are in the north temperate zone (the area between the Tropic of Cancer and the Arctic Circle), point the hour hand of your watch directly at the sun. Then draw an imaginary line halfway between the hour hand and 12 o'clock. This imaginary line points south.

Using Natural Features to Navigate

WEATHER CAN BE A VERY IMPORTANT TOOL when navigating through the wilderness, but remember: don't ever rely on just one sign. Rather, use as many as you can in combination to reduce the risk that you'll make a mistake.

If your trip preparation and planning has told you the direction of the prevailing wind, you can use that knowledge to help guide you, since wind has pronounced effects on vegetation and land forms. The growth of certain trees, called flag trees, is largely affected by wind patterns. The branches of these trees (such as white pine) will not grow into the wind but rather in the same direction as the prevailing wind. Flag trees generally point either east or west, but this is subject to regional variation.

Moss tends to grow on the north side of trees because there's less sunlight. But that doesn't mean you won't find moss on the south side of a tree or even all around the trunk. Again, it's best to look for such signs in combination. The melt-off around boulders is usually on the south to southwest side.

In the northern temperate climate, many flowers will face either south or east to maximize their exposure to the sun. The barrel cactus in the Sonoran Desert does the same.

Celestial objects are good navigation tools, particularly the North Star. Although you may think that the stars are constantly moving across the night sky, in the Northern Hemisphere, the North Star always holds its position. To find the North Star, first find the Big Dipper. Draw an imaginary line connecting the two stars that form the right-most part of the ladle. Continue the line a distance about five times greater than the depth of the ladle, which will lead you to the last star in the handle of the Little Dipper. This is the North Star. Make a marking or lay a stick on the ground pointing north (to the star). Once daylight comes, you can use this to establish your direction.

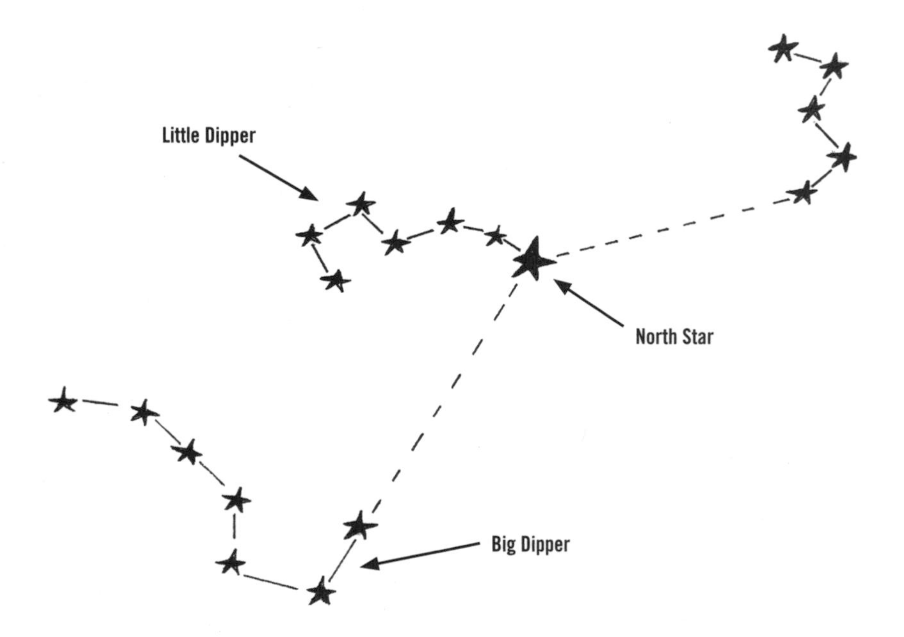

You can find the North Star by locating the end stars of the Big Dipper. Follow the line they make diagonally north and you'll find the bright light of the North Star.

In the southern hemisphere, you can use the Southern Cross (and its two pointer stars) to determine south. Start with the star that marks the top of the cross and draw an imaginary line through its long axis. Now draw a line that starts midway between the two pointer stars and comes out at a right angle to it. This line should cross your first imaginary line through the long axis of the cross. The intersection of these two lines is close to the South Pole.

You can also use the moon to navigate or at least gain a rough idea of where north and south lie. If the moon is a crescent, draw an imaginary line through the ends of the crescent down to the horizon. If you're in the northern hemisphere, the point where it touches is south; if you're in the southern hemisphere, it's north.

If the moon rises before the sun sets, the illuminated side will be west. If it rises after midnight, its illuminated side will be east.

Following beside a stream or river may seem like a logical plan, since it can lead you to civilization . . . or into endless wilderness. You can walk along gravel riverbanks with ease or find that the forest on the edge of the river is too thick to penetrate. Only solid knowledge of an area, gained during your planning and preparation stage, will help you decide what to do.

Nor are train tracks or power lines necessarily the path home. You could find a town just around the bend . . . or walk through miles of nothingness along a line no longer in use. Power lines also have a nasty habit of leading to a swamp or lake across which the wires have been strung.

While making one of my survival films, I once came upon a set of train tracks. Although I later received a lot of mail chastising me for not following the tracks to safety, at the time, I had been certain there was a highway only a few miles east of the tracks. Since I didn't have a clue where the tracks would take me, I went with the sure thing, crossed the tracks, hit the highway, and found my way home.

Global Positioning System (GPS)

GPS IS A SATELLITE-BASED NAVIGATION SYSTEM that can provide accurate locational data anywhere, at any time. A GPS unit displays your current location in latitude and longitude coordinates; if you enter the map coordinates of your destination, it will also tell you the direction you should travel. Most GPS units also have an electronic compass. Purchase one with a coil antenna that gets good signals under tree canopy and a memory card with topographical maps, so that you can track your movements and easily use the "go-to" feature to find any place on the map.

Remember, though, that GPS units run on batteries, which may die at the worst possible moment. Never rely on a GPS. You should also know how to use a map and compass.

Trailblazing

THOUGH OFTEN OVERLOOKED, an important aspect of survival travel and navigation is marking the surrounding natural features (also known as trailblazing) while you move. Other travelers may see these indicators that you've left behind, increasing your chances of being rescued. These markings are also useful if you decide that the path you're taking is wrong and you want to go back.

The best way to blaze a trail is to use a sharp object, such as a belt knife, axe, or machete, to cut a small piece of bark off a tree. You can also use the orange surveyor's tape from your survival kit.

When trailblazing, make sure you mark *both sides* of the tree (the direction you came from and the direction you're going). This way you'll

The best choice for trailblazing targets are young green trees whose bark has not yet hardened. The bark of older trees is much harder and will quickly dull your knife.

see the marks if you have to turn around. Many adventurers have gotten hopelessly lost because they forgot to do this.

If you don't have an object on hand that will slice pieces of bark, you can also blaze your trail by bending or breaking branches. Make sure you bend the branches at eye level and point them in the direction you're traveling.

Blazes are most effective when placed at eye level so that you can see them from a distance without actually looking for them. Make as many as your physical strength and circumstances allow.

Traveling in a Straight Line

MOST PEOPLE WALK IN CIRCLES WHEN LOST, generally clockwise. We often move to the right because that is the side that people usually keep to when walking down a hallway and climbing stairs. A right-handed person's right leg is usually less flexible than the left, causing the left leg to take longer strides.

As a result, traveling straight in a survival situation is not as easy as you may think. Here's a good strategy: Consciously move in alternating directions around obstacles in your path. Go around them sometimes to the right, and sometimes to the left.

Region-Specific Travel and Navigation

Arid Regions, Deserts, and Canyons

In these regions, the decision whether to move depends primarily on your current supply of water and the likelihood of your finding it somewhere else. If you don't think you have enough water to complete the journey and are not likely to find some on the way, you shouldn't go at all, unless you have no choice.

Anyone who has ever hopped their way across a scalding beach with an ice cream cone in hand will understand that walking on desert sand—no matter how good your footgear—is just as difficult. It's best to stick to brushy and grassy places where the ground is a bit firmer. Snakes and spiders also seek grassy places, so you increase your risk of being bitten, but this is still the best way to go. If there are no shrubby or grassy areas, travel on the hard valley floor between dunes, not on top of them.

If you are unlucky enough to get caught in a desert sandstorm, stop moving immediately or try to get to the leeside of a natural shelter. Mark your direction of travel, sit or lie down in that direction, cover your head (especially your mouth and nose) with a cloth, and wait until the storm abates.

When traveling through canyon country, you have to be extremely cautious around slot canyons (narrow canyons with high walls), which have seen the deaths of many unsuspecting travelers. The danger here is flash flooding, which happens with little warning. Flash floods can rip through slot canyons on perfectly calm, blue-sky days, generally because a major storm has occurred elsewhere and all the surface runoff is collecting in the canyon. The wall of water can be as high as 60 feet (18 m). A strong breeze or a sound like thunder are signs that a flash flood is approaching.

Boreal and Other Temperate Forests

The denseness of the trees often complicates travel in boreal and other temperate forests by preventing the traveler from gaining a good long-distance view of the surroundings. Your skill with a compass will come into play here, as you'll need to take frequent bearings to make your way out. You can also climb a tree to get a better view.

The rivers, streams, swamps, and lakes common in boreal and temperate forests open up the terrain and provide an excellent means of travel and navigation, provided you have a boat and the skill to travel on water.

The greatest danger in traveling in the boreal forest is overestimating how fast you're moving. It is common to travel barely a mile and feel like you have traveled several.

STROUD'S TIP

When moving through the forest (and the jungle) in a group, chances are the person in front of you will hold the branches, to prevent them from whipping back into your face. This may be a considerate gesture, but don't rely on it. There will invariably come a moment when the person in front gets distracted and *fails* to hold the branch. If you're not paying attention, you're going to get it in the eye, which can be serious. Always hold a hand up for protection or stay well enough back.

The Arctic and Polar Regions

Those who have not had the opportunity to travel in the world's polar regions are missing some of the greatest scenery on earth. The problem, especially when ice fog sets in, is that you can feel like you're traveling inside a giant ping-pong ball.

The ping-pong ball effect can be extremely disorientating and make it nearly impossible to tell the sky from the ground; everything is white. In the Arctic, I once nearly walked off the edge of a 30-foot (9-m) snow cliff. It was only at the last minute that I realized what I was about to do and stopped. I had to get down on my hands and knees before I could actually detect the difference in the landscape a few feet in front of me!

Generally, the wide-open vistas make traveling in the Arctic enjoyable and the natural land features (if there's no fog!) easy to distinguish. But bear in mind that whenever you're in a region with heavy snow cover, you run the risk of snowblindness on bright, sunny days. Snowblindness is a sunburn on your retina, and it's a debilitating injury that can last for several days.

Do not, under any circumstances, travel if a heavy snowstorm or blizzard is approaching. You should also avoid traveling when the wind, which can create bitterly cold temperatures, is strong.

Protect your eyes from the sun's UV rays with either sunglasses or ski goggles. If you don't have protective lenses, fashion what you can out of birch bark, paper, or any other fabric. Just leave a couple of horizontal slits to see through.

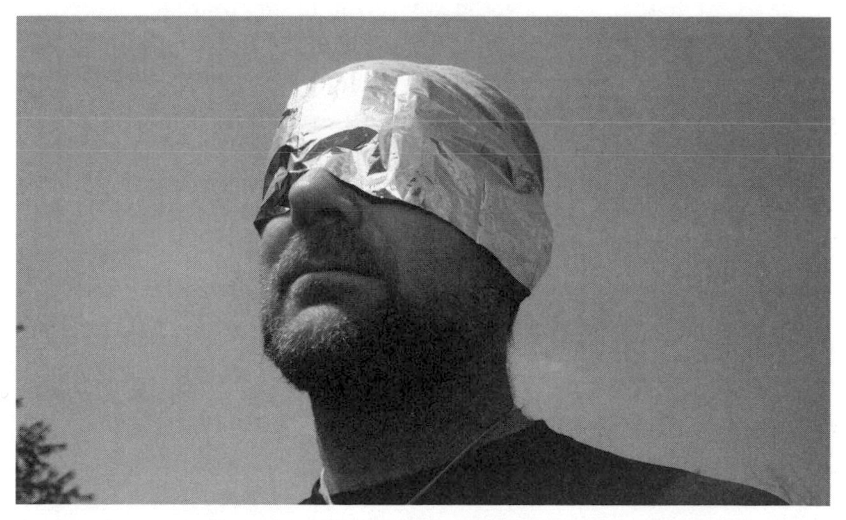

Because you can see through a solar blanket, you can use a piece of one to protect your eyes if you don't have sunglasses.

On the Sea or Open Water

When traveling on open water, it helps to be aware of the subtle signs that land may be near: stationary cumulus clouds in a clear sky (or in a cloudy sky where the other clouds are moving); a greenish tint in the sky in the tropics; lighter-colored reflection on clouds in the Arctic; and increased bird life (and sounds). Lighter-colored water also indicates shallow water, as does an increased amount of floating debris.

Jungles

The jungle is probably one of the toughest ecosystems in the world to travel through (hence the popular phrase "It's a jungle out there"). You often don't know exactly where you are or where you're going, nor do you always have the luxury of a trail or river to follow. Where possible, stick to traveling near water, as you are more likely to come upon a village.

As part of your planning and prep, bring a good machete. Slashing and cutting the growth in your way opens up a path and also keeps the many creepy crawlies from biting you or hitching a ride on you.

You also need to be vigilant about looking *up* as well as down while you walk. Snakes are found as often in trees as on the ground.

Walking across logs is very different in the jungle than in the temperate forest. In the forest, I would advise you to step over logs or around them to avoid slipping and twisting an ankle. In the jungle, the opposite is true: you're better off stepping *on* a log rather than *over* it. Many poisonous snakes like to hide just under the crux (small space or hole underneath) of the log. Snakebites occur when travelers step over a log and place their feet down on the other side, exposing their ankles to snakes.

Mountains

Streams will eventually lead you off a mountain, but this does not mean that you won't at some point find yourself at the top of a 100-foot (30-m) waterfall—that's the downside. As long as the water course is lined with trees, however, you will likely find handholds and footholds to help you make your way down.

Avalanches are the main travel hazard you'll face in the mountains, although rockslides can also occur after heavy rainfalls. Avoid ridges and mountaintops during lightning storms, and because of the risk of flash flooding, stay away from low-lying areas after major storms.

Chapter Ten

DANGERS AND HAZARDS

The wilderness may be a dangerous place at times, but we tend to play up the hazard in our minds. One of the most beneficial characteristics you can have in a survival situation is *confidence.* If you believe you can make it through the bad times and you're not intimidated by the forces of nature, you will increase your chances of survival.

To see yourself to safety, you must play both offense *and* defense. On the offensive end are proactive measures such as signaling, finding water, making fire, building a shelter, and finding food. The defensive end includes protecting yourself from the many hazards inherent to the wild. In other words, it doesn't matter how much water is available to drink if you get bitten by a poisonous cape cobra while lapping it up.

The thing to remember about the dangers of the wild (from animals to creepy crawlies to weather) is that they are not, by their nature, malevolent forces trying to do you in. To the contrary, they are just there, doing what they do. *Your* actions will determine whether these elements affect you negatively.

For example: you are rushing through the boreal forest and not paying attention to where you're going, only to run headlong into a hornets' nest or trip and snap your ankle in a hole. Now you're in some serious trouble, which you could have avoided had you simply slowed down and paid closer attention. The *potential* for danger was always there, but your actions determined how it affected you.

Or let's say you've been blessed with glorious weather for a few days and have chosen not to make a shelter. Invariably, the bad weather comes, and now you're in a desperate situation trying to keep your fire going and stay warm in the pouring rain. The weather was coming anyway. Only your choice not to make a shelter exposed you to the danger.

Remember that of all the hazards you'll face in a survival situation, it's not the big-impact things (such as predators and poisonous snakes) that are most likely to get in your way. Rather, it's the little things that you tend to ignore but which exist in abundance that will slow you down; small problems which can snowball if ignored for too long.

Weather

Of all the potential dangers you will face in a survival situation, none is more formidable than the weather. People can tell all the stories they want about dangerous animals, poisonous creatures, or getting ill from eating the wrong plant, but for me, weather is the most frightening variable of all. It's the greatest foe you'll face. I have yet to be bitten by a snake, to be stung badly by wasps, or to succumb to starvation in my travels. But I *always* have to put up with or hide from bad weather.

It could be too hot or too cold, too wet or too dry. It could be too windy or too calm. But no matter what the weather is, it's going to affect you in some way, whether it's offering you an advantage by being pleasant and giving you time to accomplish the survival tasks you need to do, or coming down on you hard as something you have to endure until you get respite.

In the Kalahari Desert, my greatest concern was the blistering heat, which I had to escape somehow. Luckily, I found a small tree (the only one for a few square miles), which I huddled under for hours. There was a 20-degree difference between areas in the shade and those in the sun, and that little tree helped me survive.

Ignore the weather and you radically decrease your chances of seeing home again; acknowledge and respect it and you've taken the first step toward survival. These are the weather events (in no particular order) that you should be prepared to deal with, depending on your region and the time of year:

- blizzards and wind chill
- extreme heat
- floods
- hurricanes
- sandstorms
- thunderstorms/lightning storms

See "Weather," Chapter 11, for a more detailed description of how to handle these events.

Predators and Dangerous Animals

NOTHING GETS AS MUCH PLAY IN THE MEDIA as people getting mauled or killed by animals. And while it may be true that people occasionally *are* killed by animals, in the overwhelming majority of these instances, the death was due not to the actions of a true predator but to what I call an "accidental predator."

An accidental predator (such as a black bear) is primarily concerned with getting its food, usually small or hoofed animals, fish, or plants. Encounters with accidental predators occur when human beings invade their territories.

True predators (such as great white sharks or tigers), on the other hand, are opportunistic and look at people as opportunities. Sometimes we serve them this opportunity on a silver platter by venturing into their territories unprotected.

Animals of every sort have an uncanny ability to sense your state of mind, whether you feel confident or fearful. Exude fear and they'll be all over you. Act confident and strong and they'll think twice about attacking. Sharks, for example, don't like the idea of their prey fighting back, so the toughest way for a shark to come at you is from the front.

Make sure you're familiar with the creatures you may meet before you head out on your journey.

Accidental Predators

The majority of the animals we fear when we head into the wilderness—including black bears, poisonous snakes, or elephants—are not predators looking for human prey at all. Creatures such as these are occasionally associated with killing humans, but these deaths are usually the result of circumstance rather than premeditation. Here's a list of what I consider the most common accidental predators:

- wolves, coyotes, and other similar canine creatures
- mountain lions, cougars, jaguars, pumas, panthers, and other similar small cats
- black bears, grizzly bears, Kodiak bears, brown bears, and other similar bears
- sharks (other than great white sharks)

Have a healthy respect for animals in the wild, but don't let that evolve into an irrational fear of them. Once your respect becomes fear, you lose your ability to act rationally in a confrontation, and you may freeze, to your peril.

Say, for example, that you have no fresh water, the localized weather conditions are poor, and you have little fuel for fire. You know from your map that there's a better spot a few miles away, but you're too afraid to move because you believe you may encounter a bear along the way. Your fear of the bear is actually hindering your ability to survive.

Generally, accidental predators want nothing to do with humans. Problems occur when we present ourselves to them in a compromising position, whether it's getting between them and their food, getting between a mother and her young, or simply getting too close and startling them. They are bigger and stronger than us, and when they react out of fear, the outcome usually is not in our favor.

Now, there have been instances where rogue animals have killed humans in a seemingly predatory fashion. Though exceedingly rare, rogue animals are dangerous, because they are unpredictable and don't act the way the rest of their species does.

Habituated animals (bears, in particular) can also prove dangerous because they have become accustomed to humans and do not necessarily see us as a threat. Habituated animals are those that have learned to equate people with food, because people do things like leave garbage lying outside the house, or feed the animals in the backyard or park to get a nice photo.

In Wyoming's Yellowstone National Park, there was a time when mothers were seen spreading peanut butter on their children's faces so that a several-hundred-pound black bear would lick it off, all for a picture!

The good news for the adventurer is that habituated animals are rarely found in remote areas.

You can prevent encounters with accidental predators by taking these steps:

- Make your presence known.
- When you're traveling in an area where you know there are accidental predators, be as noisy as possible. Sing, yell, blow a whistle, wear a bear bell . . . anything that will inform animals of your presence. If they hear you, chances are they'll take off. Early in my days of survival training, I had to walk alone in a remote area of northern Ontario. I knew the area was thick with black bears (there was bear scat everywhere), so I simply played my harmonica as I walked along. It gave me comfort on a number of levels.
- Keep your camp area clean and free of excessive food smells.
- If you come upon a freshly killed animal in grizzly territory, give it a wide berth. Grizzlies will often wander some distance from their kill, but you can be sure they sense when something else is getting close to it.
- Don't travel alone through the territory of large predators if you don't have to.

There are as many strategies for dealing with large animals as there are animals themselves. What works in an encounter with a puma may not work with a grizzly bear. However, in general terms, here's what you should do if you happen upon an accidental predator:

1. Don't panic! Turning and running may well incite an instinctive predatorial response in the animal, since you are telling it that you are prey. So if it wasn't interested in you at first, it sure is now!
2. Calmly and deliberately move away from the animal. Do not make jerky movements, which may startle it. Keep facing it, but do not look it in the eye. Some animals may interpret eye contact as a challenge. (An exception to this rule is sharks, which will take much longer to attack if you keep your eyes on them.)
3. Make yourself seem as big and threatening as possible by waving your arms over your head, making lots of noise, or joining arms with your travel mates.
4. Remember that *you* are the visitor! No matter how intent you were on heading in a certain direction, taking a certain path, or making camp in a certain spot, move elsewhere!

Many years ago, I was writing an exam for a job as a river guide on the Nahanni River in northern Canada. One of the questions on the exam asked what you should do if a bear wandered into your camp and would not leave, even after you made as much noise as possible, banged pots, and threw rocks in an attempt to scare it away. My reply was to *leave*. The examiner told me I was the first applicant in three years to get the answer right. After all, it's the animal's home and territory, not ours. *We* are the visitors.

Years of research and thousands of anecdotal accounts of encounters have shown that the only animals worth fooling by "playing dead" are the North American grizzly and Kodiak bears. For all other accidental predators, human aggressive displays tend to win the day, because these accidental predators can't afford to get injured. In one case, a woman thwarted a bear attack by reaching out and tweaking the bear's nose. That's all it took! The bear was so freaked out, it lumbered away. These animals don't know if you have the ability to seriously injure them, so they spook easy. Only the grizzly has a good handle on just how much bigger it is than you.

As the character Bearclaw replied in my favorite movie, *Jeremiah Johnson*, when asked by Jeremiah why they were hiding behind their horses even though the elk could see their feet, "Elk don't know how many feet a horse has!"

True Predators

Even the most intimidating and dangerous of animals do not come into the world programmed to kill humans, nor are they taught to hunt us. We're not on the menu of the following creatures:

- African lions
- great white sharks
- polar bears
- saltwater crocodiles
- tigers

Polar bears learn how to hunt seals; lions learn how to hunt gazelles and zebras. Predators are dependent on their physical health and strength to catch their next meal, so they have a great fear of getting injured. When they first encounter you, their instinct is not to attack you and eat you but rather to take off because you present an unknown. And in the wilderness, an unknown is usually a threat. You should be *more* scared when an animal's curiosity overrides its fear of you.

So why is it, then, that we hear stories of man-eating lions or polar bears stalking Inuit across the tundra? Because in addition to being predators of other animals, true predators are also opportunistic eaters. If something comes into their world that is soft, smelly, and fleshy (like you and me), these creatures may recognize us as a potential meal.

Here's what you can do to protect yourself in true predator country:

- Avoid detection: Humans tend to be loud, bumbling creatures in the wild. If you're in true predator terrain, move as stealthily as possible. To avoid giving the predator an opportunity, try not to attract any attention to yourself.
- Make as much noise as possible: (You're going to hate me for this contradiction!) Noise can scare animals away. This alternative is likely better attempted when you're with a group of people, as there's safety in numbers. (These completely opposite methods indicate just how difficult it is to predict what an animal will do, or how you should behave, during an encounter.)
- Create obstacles: When you're stationary for any length of time, try to use natural materials to create a buffer between you and the animal. This is particularly important for your shelter. In Africa, I built a corral from acacia thorns around my shelter. It wouldn't have stopped a lion that was intent on getting me, but it would have deterred one long enough to buy me time to plan my escape.
- Plan an escape route: Even with protection, sometimes the best route to safety is an escape route. In Africa, even with a fence of thorn bushes for protection, I made sure my shelter was built against a tree in case the pride of lions wandering the area decided to pay a visit. I hung a rope from the tree into my shelter so that I had the option of climbing the tree to get out of range.

African lions, polar bears, tigers, sharks, and saltwater crocodiles—they're all big and can kill us with little effort. It may seem that you have little chance against a 500- to 2,000-pound (227- to 907-kg) animal, but remember that perhaps more than any other wild creatures, true predators (just like accidental predators) cannot afford to get injured. Unlike benign creatures such as rabbits (which can sustain an injury but continue to forage for food), if a predator is seriously hurt, its ability to hunt—and therefore to eat—is impaired. For instance, a wolf that suffers a broken jaw from a tangle with a moose is as good as dead. Animals such as these will often retreat rather than fight.

STROUD'S TIP

Your fire may not be as effective as you thought in keeping you safe from animals. A small fire will provide warmth, light to see what is going on around the shelter, and burning logs that can be used as "weapons" to scare off animals. But big fires can attract curious predators, and also insects and scorpions. Build your fire using heavy, hard wood that will burn slowly through the night, provide long-lasting coals, and offer strong "missiles" as weapons in case of an attack.

But if a true predator attacks you, your only chance may be to fight back. If you end up in a body of salt water during a survival situation, don't create a lot of turbulence by thrashing about, as sharks are attracted to this type of behavior. While filming a TV special on sharks in the Caribbean, I was treading water with a number of lemon sharks beneath me and two tiger sharks close by (accidental and true predators). We posed the question whether it was better to swim as fast as possible to the boat or lie still and let the boat come to get me. When I made my move by swimming quickly and splashing a lot, a huge shark darted straight for me, excited by my movements.

Never enter the water if you are bleeding, as a shark can detect even the smallest amount of blood in the water. Finally, do not throw entrails or garbage into the water, as this, too, may attract sharks. Look behind any cruise ship that throws its food refuse overboard and you will see hundreds of sharks.

If you do encounter a shark, your only option is to defend yourself. A shark's most sensitive place is its nose; direct your blows there. Remember that sharks like to attack from behind, so try to face the shark at all times. Keep your back against a coral reef or wreckage, if there is any. Go back-to-back with your dive buddy and put any object you have, your underwater video camera, for example, between yourself and the shark. Oh . . . and get out of the water!

Swimming with Caribbean reef sharks in the Bahamas was thrilling, though intimidating.

Secure Your Shelter from Predator Attack

In making my survival films in the African plains and the Kalahari Desert, I had the wonderful opportunity to learn from Koos Moorecroft, Raphael Gunduza, and Douw Kruger, three of the most knowledgeable survival experts in Africa. I asked Douw to give me his thoughts on dealing with the wild animals of Africa:

Surviving in the African wilderness means that you must take precautions to limit encounters with animals like lions, leopards, and hyenas, especially at night when a survivor in a shelter is nothing more than a sitting duck.

This is not to say these predators will come after you like man-eaters, but they are curious animals and might investigate for an easy meal. Their senses are extremely well developed and they will smell your presence from a distance and see your movements easily at night.

These animals all move very quietly, so it's not easy to hear them. The best you can (and must) do is secure your shelter or sleeping place, and plan an escape route for an emergency situation. You can also install an early-warning system to wake you up when something is moving around the shelter.

Securing your shelter should be planned and done properly, as you are dealing with powerful and clever predators. If not, you will have nothing more than a false sense of security, which may end up as a nasty surprise. Spending a little extra energy securing your shelter properly will provide a safe place, which will reward you with a good night's sleep.

Create an Early-Warning System

When alone at night in a survival situation, you'll have better peace of mind if you've put up something that will warn you in advance of a predator's approach. Use a long, thin piece of string or fishing line as a trip line around the perimeter of your shelter, about a foot and a half (0.5 meter) off the ground. Connect the line to anything that will make noise when moved or banged together.

Even a small rock balanced on a piece of wood over a larger rock will wake you if it's knocked over in the quiet of the night. You can also use any number of trapping trigger mechanisms to get a big log to fall on a dry, thinner log to create a loud cracking sound.

Tips on Dealing with Dangerous Animals

There are numerous theories as to the best way to deal with dangerous animals, but here are a few tips:

- Prepare properly, as if you are expecting an unwelcome visitor.
- Do not keep meat or other smelly stuff in or near your shelter. Suspend food by a rope from a tree branch 50 yards (46 m) or more away.
- Do not leave anything outside your shelter, as it will be chewed up and carried away by lions and hyenas.
- Do not build a large fire, as it will attract some animals and insects.
- Urinate on the bushes around the outside of the shelter during the day. It can be smelled from a greater distance than if you urinate on the ground, and the odor may help to keep animals away.
- Do not leave your shelter at night!

Angry Ungulates

Despite the bad press animals such as bears, cougars, and lions get, there's another group that's rarely written about or discussed in this vein, and yet they can be some of the most dangerous creatures you'll ever cross paths with in the wilderness (even if they won't eat you): ungulates, or hoofed mammals.

In the rutting (mating) season, a bull moose can turn into 1,500 pounds (680 kg) of testosterone-driven rage. They've been known to attack vehicles. Get too close to one during this time and you may never live to tell the tale. For that matter, all ungulates—even the seemingly gentle elk—pose a significant danger during the rut.

The females of these species can also be formidable foes when they're with their young and can kill a person with one kick of their hooves.

Other Dangerous Animals

- elephants: Need I say more?
- buffalo, musk oxen, water buffalo: Powerful and very smart, those in Africa are considered to be the most aggressive animals you will encounter.
- hippopotamuses: Surprisingly, hippopotamuses are responsible for more deaths every year than lions.
- rhinoceroses: Nervous and defensive, each of these animals has an oh-so-big horn.
- ostriches: An ostrich protecting its nest can slice open your rib cage with one swipe of its claws.

Creepy Crawlies

CREEPY CRAWLIES ARE ALL THOSE STINGING and biting creatures that give most of us the shivers. This group includes snakes, lizards, spiders, scorpions, ants, bees, ticks, and leeches. It is important to know something about these creatures and how to travel safely through their world.

As nasty as creatures like the tarantula may seem, creepy crawlies abide by the same guidelines as their kin in the animal world: except in the case of rare exceptions like leeches and ticks, they want nothing to do with you and are *not* on the lookout for you. Solid pre-trip research will tell you what *you* need to watch out for.

The only ways you will get bitten or stung by creepy crawlies is if you abruptly enter their space and scare them, if they enter your space and get scared (usually in camp or at night), or if you provoke them. For that reason, slow, deliberate movement is essential at all times.

You are at much greater risk from creepy crawlies than from predators and other dangerous animals, due to their numbers. I once spent seven days alone in the jungle and although I encountered no snakes, I saw lots of monster-sized poisonous ants, a couple of spiders, and a poisonous frog.

The rule of thumb when it comes to creepy crawlies is to minimize your exposure to them. In the desert, for example, where there are lots of scorpions around, I build my bed up off the ground so that I won't find one in with me when I wake up.

Most creepy crawly encounters occur during the night when creatures such as scorpions, snakes, and spiders seek out warmth, and you represent nothing more to them than a large mass of radiant energy. So as ridiculous as it may seem, they really just want to snuggle up with you. It's only when you move quickly, accidentally or out of panic, that you get bitten. You could literally sleep through the night and not even realize that a number of poisonous creatures had crossed your skin.

A man in Africa once had a black mamba (arguably the most aggressive and dangerous snake in the world) slither down into his sleeping bag to get warm for the night. The man was nearly hysterical when he realized this and was convinced the snake would bite him. His camping mates decided that in one swift motion two of them would yank him out by his shoulders while two others whipped the sleeping bag off his feet. They did just that, and in the few seconds it took to complete the task, the snake bit the man 13 times, killing him. Chances are the snake eventually would have left if the man had lain still and waited it out.

When it comes to avoiding creepy crawlies, a little local knowledge goes a long way. Learn before you head out what you need to watch for and where it lives. Generally, you should follow these rules to minimize contact with creepy crawlies:

- Keep your hands and feet out of dark places such as rock crevices, heavy brush, or hollow logs. If you need to get into such places for supplies or shelter, first use a long stick to probe the area and scare out any problem critters. Indeed, any time you slam your foot down beside a crevice, crack, or hole, you're risking a bite, because these are the places where snakes like to curl up. Bringing your foot down right beside one might be enough to get you bitten.
- Close up your pants, sleeves, and necklines tightly.
- Get up off the ground when you sleep. If you have bug netting, wrap yourself in it (rather than just placing it on top of you).
- Don't leave your clothes or shoes lying around on the ground while you sleep, and always shake them out and check them before you put them back on. Most scorpion stings occur on the foot after a scorpion has spent the night in a traveler's shoe or boot.
- Wear protective clothing if possible. Most snakebites occur at the ankles, so leather boots that cover this area can help. Bug jackets and pants, as well as general mosquito netting, help fend off most flying, biting insects.
- Pay attention! Creepy crawlies are not that easy to spot, so stay alert as you move through their world. Look up. You don't want to walk headlong into a hornets' nest, or grab a branch that's covered in stinging ants. Look down if you're walking through heavy brush or tall grass.
- Don't bother them and they won't bother you. In the Amazon jungle, a Waorani man toyed with a spider by poking it with a stick. He just kept poking and poking, and eventually the spider decided it had had enough, jumped 5 feet (1.5 m) at the guy's face, and sank his fangs right into his nose. He later told me it was one of the most painful things he'd ever experienced.

Poisonous Plants

As those of us who have suffered through a bout of poison ivy can attest, coming into contact with a poisonous plant—let alone ingesting it—can be an extremely unpleasant experience. Poisoning from plants can result in anything from minor irritation to death.

An important part of your trip planning and preparation is to learn which plants you'll encounter when you're in the wild, especially since many edible plants have poisonous look-alikes. Also, don't believe the following misconceptions about poisonous plants:

Misconception: "Eat what the animals eat."
Fact: Not true. Animals sometimes eat plants that are poisonous to the rest of us.

Misconception: "If I boil the plant, the toxins will be removed."
Fact: In some cases, boiling doesn't remove all toxins.

Misconception: "Red . . . you're dead."
Fact: Some red plants are poisonous, but not all.

Misconception: "White . . . just right."
Fact: Many white plants and berries *are* poisonous.

If you don't know what a plant is, don't touch it or eat it. Eating the wrong plant can kill you. Nausea and vomiting, diarrhea, abdominal cramps, depressed heartbeat and respiration, headaches, and hallucinations are all symptoms of poisoning.

If you suspect you've eaten a poisonous plant, immediately induce vomiting. This will bring up some of the toxic matter, but not all. After vomiting, if you have an ample supply of water, drink as much as possible to dilute the poison.

When you have no knowledge of a plant, suspect it's edible, and have no other choice but starvation, then you need to do an edibility test before you ingest any quantity of it. (For more on edibility tests, refer to "Food," Chapter 8.) However, never eat mushrooms! Identifying mushrooms is a very exact science, and if you eat the wrong one, it can kill you quickly. Mushrooms offer little nutrition in return for the chance you are taking.

My friend in survival Dave Arama has this to add: "In a survival situation, and on an empty stomach, even a mildly toxic plant can kill you. With a full stomach as in our everyday lives, ingesting a mildly toxic plant will probably result in a stomach ache or in the worst-case scenario a quick visit to the hospital."

If you suspect that your skin has come into contact with a poisonous plant, your first course of action should be to try to remove the oil by washing the area with soap and cold water. If there is no water nearby, use dirt or sand to wipe your skin (but not if blisters have already appeared there).

The toxin and the infection can be spread by touching the infected area and then touching another part of your body, so resist the urge to scratch! Bandage the infected area to prevent any other part of your body from coming in contact with the infection.

Aside from the dangers of touching and eating unknown plants, there is another little-known way that plants can be harmful: if you burn them. People have experienced life-threatening health issues from burning piles of poison ivy and inadvertently breathing the smoke.

Plants can prove hazardous through more than just their poisons, too. Many are covered in spikes, spines, barbs, or thorns that can cause excruciating pain that, if left unattended, can result in festering wounds. One unfortunate hiker who was walking carelessly through the desert tripped and held out his hand to break his fall. He landed on a saguaro cactus, and a 4-inch (10- cm) spine went right through his palm and out the other side.

Some plants can be hazardous because of the insects they host. Certain plants and insects help each other out. For example, there is a bush in the Amazon jungle that is home to a very protective type of ant. Get too close to the bush and the ants will actually jump out and attack you. Grab the bush and all bets are off. For this reason, wear gloves when possible and tuck your pants into your socks whenever you travel in creepy-crawly country, no matter how uncomfortable it may be.

Don't overlook the importance of footwear as protective clothing. One time in Arizona, I stopped in the middle of a hike because of excruciating pain on the top of one foot. It turned out to be a teddy-bear cactus making its way through my leather boots. The only scorpion sting I ever got was while wearing sandals in the desert. The scorpion also stung me on my index finger as I pulled it off my foot (and the numbness lingered for nearly two years).

Lack of Sleep

It may seem benign in the context of huge weather events, predators, and deadly plants, but lack of sleep may well pose a more significant threat than any of these other hazards. Though it takes significant sleep deprivation to kill a human, the risk from it lies in how it affects your ability to function in the wild. Lack of sleep has been shown to adversely affect brain function, growth, healing, and general ability.

We tend to sleep poorly in survival situations, but it is important to try to get as much sleep as possible. Sleep keeps you fresh, alert, and well-functioning, and it cuts down on your energy requirements when you are awake.

As survival instructor Dave Arama likes to say, "If you don't have to walk, sit down, and if you don't have to sit down, lie down." To that I add that if you don't have to be awake (particularly to signal for rescue), sleep. My most restful naps happen at around 2 p.m., during the warmth of the day. It's the wrong time to sleep if you want to be rescued, but when sleeping at night is often so difficult, I'll take what I can get to keep my sanity.

Starvation

Human beings certainly need food to survive, but most of us overestimate the significance of food in a survival situation. This, I've found, is one of the greatest risks you'll encounter regarding food in the wild: thinking you need three meals a day to function properly.

The truth is, you can survive for a very long time without food, sometimes as long as a month. You won't be functioning very well after the first couple of weeks, but you won't necessarily die, either.

While making my survival films, the primary issue I face due to not eating is lack of energy. I work for 20 minutes, then have to sit down and rest for the same amount of time. Then I work again for another 20 minutes until I am exhausted and need to rest again. This continues until I somehow get something to eat. See "Food," Chapter 8, for more information.

Dehydration

THE DECISION AS TO WHETHER TO DRINK UNPURIFIED WATER comes down to a question of risk. Can drinking unpurified water kill you? Definitely. But with a few exceptions, it can take a week or more before the effects of drinking bad water are felt. Dehydration, on the other hand, will kill you more quickly; after only three to four days your ability to function well is reduced.

Clearly, your first choice should be for clean or filtered water. But if you have no other choice, drink the unpurified water and hope that you can reach safety in time to deal with the water-borne illnesses you may have contracted as a result.

Use some common sense when you see a tainted water source. Can you get to other water? Is it contaminated with something you think could be deadly, or is it just dirty? Remember, sparkling clean water can hide some pretty nasty diseases too. See "Water," Chapter 5, for more information.

Cold Weather

WHILE FILMING A SPECIAL FOR THE DISCOVERY CHANNEL on surviving in Alaska, I had the distinct pleasure of jumping through an ice hole cut in an Alaskan lake and spending 13 minutes immersed in frigid water with one of the world's renowned experts in the study of cold on the human body. I asked my friend Gordon Giesbrecht, PhD, professor of thermophysiology, to pen the following sections on hypothermia and frostbite.

Hypothermia

When people play in the wilderness, one danger they commonly recognize is hypothermia, the lowering of the body's core temperature from its normal level of 98.6°F (37°C) to 95°F (35°C) or lower.

The onset of hypothermia is slow and usually undetected by the victim. Even in ice water it may take 30 minutes or more to become hypothermic. In cold air, it takes hours or even days.

If you are stranded in a cold air environment, the cold/wet/wind triad can be deadly. Many folks set off on a pleasant day with minimal extra clothing and supplies, only to be overtaken by wind and rain. These conditions can be deadly if you don't have a day pack with some extra clothing. Traveling partners need to watch each other for signs of hypothermia, which can be described as the "umbles": grumbles, fumbles, stumbles, and tumbles. Change in personality, loss of fine and gross motor movement, and shivering are potential signs that you are too cold. Get into a shelter, rest, and ingest high-calorie drinks and foods until you feel better.

Frostbite

Frostbite is the freezing of tissue. Mild frostbite involves freezing superficial layers—skin—while severe frostbite involves freezing flesh below the skin. Obviously, the deeper the freezing, the more damage is done.

Water within tissues freezes and forms ice crystals, and these sharp fragments damage the tissue (one reason why you should never rub the site of frostbite). The major problem resulting from frostbite is the destruction of capillaries. These small vessels are responsible for the exchange of oxygen and nutrients between the blood and tissue. Once tissue is thawed, the frostbitten area can become flushed as blood flow returns to it. But because the capillaries have been destroyed, the blood cannot provide life-giving oxygen.

Our advice to outdoors enthusiasts is this: Never accept numbness. As nerves get progressively colder, sensations progress from cold, to pain, to numbness, to nothing. Numbness is a warning that tissue is nearing the freezing point. At that point, you must get the numb body part out of the cold or add insulation. Simply putting your hands in your armpits can all but guarantee that they won't freeze. If your fingers freeze even when they are in your armpits, your biggest problem isn't frostbite.

"Professor Popsicle" Gordon Giesbrecht and I spent nearly 13 long minutes submerged in the frigid waters of a remote Alaskan lake to test my body's reaction to hypothermia.

Region-Specific Hazards

Arid Regions, Deserts, and Canyons

By far the worst danger in the world's warmer and drier regions is the sun, but it's not the only hazard. You will also find yourself exposed to poisonous creepy crawlies, thorn-covered plants and cacti, contaminated water, and eye irritation from the constant dust and blowing sand.

Extreme heat can affect you in several serious ways. Heat cramps and heat exhaustion are caused by a shortage of water and salt in the body. Symptoms include headache, profuse sweating, weakness, dizziness, irritability, cramps, and sometimes even mental confusion. If you experience any of these symptoms, get into the shade to cool off. Sprinkling water on your body may also help.

Heat stroke is more severe than heat exhaustion and begins to impede the body's natural ability to cool itself. If not treated quickly, it can lead to death. Symptoms include hot, dry skin and a visible lack of sweat, as well as headache, dizziness, confusion, nausea, and vomiting. If you suspect heat stroke, get into the shade and pour water on your body if possible (even if the water is contaminated). Consume water every few minutes, but only in small quantities; large amounts will bring on vomiting.

My most dangerous survival moment occured in the Kalahari Desert. Two days of drinking hot water and having the sun and wind suck the moisture out of me brought me frighteningly close to heat stroke. It was 117°F (47°C) in the shade and 142°F (61°C) in the sun. By midnight I actually had the sensation that I was getting hotter, though the sun had long since disappeared. Only careful attention to staying immobile and constantly wiping my neck and head with a damp bandana kept me alive. Heat stroke can hit you fast and can kill.

Dehydration is another risk in these regions, particularly when there's wind. The combination of heat and wind will suck the moisture right out of your body. Seek protection from the wind as well as the sun.

The most significant weather event you'll encounter in the desert is a sandstorm. If you have the misfortune of being caught in one, try to get downwind of a shelter. Cover your mouth and nose, and wait. Sand in some deserts can be alkaline and irritating if it finds its way into your many orifices. Breathing in the salty air that blows up from the salt "pans" in a place like the Kalahari Desert can cause serious sinus and lung irritation.

Finally, remember that mirages can and do occur in these regions and they present a hazard (they've also been known to occur in the Arctic). The greatest risk is that a mirage will create optical illusions of what seems to be water in the distance. These illusions can entice you to travel in a direction you otherwise wouldn't or shouldn't go. Be skeptical of the big lake you see in the distance.

Boreal and Other Temperate Forests

Forest fires have become more frequent in the last few decades. The upside of finding yourself close to one is that fires attract firefighters, increasing your chance of rescue. The downside is that you may die. Move in the opposite direction from the fire by determining the prevailing wind. If possible, make your way to a lake. Remember that fire travels faster uphill than downhill.

Underestimating the difficulty of travel in a forest can be a real threat as well. It might seem like your destination is only a mile away, but a mile through some types of thick forest can be hours of pure hell.

The Arctic and Polar Regions

At the top of the list for polar dangers is the weather. Blizzards have taken the lives of many very experienced Arctic travelers. Do not, under any circumstances, travel in a blizzard. If a blizzard strikes (or is imminent), return to your shelter immediately. If you don't yet have a shelter, build one right away. If you don't have time to do this, at least get out of the wind.

Frostbite is another ever-present danger in the world's cold places. Proper clothing is your first line of defense in preventing frostbite, but protecting yourself from the elements—especially the wind—is equally important. See "Survival First Aid," Chapter 13.

Snowblindness, which is essentially a sunburn on your retina, is also a real hazard in these parts. On sunny days, the sun's rays reflect off snow and ice and come at you from all directions. Snowblindness causes excruciating pain and can leave you without proper vision for as long as three days. Protect your eyes in any way you can.

On the Sea or Open Water

As with snowblindness in the Arctic, *sunblindness* is a sunburn of the retina caused by the reflection of the sun's rays on the water.

Seasickness is a malady that affects some people and doesn't touch others at all. If you're prone to it, bring seasickness medication in your first-aid kit. When you're on the open water in a sizable vessel, staying above deck may help. Some say that looking across the horizon instead of at the waves can help. Focusing on small, dexterity-associated tasks, on the other hand, may promote seasickness.

If you do get seasick, allowing yourself to vomit may provide almost immediate relief.

Jungles

Freshwater rivers and lakes in the jungle can host a number of dangerous creatures such as alligators and crocodiles, not all of which are visible from the shore or your boat. Many of these animals have been known to attack boats and other vessels, so plan your trip carefully by avoiding proximity to them whenever possible.

You'll find many smaller, though no less hazardous, critters along the way. The black piranha is the most dangerous freshwater fish in the world.

Limited to northern South America, they are small but have very big teeth, and they travel in large schools capable of devouring a person in minutes. They are most dangerous in shallow waters during the dry season.

Electric eels—which can be 6 ½ feet (2 m) long—are usually found in South America and are capable of generating up to 500 volts of electricity. Large freshwater turtles may seem like an easy meal, but the snapping turtles of North and South America have been known to bite the fingers and toes off unsuspecting people. Even the platypus, which is found only in Australia, has a poisonous spur on each hind foot that can inflict intensely painful wounds.

Far less dramatic but no less a hazard are falling coconuts, silly as that may sound. More people are killed in the tropics every year from falling coconuts than from shark attacks. Victims are usually at the base of a palm tree when it happens. Be careful where you decide to sleep; most of these deaths occur at night.

Rising river levels pose a real threat in the tropics, even if a storm is not apparent in your immediate area. Jungle rivers can rise by as much as 20 feet (6 m) in a few hours, even though the rise is caused by storm systems many miles away.

I think the jungles of this planet are home to more dangers than any other region. An entire book could be dedicated to the subject. From caterpillars to freshwater stingrays, from a deluge of rain to killer ants, from roaming jaguars to wasps as long as pencils, jungles are home to a bewildering array of events and creatures that can hurt or kill you. Yet, jungles are amazingly beautiful places to experience, and they are still my favorite ecosystem for adventuring. They can be for you too, if you're careful.

Coastal Regions

Oceans rival jungles for the most hazards to travelers. Salt water is home to numerous threatening creatures, none as feared as the shark. Shark attacks are rare, however, and usually considered accidents. You can best avoid shark attack by avoiding shark *habitat*.

In shallow waters, you'll find many creatures that can inflict pain and cause infection to develop if you happen to step on them. Invertebrates such as jellyfish are capable of injecting venom by biting or stinging, or through spines located in their fins and tentacles. Although jellyfish-related deaths are relatively uncommon, invertebrate bites or stings can be fatal.

Wear protective footwear when wading near the shoreline. Shuffle your feet along the bottom of the water body (rather than raising them up and stepping), as most of these critters sting from the top rather than from the side. Stingrays, especially those of the tropical variety, can be quite nasty in the shallows.

If you are fishing in these areas, remember that not all fish can be eaten. Though there are no hard-and-fast rules to distinguish edible from poisonous fish, most of the poisonous ones live in shallow water around reefs or lagoons, have box-like or round bodies with shell-like skins covered with bony plates or spines, and have small, parrot-like mouths. As is often the case, being informed about the potentially dangerous creatures in a region can go a long way toward preparing you.

Like mountain areas, coastal regions can be susceptible to fast, violent weather changes. Storms can blow in seemingly without notice; be prepared to seek appropriate shelter.

If you're planning on traveling by water, you should have a working knowledge of local tide patterns, including currents and rip tides. If you're on land, make sure you build your shelter beyond the high-tide mark.

Very low on the probability scale but high on the danger scale are tsunamis, series of waves generated by undersea disturbances such as earthquakes. Tsunamis can cause waves to travel as fast as 450 miles (724 km) per hour, reaching heights of 100 feet (30 m). Tsunamis are sometimes preceded by rapid changes in water level; they typically arrive as a series of successive crests (high water levels) and troughs (low water levels).

If you suspect a tsunami is approaching, move to higher ground immediately. Stay away from the shore. Finally, do not assume that the danger has passed if a lengthy period of time elapses between waves. Tsunami crests can be 90 minutes apart.

Mountains

Full-blown rockslides and mudslides are significant hazards in mountainous country but are fairly rare. Much more common is the rockfall, which can occur at any time. Take extra care when traveling at the base of rock walls, cliffs, or rocky slopes.

When snow is present, the risk of an avalanche occuring is a real one. Stay away from open, exposed slopes that are bare of vegetation, as this is a sign that avalanches regularly rip through the area. The most dangerous slopes are ones that are 34 degrees to 45 degrees, as these hold lots of snow but are steep enough to let it go frequently. The more trees that are present (and the larger they are), the more likely it is that the area is relatively safe from avalanches.

If you get caught in or near an avalanche, seek shelter (if possible) on the downhill side of boulders or trees. Crouch low, face away from the slide, and cover your nose and mouth. Experts recommend using a swimming motion, which may keep you near the top of the slide. If you have the ability to do so, try to make your way to the top of the slide while it is slowing down but still moving. I highly recommend wearing an avalanche beacon when traveling in the mountains.

The upper regions of mountains can also be prone to sudden weather changes. Lightning may also be present; if so, seek shelter and stay off ridges.

Group Versus Solo Survival

As with most aspects of survival, being in a group helps because you benefit from the combined knowledge of the members. Somebody in the group may know about the specific hazards present in a region, which should help you stay well away from the danger.

Chapter Eleven

WEATHER

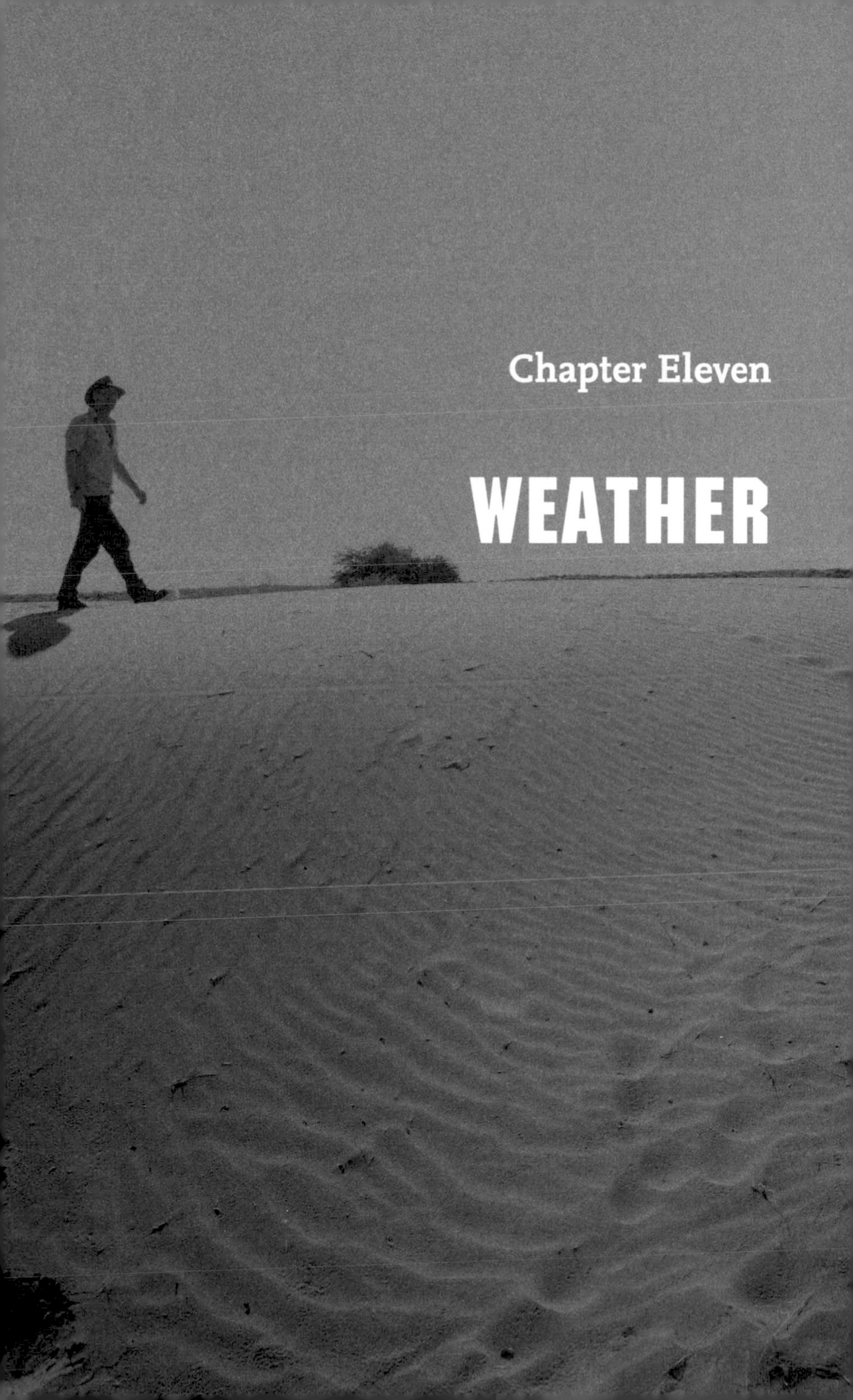

To a certain extent, you can control many aspects of survival—water, fire, shelter, and food. But weather may be the toughest challenge you face in a survival situation because it is one of the few things you *can't* control.

Understand one truth of the wilderness: No matter how beautiful a day it is, the weather will eventually get bad, often quickly and sometimes violently so. And if you're not prepared for the worst, you reduce your chances of making it home alive.

In our day-to-day lives, most of us are ill-prepared for bad weather. Why should we worry? We can always go home or duck into a coffee shop if things get bad. But there is no relief from bad weather in the wilderness. You're either ready for it or you're not. And the stakes are high: rough weather can kill you. Weather is the most important "flow" to go with when lost in the wild.

Prepare to Stay Alive

If you're in a remote area and have failed to anticipate bad weather, you're stuck when it hits. Searching for firewood, trying to build a shelter, or looking for food and water in driving rain or snow can be deadly.

Preparing for bad weather, therefore, is a high priority for the adventurer. Preparation may be as simple as moving your firewood to a dry spot or as complex as building a shelter that will protect you against a coming blizzard. Whether I'm in a survival situation or just on a camping trip, I'm always doing one of two things regarding the weather: taking advantage of the good weather to prepare for the bad or hunkering down during bad weather and doing what I can "inside." Bad weather can present a perfect opportunity to take care of little jobs that don't require you to be outside. Given the proper amount of materials, space, heat, and light, you can accomplish tasks like sharpening knives, building traps and snares, creating fishing implements, mending your clothing, or working on a signal device while a storm rages around you.

Once the weather brightens up again (and it will), you will have your chance to gather those wild berries you know are in a particular spot, travel to another location, hunt, or fish.

Weather Versus Climate

WEATHER AND CLIMATE ARE TWO DISTINCT BEASTS. While weather can change on a dime, climate is the average weather that predominates in an area over a long period of time. It's a variable that's largely known and understood, and one that can and should be prepared for well in advance of your trip. Preparation could mean the difference between life and death.

STROUD'S TIP

If your local research uncovers the fact that weather can change quickly in a region, don't underestimate it. Be ready.

I knew before visiting the Amazon jungle that it rained a lot. There are basically two seasons: wet and wetter (it is, after all, a rain forest). Though I visited during the "less wet" season, I discovered that it could still rain for three days at a time. The pre-trip research I did on the climate made a huge difference to my survival for the next seven days. I also heeded warnings that rivers could rise 20 feet (6 m) in a few hours. I tied my dugout canoe to a spot on a tree 8 feet (2.4 m) off the ground, and still the force of the flood threatened to snap the tether rope!

In the jungle, don't assume water levels will remain static for any period of time. I almost lost my dugout canoe—and my primary mode of travel—to a swollen river.

Ways to Predict Weather and Interpret Weather Signs

PREDICTING WEATHER OFTEN BOILS DOWN to one basic question: How long is the good weather going to last? The answer will tell you how long you've got to complete the other tasks important to your survival, particularly if you're planning on traveling. Learning some basic forecasting methods could save you from being caught out in a storm.

Local Guidance

Since weather is so area-specific, the best way to discover natural predictors is to talk to locals. They will know the subtle signs in their environment that are almost impossible to relate in the pages of a book. You may have someone say to you, "If you notice that all the birds suddenly stop singing while you're out there, bad weather is coming." Listen to the experts.

Barometers

If you're lucky enough to have one, a barometer makes predicting weather a heck of a lot easier. Decreasing air pressure usually indicates the approach of a low-pressure system, which brings clouds and precipitation. Increasing air pressure, on the other hand, means that a high pressure system is approaching, bringing with it fine weather.

Wind and Wind Patterns

To predict wind patterns, start by gaining an understanding of the prevailing winds for an area. You can then detect if a wind is coming from a different direction. If this occurs, or if winds are beginning to swirl around every which way, a change in weather may be coming.

Clouds

I still have a hard time naming all the different types of cloud patterns, whether they be cumulonimbus or nimbostratus. I can, however, make a pretty good guess as to what they foretell, and that's largely based on a few general characteristics:

- The darker and lower the clouds, the more likely they are to carry precipitation. The higher and finer the clouds, the better the weather will be (though it may become windy).
- A general increase in the density of clouds may indicate a change in the weather. I've been in many situations where this was an indicator that a system was developing.
- The approach of a long bank of clouds on the horizon on an otherwise fair day may also indicate that foul weather is on its way.

Fireside Smoke

You can actually use the smoke from your fire to help make very rough weather predictions. If the smoke rises steadily with little change, the pleasant weather you're currently enjoying should stay for a while. If you see that the smoke begins to swirl after rising a little way, or if it seems to be beaten down, a storm or shower may be on its way.

If you're near a lake and notice that the smoke hangs low over the water, rain may be approaching.

The Sky

There is a reason why adages persist through generations: they're largely true. "Red skies at night, sailor's delight; red skies in the morning, sailors take warning." This is more of a short-term indicator but a good one nonetheless. A red sky at dusk indicates that the weather will stay fair for at least the next few hours; if the sky is red at dawn, however, beware: a low-pressure system (and possibly a storm) may be on its way. Don't confuse a red sky with a *red sun* in the morning. If the sun is red at sunrise but the sky is normal in color, the day should be fair. If you find yourself in hilly or mountainous terrain, pay attention to how the early-morning mist moves. If it lifts early in the morning, you will likely have a fair day. If it has not moved by early afternoon, it likely won't, and you may experience some precipitation later.

The night sky can also help you predict the weather. If it is clear at night, the weather should stay calm. If you can't see many stars one night after a few clear ones, you may be in for a change.

Dangerous Weather

DANGEROUS WEATHER EVENTS MAY WELL BE RESPONSIBLE for killing more people in survival situations than any other danger or hazard. Familiarizing yourself with weather events will help you prepare for them and know how to react when they hit.

Hurricanes

Hurricanes occur in relatively few places on this earth, but when they do, they can be devastating. It's not likely that your little stick shelter could withstand the force of a hurricane, so if one is on its way, seek out something more substantive, such as a cave.

If you're in a coastal region, perhaps the greatest risk from hurricanes is the storm surge, a dome of ocean water that can reach as high as 20 feet (6 m) and 50 to 100 miles (80 to 160 km) wide.

Thunderstorms and Lightning Storms

Most of the time, thunderstorms give notice of their impending arrival with dark, threatening clouds and distant lightning and thunder. You can estimate your distance from an approaching thunderstorm by counting the number of seconds that elapse between a flash of lightning and the next clap of thunder. Divide this number by five and you have a rough idea of how many miles away the storm is.

All thunderstorms are accompanied by lightning, which is one of the primary risks of being outside in a survival situation when one hits. The best thing you can do during a thunderstorm is hunker down and hope your shelter is strong enough to withstand the onslaught. If you do get caught outside, avoid natural lightning rods such as tall, isolated trees in open areas; stay away from hilltops and other high, exposed places. And remember that dead or rotting trees and branches can fall during severe thunderstorms.

At one point while living in the boreal forest for a year, my wife, Sue, and I were holed up in our tipi during an intense storm. The wind was so strong that our tiny lake even had whitecaps on it. That's when we noticed that the tree we had built our shelter beside had nearly blown over. Had it done so, the entire root system would have lifted up right in the middle of our shelter and ripped it apart. We were also worried about lightning striking the tree. Our poor location choice for the shelter, made on an earlier, sunny day, resulted in our holding on to our walls and our wits that day and waiting out a potentially devastating storm. We got lucky, that time.

Blizzards and Wind Chill

Never go out in whiteout conditions, when you can't see more than a few feet in front of you! If you have no choice but to do so, make sure you layer your clothing so that you can remove items as you warm up. Try not to sweat profusely, as this will only soak your clothes and make you even colder.

Wind chill can often accompany a blizzard, though not necessarily. Wind chill is a calculation of how cold it *feels* based on temperature and wind speed. If the temperature is extremely cold and there is a steady wind, stay inside. Wind chill is the culprit in most cases of frostbite or hypothermia.

Sandstorms

Sandstorms are exclusive to deserts and can be devastating when they occur. If you see one approaching, get downwind of a shelter, cover your mouth and nose, and wait it out.

Region-Specific Dangers and Hazards

BECAUSE WEATHER CAN BE LOCALIZED to very small geographic areas, the best way to learn about prevailing weather patterns is to do serious research before departing on any trip. Locals will be your greatest source of information here, so try to spend time, either before or at the beginning of your trip, with someone who has been on the land.

Arid Regions, Deserts, and Canyons

Though more of a climatic concern than a weather event, extreme heat can be a serious problem in these regions. Extreme heat can cause cramps, exhaustion, and even stroke. If you're becoming overcome by the heat, get out of the sun and try to pour some water on your body. Consume water in small amounts. Extreme heat kills and does so by pushing your body beyond its natural limits. Under normal circumstances, your body deals with heat by producing perspiration to cool itself through evaporation. In instances of extreme heat (and humidity), however, this evaporation process is slowed, forcing your body to work harder to maintain a normal temperature.

The Arctic and Polar Regions

Wind chill is the result of cold temperatures and wind. Do not expose yourself to these elements in combination for any length of time.

Jungles

River levels can rise as a result of a distant storm. Tropical rivers can rise by as much as 20 feet (6 m) in a few hours. If you see the water level rising, get as far away from the river as possible, preferably to higher ground.

Coastal Regions

Coastal regions are susceptible to sudden, violent weather changes. Thunderstorms can arrive with little notice; hurricanes are far less likely, though more dangerous.

Tsunamis are even less likely, though utterly devastating when they occur. If you see that the entire ocean has receded in what seems like a crazy, extremely low tide, it is a sign of an impending tsunami . . . so head for the hills!

Mountains

Sudden weather changes, including lightning, occur in the upper regions of mountains. In winter, mountains are subject to significant amounts of snowfall, and blizzards are also common.

Chapter Twelve

CLOTHING

Before you have time to build that first shelter, before you have the time to make a fire and even before you have the time to figure out what you're going to do next, your clothing is already working for you. Your clothing is your first shelter and therefore your primary defense against the elements.

Yet despite its importance, most travelers don't give clothing the attention it deserves. Remember that people have died simply because they wore the wrong clothing. Never underestimate the value of the right clothes.

In choosing clothing for your expedition or adventure, you need to ask yourself this question: "What does my clothing have to do?" It must protect you from the wind and the rain, from the dry, from the cold and the heat, from poisonous plants and creepy crawlies. It has to get you through the various stages of the day and the night, and to be of a construction and weight that allows you to travel without it becoming a hassle.

Research and Planning

Researching and planning what clothing (including extra clothing) you're going to take with you on a wilderness adventure is as vital as any other preparation for your journey, including planning your route and the food required. What could be more important than the clothes on your back?

To figure out the most appropriate clothing to take, spend time talking with the people who know. Whether it's the staff at the closest outdoors store, your experienced outdoorsy friends, or local guides at your destination, try to get as much information as you can from people who have first-hand experience with the area you'll be visiting or the activities you'll be doing.

In the case of boots or shoes, you can help prevent blisters by wearing them around town to break them in before you go on your trip. You want to know before you go whether they'll actually work for you. The same goes for your clothing. Find out now whether your new raincoat will keep you protected in a downpour.

STROUD'S TIP

Dressing for survival is easy when you're taking a survival course, because you know what's coming. The trick is to dress appropriately for your adventure activities (hiking, fishing, hunting, kayaking, et cetera) and still be prepared if you end up in a survival ordeal. It's a matter of fashion versus function. A lot of high-tech clothing is not adequate when you're fighting to survive.

In the Arctic, I arrived with all the high-tech gear I could get my hands on. In the end, though, I traded it to a local Inuit hunter for his caribou parka and pants. It was then that I truly realized how clothing can act as your first shelter, your primary line of defense against the elements. In those clothes, I could literally stand still in the wind and cold and not feel a thing. The clothing *was* my shelter. So don't close your mind to the effectiveness of traditional clothing, which though it looks rustic, may work better than anything you could buy in a store.

What you wear really depends on where you are going, the activity, and the season. But with few exceptions, layering (as opposed to using just one layer, like a snowmobile suit) is the best bet. With layering, which means three to five layers of clothing from your skin to your outer shell,

Perhaps the greatest cold-weather clothing ever conceived: full caribou parka and pants.

you can strip down or dress back up again depending on the weather and how you are feeling. Layering is a hassle, because it takes time to put on or take off several pieces of clothing to get warmer or cooler, but it could save your life. Perhaps the best thing layering does for you is help to prevent sweating, a factor critical to survival. Peeling off layers allows you to cool yourself down gradually as you work or travel, while still keeping you as warm as you need to be.

In the gung-ho early years of my survival training, I would merrily work for hours to make a robust shelter, no matter what the weather. Soon I'd be soaked in sweat. As night fell and temperatures dropped, I often found myself without enough time to dry my clothes, even if I had a fire. The chills I felt were devastating. If I had had the foresight to layer my clothes, I would have staved off hypothermia-inducing chills.

When doing strenuous labor in the cold, don't sweat! Staying dry will keep you warm later, but if you sweat, you'll feel the chill for hours after.

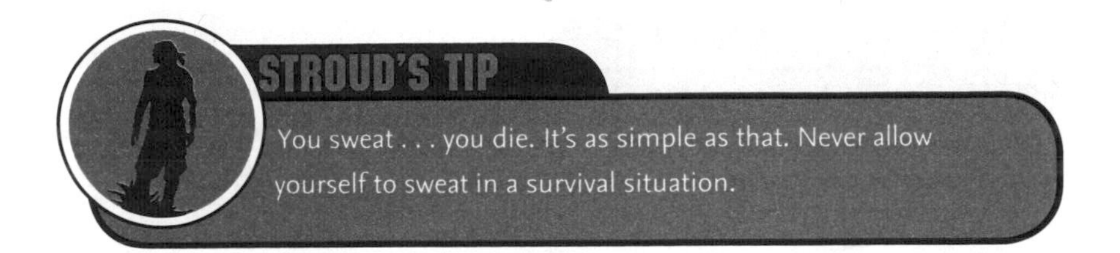

Layering is vital in every type of climate. Even deserts are notorious for cooling at night; you don't have to be in a cold climate or season to become hypothermic. In fact, many cases of hypothermia occur every year in the fall and spring, when people are fooled by a nice day followed by a cold night. Wearing enough layers can make the difference in a survival circumstance.

Traditional or High-Tech Gear?

In my adventuring, the question often is whether I should wear high-tech or more traditional gear. High-tech clothing is usually light and warm, brightly colored, and easily packed and transported. However, should the worst happen and you find yourself in a survival situation (like a canoe dumped in rapids in the middle of northern Canada), such clothing rarely stands up to a few days spent in a bush shelter or sleeping beside a fire.

Take Gore-Tex as a perfect example of the conflict between rugged and high-tech. Gore-Tex is a fantastic material. It will keep you fairly dry in damp conditions because it sheds the rain and still breathes. But try sleeping beside a fire in it: one spark, one touch of an ember, and Gore-Tex melts. So high-tech clothing may be great for outdoor adventuring, but it's less than ideal in survival situations.

Not so with wool, cotton, or canvas-like materials, which are tough and can handle the rigors when you're pushing through dense forest to get firewood or food. With these materials, an ember will burn a hole only in the spot where it lands, and often not before you can flick it off. On the other hand, cotton is horrible if it gets wet because it takes so long to dry. Wool is very heavy, especially when it gets wet, yet it retains 80 percent of its insulating value.

In the end, the best option in a survival situation is to have a combination of lightweight, high-tech clothing for your under-layers and some

STROUD'S TIP

If you plan on taking survival courses and don't want to drop a fortune on new gear, go the other route: buy second-hand clothing such as wool sweaters.

rugged traditional clothing for your outer layers. But this usually applies only for survival courses or hunting and fishing trips, not sea kayaking, mountain climbing, hiking, or other similar adventures. For anything that requires a high level of physical activity, the lighter, high-tech gear wins out.

When Clothing Kills

CLOTHING DOESN'T ALWAYS FIT OR WORK the way it's intended to, which can be deadly in a survival situation. If you begin to feel any kind of chafing or rubbing from your clothes or shoes—especially on your feet—stop and deal with it *immediately*. When you're fighting to survive, you're not going to finish the day in the comfort and cleanliness of your home, where you can take a bath, throw your clothes in the laundry basket, and tend to your wounds. In the wild, you can't afford to wait.

Perhaps nobody better understands the urgency of such situations than adventure racers. They know that they have 1 to 10 days of nonstop tromping through the bush ahead of them, so if they begin to feel any type of hot spot developing, they stop and do whatever they can to prevent it from getting worse. If they don't, it could cripple them. Remember, you can't walk on a foot full of blisters, and if you can't walk, you can't perform any of the tasks necessary to survive.

Keep It Dry and Clean

IN A SURVIVAL SITUATION, YOU SHOULD STRIKE a symbiotic relationship with your clothing: It protects you, and you should also protect it.

To the best of your ability, keep your clothing dry. Now, that doesn't mean you shouldn't crawl into that old rotting log to sleep for the night, especially if that will keep you alive. But if the opportunity arises the next day to dry some of your clothing, take advantage of it. Clean and dry clothing will last much longer than wet clothing, which will rot and disintegrate. Dirt and dampness also reduce the effectiveness of clothes as insulation.

Keeping your clothing clean also reduces the possibility of skin infection. If you don't have a way to wash your clothes, at least shake them out and leave them in direct sunlight for a couple of hours. If possible, never go to bed wearing damp clothing, as this increases your risk of hypothermia.

Extra Is Always Better

CLOTHING TENDS TO GET PRETTY BEAT UP in survival ordeals, so the more you have with you, the better. You can never have too much clothing, unless its bulk or weight prevents you from traveling to safety. If you end up carrying so much clothing and gear that it takes your energy away from looking for food and water, then it's time to make the difficult decision about what you're going to leave behind.

Making Clothing

THOUGH THIS IS A FAVORITE TOPIC OF SURVIVALISTS, the fact is that you're not going to make clothing in a survival situation. Making clothing from the bush is camp craft and it takes many months. Sure, you can make a coat out of cedar bark; you can kill an animal and tan its hide. But that is about wilderness living, not survival. If your survival situation lasts long enough for you to make clothing from natural materials, you're probably past the survival stage and have decided to call the wilderness your home.

There are a couple of materials, however, that you may be able to use to make emergency clothing if necessary and that don't require too much time or expertise. The first is birch bark. If you are able to peel off a large enough strip of birch bark, you can fashion it into a crude hat or rain poncho. But it's not easy. Native North Americans were able to peel new birch bark cleanly only in the spring; try to peel bark from dead trees, when they are rotting but hopefully not too far gone.

If you are a skilled hunter or trapper, or are fortunate enough to catch an animal, you can use the animal skin as a primitive form of clothing. The skin of a snowshoe hare peels easily off the carcass. Cut only along the bottom end, from foot to foot, and then roll it back like you are pulling off a wet sock. With the fur on the inside, you can use the skin as a mitt or a sock. If you have the skin of a larger animal such as a deer, you can cut a head hole and slip the skin on like a poncho, with the fur facing in toward your body.

Before doing that, though, remember that most animals also carry pests such as ticks, lice, and fleas. If you have enough water available, wash the skin or even smoke it over a fire; if not, just give it a good shake. Try to remove as much of the fat and meat as possible, and dry it out before you wear it.

Another thing you can quite easily do using natural materials is boost the insulation abilities of your existing clothing. If you have loose-fitting clothing and have remembered to layer, you can stuff the various layers

When using leaves or other plant matter for insulation, look for the driest materials you can find. These natural materials will increase the insulating abilities of whatever you are wearing.

You Sweat, You Die

It was –10 degrees celsius in the dead of winter when his snowmobile ran out of gas. He had no food, water, or matches, and was completely lost in the northern Manitoba wilderness, a vast expanse of isolated bush hundreds of miles from any urban centre. But Christopher Traverse, a 24-year-old construction worker, had a survivor's instinct, and he remembered some tips he had learned from watching my survival films.

With the temperature dropping steadily on that first bone-chilling night, Chris modeled a shelter after one he'd seen me construct, fashioning a makeshift bed and enclosure out of the scant resources he had at hand—spruce branches and his snowmobile. And that's how he survived the massive blizzard that descended later that night.

The next morning, he began a three-day trek through waist-deep snow, which he often ate. He would later tell me that he remembered how I point out that as long as you eat snow during the day while you're working (and not later as you cool down), you can keep yourself hydrated without increasing your risk of hypothermia.

Far off on the horizon, Chris spotted the glowing beacon of the Devil's Lake communication tower. He was determined to make it there. Walking 12 hours a day, he also recalled another of my favorite survival tips: "If you sweat, you die." So Chris was careful to air out his socks every night to keep the sweat from freezing his feet, and he wisely reserved one layer of dry clothes for sleeping.

An eagle followed Chris overhead everyday, and he began to think of it as his elder guide, coaxing him to carry on. Search crews also soared above him, but despite his best efforts, he couldn't get their attention. They couldn't see him through the heavy snowfall. He kept walking.

After five grueling days, Chris found a highway, flagged a Greyhound bus and made it to the aptly named Last Resort »

Convenience Store. There, he was picked up by the RCMP, who were astonished to find him in such good condition. When asked how he'd managed to survive, Chris responded, "I just held my composure. I didn't let fright pull me down."

When Chris and I spoke after his ordeal, we knew immediately there was something in his story, similar to so many of mine, something that he could only ever share with people who have had similar experiences. Spending the majority of a cold, dark night jumping up and down trying not to freeze to death in the middle of the bush is not something most people can relate to. But using his wits and a few survival skills he'd seen on my shows, Chris had made it out of the wilderness . . . alive.

with light, airy materials such as leaves or cattail fluff. In essence, you are creating a down-like layer in your clothes, which will greatly increase their ability to keep you warm.

Footwear

THE IMPORTANCE OF PACKING AND wearing the right footwear cannot be overstated. All it takes is the wrong footwear to make walking nearly impossible. Simply put, if you can't walk, you may not survive. Blisters, foot fungus, and swollen feet can often be prevented with the right pair of shoes, sandals, hikers, or boots. Solid ankle support is important for rough bushwhacking or hiking. In the jungles, you have to strike a balance: wearing boots to protect yourself from poisonous bites and yet avoiding foot fungus caused by wearing hiking shoes that are too hot or constricting. The best thing for cold weather is footwear that is just slightly too big—big enough to be able to wriggle your toes to help keep the circulation flowing for warmth.

Region-Specific Clothing Considerations

RESEARCH, RESEARCH, RESEARCH. Nothing will better prepare you for the different types of clothing you'll need in various parts of the world like checking with people who know that area.

Boreal Forests and Arctic Regions

Because of the sometimes-dramatic temperature swings in these areas, the most important consideration is layering. Make sure you have enough items of various weight to deal with both cold and heat.

Arid Regions, Deserts, and Canyons

You lose much less water from your body if you wear a light-colored, loose-fitting shirt, which will protect you from the moisture-sucking properties of the wind. It's not always easy to keep clothing on when the air is so hot, but remember that it will keep you alive in the long run.

Whenever I've underestimated clothing requirements, it's been in the world's hot and dry places. My initial thought would be, "I'm going to be in a desert, I don't need much clothing." But in the Kalahari—where the temperature on the surface of the sand in the sun hits 150°F (67°C) during the day—I still found myself cold at night. There can be a 50°F difference between daytime highs and nighttime lows, and a person's body doesn't handle the great difference in temperatures very well.

Add to this the fact that you might be sleeping on the ground—which will draw the heat right out of you—and the potential for a cold wind, and there's a possibility that you could become chilled and hypothermic. And at the very least, the cold will prevent you from sleeping at night, which will make the rest of your survival experience more miserable than it needs to be.

Jungles

Clothing in the jungle needs to be protected from the never-ending dampness. Cotton rots alarmingly quickly in this sort of area. Try to dry clothing whenever the rain subsides and the sun comes out.

Because there are so many poisonous things to bump into in the jungle, your clothes should also afford you a layer of protection from them.

This means covering your body to keep it safe from the biting, pricking, blood-sucking, and stinging things that lurk there.

Long pants work better than shorts, and long pants that are tucked into socks work better than ones that hang loose. Jungles by their very nature are hot and humid, however, and the last thing you want to do is tuck in your long pants. So when packing, choose pants you can see yourself wearing tucked in for the duration of your journey. Beware of the "zip-off" pants that change from long to short; the zipper around the thigh can severely chafe in the heat of the jungle.

At the opposite end of the spectrum are native peoples, such as the Waorani, who live in the Amazon jungle. They spend a lot of their time naked, because clothes rot so quickly. And clothes take a long time to dry after hours of jungle rain; naked skin does not. The biggest difference between the Waorani and us is that they have generations of knowledge about the jungle in which they live. They know every plant and creature that can hurt them as they run naked through the thick growth. (They still end up with numerous bites and stings!) I wouldn't take the chance on the naked approach, not without years of jungle living under my belt, so to speak.

The Waorani men also wear a string around their waist. It is tied to their foreskin to keep their penis out of the way while they travel through the jungle. Their cultural belief is that when you wear the string around your waist you are "clothed." When you don't wear the string, you are naked, and this is considered shameful. I wore my pants.

On the Sea or Open Water

Similar to snowblindness in the Arctic, sunblindness can affect you out on the open water. Always carry a brimmed hat and sunglasses for water travel.

Chapter Thirteen

SURVIVAL FIRST AID

Like the animals, you will soon realize that nothing limits your effectiveness in the wild more than an injury. What separates us from the beasts, however, is that we can *treat* ourselves (although there is evidence to suggest that some animals treat themselves with herbal medicines by eating certain plants when they have upset stomachs).

Although you have a responsibility to yourself and your travel mates to know as much about wilderness first aid as possible, this is something that can't be mastered by reading a book. I strongly recommend you prepare for your adventure by taking a wilderness first-aid course.

Even then, for all the first aid you may know, a more important factor in survival is injury prevention. All your movements should be planned, methodical, and cautious. If you want to be a TV stuntman, go ahead and leap from cliffs and dash across raging rivers. If you want to survive, then protect yourself against injuries in the first place.

Your Survival First-Aid Kit

Among the most important components of your survival kit are the first-aid items. Ensure too that you are familiar with the kit's contents and know how to use them. See "Survival Kits," Chapter 2.

Like your complete survival kit, your first-aid kit should be customized for the area you're visiting and (to a lesser extent) the activity you're doing.

Herbal Medicines and Healing Plants

WHILE IT'S APPEALING TO THINK that you might be able to heal yourself with plants in the wild, the chances of your doing so are even slimmer than the chances of your finding safe plants to eat. Nor is using plants to heal as simple as picking the plant and either eating it or applying it to your skin. In many cases, complex concoctions require careful preparation.

Healing plants are also region specific and the product of generations of experimentation and use. Near Georgian Bay, Ontario, jewelweed grows right alongside poison ivy and can be a great traditional remedy as a preventative wash for poison ivy. But to use it effectively, you need to learn how to recognize both plants. When I was in the Amazon, Waorani medicine was helpful in curing the fungus on my feet, but it came from a native woman who drew on her own experience and that of her people.

The Importance of Hygiene

SURVIVAL IS DIRTY, but that doesn't mean you should ignore basic hygiene, which is an important way to ward off infection and disease, and to prevent minor injuries from becoming major.

If water is available, try to wash yourself daily, with or without soap. Your hands, hair, feet, and armpits are the likeliest areas of infestation and infection; pay special attention to them.

Always keep your hands clean, since germs found there can infect you and your food. Wash them frequently, especially after a bowel movement. Your hair should also be kept as clean as possible to prevent infestation by fleas and lice.

Another significant aspect of personal hygiene is keeping your clothes clean. This may mean making like your ancient ancestors and scrubbing clothing in a river with rocks. If you don't have a water source nearby, shake your clothes out (especially your underwear and socks) and leave them to dry in the sun for a few hours whenever possible.

Prevent mouth infections and abscesses by brushing your teeth daily, whether or not you have toothpaste. Improvise a toothbrush with a young, green twig, assuming you are sure it's not poisonous (based on all the excellent pre-trip training you did on the local flora and fauna!). Peel the bark off the end of the twig and chew it until the fibers begin to separate. You can use these fibers to dislodge any food bits that accumulate in your teeth. You can also wrap a piece of cloth around your finger to brush your teeth; small amounts of baking soda, sand, or salt can act as abrasives. Fishing line can double as dental floss.

If you find yourself getting damp and musty but don't have sufficient water on hand, strip and let your body dry in the air for at least an hour, while wiping yourself (especially the areas I just mentioned) with a clean rag. Be careful not to let yourself cool down too much. It's better to do a wipe-down early in the day or when the day is at its warmest.

STROUD'S TIP

The four body parts you should protect in survival situations are your eyes, feet, hands, and stomach. All these are vital parts of the body, needed for survival.

Finally, do not soil your site with urine and feces. Choose an area at least 100 yards (91 m) from your camp that will serve as your "outhouse" and use it. Dig as deep a pit as possible and deposit your feces into it, covering it up afterward.

Prioritizing Survival First Aid

One of the most stressful tasks you may have to take on in a survival situation is prioritizing first aid, also known as triage. This is where you choose to treat the person with the most life-threatening injury, working your way down the line to the least severe injury.

If you are treating only one injured person, you should take the following steps:

1. Check breathing: Check the victim's airway. Make sure it's open and the victim is breathing. If not, start mouth-to-mouth resuscitation.
2. Check for unconsciousness: If the victim is unconscious but breathing, place him or her on one side with the top leg at a right angle to the body. Use his or her hand to support the head and tilt the head back to ensure an open airway.
3. Check for bleeding: Stop any bleeding.
4. Check for shock: Treat shock.

Major and Minor Injuries

WILDERNESS INJURIES USUALLY FALL into one of two general categories: major or minor. Luckily, most are minor. Although these will not stop you in your tracks, remember that any minor injury left untreated in the wilderness can quickly become a major one. For this reason, *all* injuries in the wilderness should be taken seriously.

For example, if you're in the Amazon and suffer a small cut, you'll still be able to function normally. However, that little cut can rapidly grow infected and become a major problem. If you are walking and get a blister on your foot, you may be able to keep up the pace (and endure the pain) for a day or two more. But left untreated, that blister can virtually cripple you, preventing you from reaching safety.

I was once in an adventure race with three other teammates, when one of the members of our group began to experience irritation and chafing in her groin. We had to keep moving and didn't treat her when it was still a minor discomfort, and as a result, within 24 hours it turned into a full-blown infection, to the point where she could no longer walk.

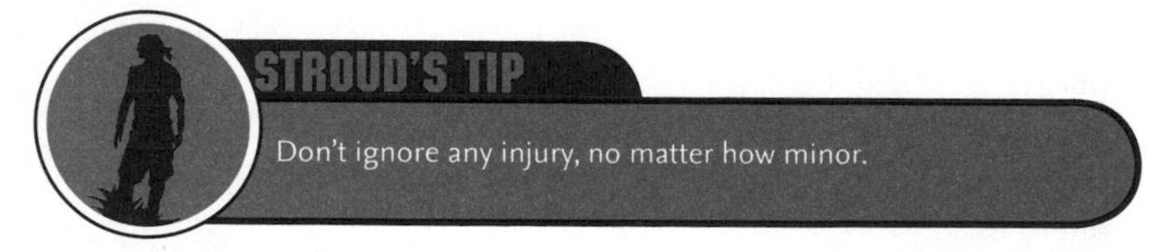

Major Injuries and Illnesses

THE KEY TO DEALING WITH MAJOR INJURIES AND ILLNESSES is to prevent them from occurring (to the extent that you can). Should you or anyone in your party suffer from the following maladies, you need to act quickly and decisively; in the wilderness, injuries and illnesses can become life-threatening very quickly.

Dehydration

Dehydration is a serious risk in the world's hot and dry regions, and one that can kill you within a few days. Finding protection from the wind and sun will slow the rate at which you lose water, but you will eventually need to get to a water source. If your only choice is to drink unpurified water, do it. I'd rather take my chances with parasites than die of dehydration.

Since you also lose valuable salts when you dehydrate, you should consider including an over-the-counter electrolyte replacement product in your first-aid kit. If you don't have one, add a quarter-teaspoon of salt to a quart (liter) of water.

Dehydration victims should drink frequently, and in small amounts.

Hypothermia and Frostbite

Once again I have asked my friend Gordon Giesbrecht, PhD, professor of thermophysiology, to chime in on how to handle hypothermia and frostbite:

Hypothermia: A hypothermic victim takes a while to become that way (anywhere from one hour to several days). It is critical to treat a cold victim as gently as possible. Quick, rough actions could be fatal due to changes in core temperature, blood pressure, and work required by the heart. Follow these steps:

1. Handle the victim as gently as possible.
2. Keep the victim horizontal.
3. Don't let the victim walk or struggle.
4. Get the victim to shelter as soon as possible.
5. Once in shelter, consider removing the victim's wet clothing, usually by cutting it off.

6. Place victim in as much insulation as possible (sleeping bags, blankets, et cetera).
7. If you have any source of heat, apply it to the chest and armpits. This could include a heat pack (fueled by electricity, chemicals, or charcoal, for instance), warm water bottles, or a healthy (that is, a warm) member of the group.
8. If possible, wrap the victim loosely in a vapor barrier such as plastic.
9. Only if the victim is awake and alert, give him or her food or drink with high caloric value (for example, hot chocolate or a chocolate bar). Monitor the victim for problems breathing and signs of worsening condition. Also check the feet and hands to make sure they are not getting cold.

Frostbite: Frostbite can have devastating effects, especially if treated improperly. For more than 200 years, the common remedy for frostbite was to rub the frozen area with snow or submerge it in cold water. This was an overreaction and is no longer recommended. Here are the do's and don'ts of frostbite treatment:

- Never rub frostbite.
- Never expose frostbite to anything cold.
- Never try to warm frostbite with dry heat from a fire or over a stove.
- Never rewarm a frostbitten area if there is a chance it could freeze again (e.g., if you are out in the mountains with several days remaining to walk to safety).
- Warm a frostbitten area either by contact with warm human skin or by immersion in warm water at about 99°F (37°C).
- Do not burst any blisters that may develop.
- Resist amputating dark or even black tissue; in many instances much or all of the tissue may survive, given enough time and tender care.

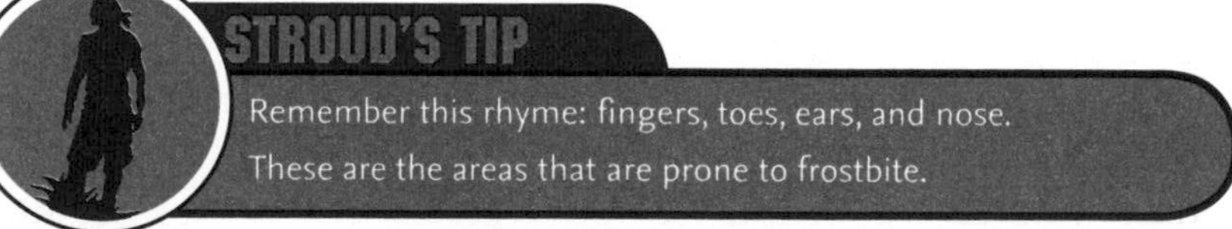

Shock

Shock is a natural reaction that occurs in most seriously (and even not-so-seriously) injured people. It can affect you on two levels. The first, the good reaction, is the one that provides you with potentially superhuman strength and helps you get out of potentially dangerous situations. This is the characteristic of shock that lets a person with a broken femur crawl for miles to safety or lift a car to free a trapped child. It's also called an adrenaline rush. The dangerous part of shock is what comes afterwards—the debilitating part that renders you unable to help yourself.

To treat shock, lay the victim on the ground, insulated from the ground, if possible. If the victim is conscious, elevate the legs about 12 inches (30 cm). If the victim is unconscious, roll him or her onto one side to prevent choking on vomit and other fluids.

Maintain the victim's body heat, either by protecting against the elements or adding external sources of heat. Give the conscious victim small doses of sugary solution to drink if he or she is able to drink, and if possible, make sure the person rests for at least 24 hours.

Burns

Burns can be dangerous in the wilderness, and are a very real risk, given the importance of fire to your survival. The worst burn I ever saw was on a camping trip when a girl lifted a frying pan with bacon and dumped the grease down her arm.

These types of burns (from oils and grease) are especially serious because they will continue to "cook" under the skin even after you've removed the burning material from the body part. Regardless of the cause of the burn, the first thing to do is immerse the area in cold but not freezing water. If you need to cover the wounds (for transporting a victim), apply dressings and rags that have been soaked in cold, clean water. If not, keep drizzling water over the wounds until rescue arrives.

With wilderness burns, there is risk of infection. After cooling, treat all burns as you would an open wound. With a covered wound, change or sterilize dressings daily by boiling. But it is best to keep the burn uncovered and to drizzle cool water on it constantly.

Finally, never apply butter or similar salves to burns. The only creams you should use are antibiotic or burn creams.

Joint Injuries

Joint injuries include fractures (breaks), dislocations, and sprains. They can be among the most debilitating wilderness injuries, since they will prevent you from one of your most important survival goals: moving. Prevent joint injuries by exercising caution at all times.

Fractures: Fractures are the most serious of joint injuries, more so if they are open or compound fractures, where the bone protrudes through the skin. In these cases, it's obvious immediately that a bone has been broken. If the bone does not break the skin, signs of fractures include extreme pain and tenderness, loss of function, swelling, general deformity of the area, and a grating sound or feeling.

To treat a fracture, you must immobilize and splint the broken bone. A splint is a solid surface, such as a stick, that you tie to the area to keep the bone immobilized.

A stick or pole is best for making a splint, although even rolled-up towels or clothing can work.

Try to pad the splint where it contacts the skin to prevent chafing; tie it tightly enough to secure it, but don't cut off blood circulation.

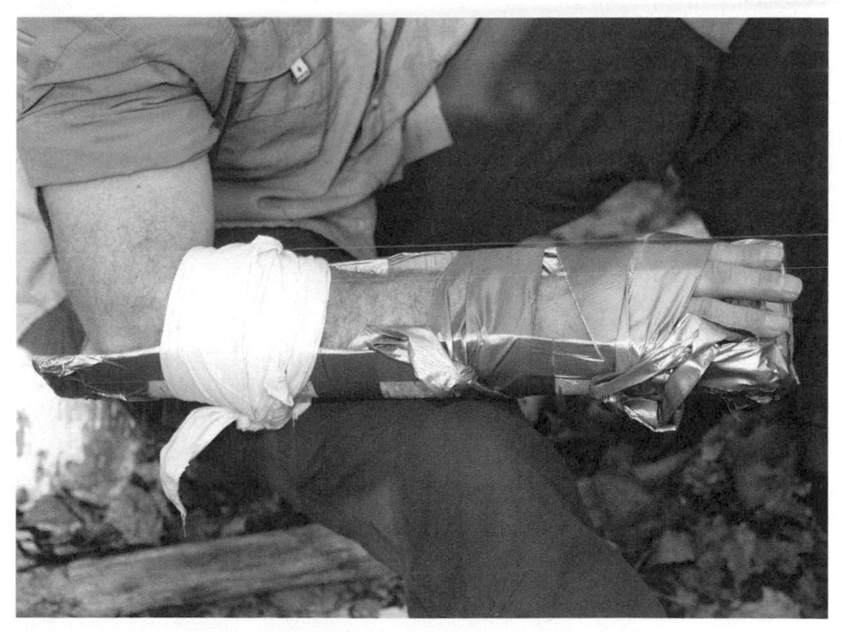

Make sure the knots are against the wood and not the skin.

Dislocations: A dislocation is the separation of a bone joint causing it to move out of alignment. This type of injury needs to be treated as soon as possible, to prevent the muscles from seizing up around it. The most complete way to treat a dislocation is to "reduce" it, which means setting the bones back in their proper alignment. Reductions are very painful, but worth the pain if done properly. Even the inexperienced should try to reduce a dislocation, as the alternative is a useless limb.

The only way to tell if a reduction has been successful is by comparing the look of the injured joint to the joint on the opposite side. Other than reduction, your other option is to immobilize a dislocated joint by splinting it.

Sprains: These occur when tendons and ligaments are overstretched. The most obvious signs of sprain are excessive swelling, bruising, and tenderness. Sprains are best treated with the RICE method: Rest, Ice, Compression, Elevation:

1. Rest the area for as long as possible.
2. Ice for 24 hours, followed by heat. Chances are you won't have ice with you, so search for anything that will cool the area. Water from a cold stream, river or lake works well.
3. Compress by wrapping the area snugly to prevent movement without cutting off circulation.
4. Elevate the area whenever it's not being used, to minimize swelling.

Heat Exhaustion or Stroke

Heat stroke impedes the body's natural ability to cool itself, and can lead to death if not treated quickly. Symptoms include hot, dry skin, and a visible lack of sweat, as well as headache, dizziness, confusion, and nausea/vomiting.

If you suspect heat stroke, it's important to get the victim into the shade. Remove restrictive clothing to allow evaporation to occur, which helps to cool the skin. You must then cool the body by pouring water on it, even if the water is contaminated. Allow the water to evaporate off the skin; you can speed the cooling process by fanning the victim. As with dehydration, the victim should consume water in small amounts every few minutes; large amounts bring on vomiting.

To treat shoulder dislocation, heavy objects can be used to pull the bones back into place. This can be extremely painful but allows for the quickest recovery. Do not attempt this procedure unless you have had proper wilderness first-aid instruction.

The key areas to cool during heat stroke are where there are major arteries: the neck, wrists, armpits, groin, and head. Cooling the back of the knees is also a good idea. You can also massage the victim's limbs to move cooled blood from the extremities to the internal organs.

Bleeding

If not stopped, major bleeding can quickly lead to death. Bleeding can be controlled with direct pressure, elevation, or (as a last resort) tourniquets.

The most effective of these strategies is direct pressure applied to the wound. Elevate and hold the wound long enough to not only stop the bleeding but to seal off the wound.

If you've injured an extremity, elevating it as high as possible above the heart will slow blood loss. Note that this method doesn't stop bleeding completely; you need to use it in conjunction with direct pressure.

Although some people recommend tourniquets for bleeding, these should be used only for life-or-death situations, when no other method can control the flow of blood. Tourniquets present a high risk because if they're left on too long they can cause gangrene and lead to the loss of the limb below the tourniquet.

Minor Injury and Illness

At first blush, minor injuries and illnesses may not seem as important or dire as their major counterparts, but they deserve as much of your attention. These are insidious injuries. Ignore them for too long and they will likely become major before you know it.

Headache

Headaches are a common and potentially debilitating aspect of survival, so carry some ibuprofen or acetaminophen in your first-aid kit. Drinking lots of water and massaging the aching area can also help.

Sickness and Disease

Sickness and disease can be major or minor, but once your defenses are down and your immunity starts to plummet, you're more susceptible to both.

Once you become sick, your energy levels suffer, as do your survival efforts. The result could be a dangerous snowball effect. If you don't have the energy to build a shelter, for example, you will increase your exposure to the elements and your susceptibility to conditions such as hypothermia. What you do to treat yourself now will affect what happens in the minutes, hours, days, and weeks to come.

Bites and Stings

Since bites and stings range from very minor to very major events, the best approach is to avoid them by wearing proper clothing and not putting your hands or feet in dark places without first investigating. Check yourself daily to make sure no strange creatures are hitching a ride on your body. Try not to scratch bites and stings, as they may become infected.

For bee, wasp, and hornet stings, the most important consideration is whether you or someone in your group has a severe allergy. If so, you should carry an epinephrine ("epi") pen and antihistamines.

You can get an EpiPen prescription from most physicians; just explain that you're traveling to a remote area and there's a chance you may get stung by an unknown insect. Be warned, however: if you have a true anaphylactic reaction to a bite or sting, an EpiPen will only help to prevent your throat from closing for about 15 minutes or so, the time it would usually take to get a victim to a hospital. EpiPens are expensive and expire after 12 to 18 months, so keep your first-aid kit updated. Carrying two EpiPens is a good idea. Note that while epinephrine opens up the airway, it does not stop the cause of the constriction. You must also take antihistamines to counter the body's production of histamine, which is what closes up your airways in the first place.

If you get stung by a bee or other similar creature, remove the stinger immediately. This can usually be done by scraping up and away (not pulling out) from the area with a fingernail or knife blade.

Being bitten by a spider or stung by a scorpion is more serious, and little can be done in the way of treatment unless you're lucky enough to have an antivenin on hand. If a member of your group is bitten or stung by one of these, watch for anaphylaxis, clean and dress the area, and also treat the victim for shock, vomiting, and diarrhea, should they occur. Some spider bites result in ulcerated areas that refuse to heal. Dress the ulcers to prevent infection.

Snakebites can also be serious, if not deadly, though the majority of snakebite victims suffer little or no effects from poisoning. Infection is a real concern, however, due to the bacteria in the snake's mouth, so clean and disinfect the area immediately. Try to calm the victim and treat for shock, if necessary.

Staying calm after a snakebite is easier said than done. I can't imagine what I would have done if bitten by a snake in the Amazon. I was miles away from anywhere and it would have been difficult to get out. And that's the paradox: When you're bitten by a snake, what you want to do is run for help, yet it's the one thing you cannot do because it only serves to increase the rate at which the venom spreads through your system.

Try to determine if the snake was poisonous or not. If in doubt, assume it was! Give the victim as much fluid as possible, and remove constricting items such as belts, watches, and bracelets.

In treating snakebites, avoid the following:

- Cutting: Opening the wound is ineffective in removing the venom, and the open wound might become infected.
- Alcohol: Similarly, this is ineffective for wound or patient.
- Tourniquet: Constricting the bite might cause more damage and pain, and even after the loss of a limb if applied incorrectly.

To treat snakebite, follow these steps:

1. Calm the patient and keep him or her still.
2. Apply a broad bandage (crêpe) tightly around the whole limb, as for a sprained ankle. This will retard absorption of the venom but still let blood through to supply the bite-wound with needed blood.
3. Check vital signs.
4. Immobilize the limb with a splint.
5. If it's not possible to reach a doctor within hours and you have antivenin, test for allergic reaction first by injecting a little under the victim's skin or inject antihistamine first. (Always carry an injectable antihistamine in your first-aid kit.)

Diarrhea

Diarrhea is common in survival situations and is another minor sickness that can become major.

There are two important things to understand about diarrhea. First, diarrhea is your body's way of ridding itself of an irritant. Let it run its course for 6 to 12 hours. However, diarrhea can also rapidly lead to dehydration. Through it, you lose valuable water and electrolytes, which need to be replenished.

The best way to replenish yourself is to drink some water, preferably clean and purified. Drink small amounts frequently (which will help your bowel absorb the fluid) rather than drinking a huge amount at one sitting (which will overwhelm your stomach and trigger more diarrhea).

If you're in a group, keep in mind that diarrhea can be embarrassing for the person who has it, so try to create an environment of understanding and comfort. You might also designate a private place for that person to go, to reduce awkwardness.

Charcoal is an effective remedy for diarrhea because it is highly absorbent, and will absorb drugs and toxins from the gastrointestinal tract. Grind a teaspoon of charcoal from your fire and mix it with water. Consume this a few times a day, as necessary.

If you have electrolyte replacement powders in your first-aid kit, they will help replace the electrolytes lost through diarrhea. Loperamide is also useful to have in your kit; it can plug you up in cases where the diarrhea just won't stop. I'd let the diarrhea run its course for at least a day before resorting to loperamide.

Blisters

Blisters also rank high on the list of problems that start out minor but can become major. The best way to treat blisters is to prevent them from happening in the first place, by keeping your socks and feet dry and clean.

If you do develop a blister—particularly on your foot—do not puncture it or otherwise open it, as this makes it susceptible to infection. Rather, apply some sort of padding to relieve pressure and reduce friction. Stay off your feet as much as possible until the blister subsides. If you have a blister that breaks open, treat it as an open wound.

Wounds

Wounds can be minor or major. If they're major, the biggest risk is excessive bleeding. The most significant risk from minor wounds is infection, so clean the wound immediately and cover it with a clean dressing. Change the dressing at least once a day to prevent infection. If you don't have any extra clean dressing material available, you can reuse the existing dressing by boiling it for at least three minutes to sterilize. Allow it to cool before applying. Let the wound air dry during that time. Gaping wounds can be closed with the butterfly sutures in your first-aid kit.

If you have antibiotic cream, apply it to the wound. Antibiotic pills should be used only for treating wound infections, not for preventing them.

Infections

In a survival situation, there's a very good chance that a wound may become infected. You can tell by the redness that appears around the wound and the consistent discharge of pus.

Treat infections by applying warm compresses on the area for 30 minutes three or four times daily. Change the compress as it cools. You can also drain the wound by opening and poking it with an implement you've sterilized, such as a knife tip held in a fire and then allowed to cool.

Altitude Sickness

Depending on how high you are, altitude sickness can range from mild discomfort and shortness of breath to life-threatening cerebral edema. Symptoms range from drowsiness and weakness to persistent rapid pulse and vomiting.

The best way to cure altitude sickness is to get the victim to lower altitudes immediately. Some victims of mild altitude sickness can control symptoms by consciously taking large, exaggerated breaths.

Group Versus Solo Survival

IF YOU'RE INJURED, YOU'RE FAR BETTER OFF in a group because you'll have people around who can help you. Members of the group can lift and move a sick or injured person.

One difficult decision you may have to make in a survival situation is whether to leave an injured person or stay with them. If you are in a group of two, leave only if your travel partner's injuries are life-threatening, you can't help him or her, and you know where safety and help lie. Before leaving, stabilize the victim, place him or her comfortably in a shelter, and mark the area so that you can find it on your return.

In larger groups, send the fastest and most capable travelers for help while others stay behind to tend to the wounded. Again, those who leave should do so only if they are *sure* they will be able to reach help.

Chapter Fourteen

ESSENTIAL SURVIVAL SKILLS

Like your prehistoric ancestors, you have the ability to harness those great human qualities of adaptability and ingenuity that could save your life during a survival situation. Whether it's making a fish hook from the bones of a decaying animal or a crude knife from a piece of rock, the ability to improvise and create survival tools from materials at hand will help you when you've got nothing else with which to work.

Think Like a Sculptor

ALTHOUGH MOST OF US ENVISION WILDERNESS as being completely untouched by humankind, the world is not that big anymore. In many ways, this is not a good thing, but it may help you in a survival situation because you are more likely than you think to come across abandoned junk that may be useful.

Some of the best places for finding useful odds and ends are coastal regions, where the sea often washes up intriguing bits. You should look upon this stuff as if you were a sculptor: Don't consider what it *is*, but what it *could be*. That piece of scrap metal might look like a piece of garbage, but if you change your lens you might see six fish hooks, a knife blade, and a pot for melting water. When I was in Labrador, I came upon an empty can of naphtha gas. After a little cutting, bending, and reshaping, I had changed it into a simple wood stove.

In the Kalahari Desert, the most effective "junk" I found included a few jars and cans in an old truck. They worked like a charm to trap scorpions, which were the basis for my diet there. In Alaska, the roof of my shelter was two big pieces of plastic that I discovered under a couple of rocks. All of it started as garbage, but for me it meant survival.

Think Simplicity

ALTHOUGH THERE IS A DESIRE AMONG HARD-CORE SURVIVALISTS to make elaborate and sophisticated tools in the bush, I've found that the best manmade survival tools are the most basic. A simple snare, a simple fish hook: these are often the most effective things you can make. Creating complex traps, snares, and shelters is fine when you have time and energy, neither of which you typically have in abundance in an emergency!

Survival is a humbling situation. Any notions you may have entertained about building incredible tools will be swept away quickly (right behind those ideas you once had about the importance of staying clean).

Attempting to construct complex survival tools can lead to immense frustration as well. The worst thing you can do in a situation like this is spend hours trying to build something, only to find that it doesn't work. A simple version often suits the purpose but takes only a fraction of the time to make.

While my wife, Sue, and I spent the year living off the land in northern Ontario, we wanted to make a blanket of rabbit pelts. We figured we'd need about 100 pelts, and my first thought was to build an elaborate set of snares and traps. In the end, though, over a few weeks, I set out a couple dozen simple snares, which were really effective and took very little time to construct. I'm sure I wouldn't have had any better luck with a more elaborate setup.

Get Over the Squeamishness of Destruction

One of the things that many people struggle with, even under the most dire circumstances, is destroying something they cherish to make a survival tool. But there's really no other choice: if it's ultimately going to save your life or limbs, *do it*. Whether this be cutting your credit card into pieces, filing your house key to a point, cutting up your car seats, or burning the spare tire in your car to attract attention, recognize that these are actions born of necessity.

At the same time, however, you must have the foresight to visualize whether the object you're destroying may be more useful to you later in its original form. You don't want to sacrifice your snowmobile's windshield, only to get the machine going later and suffer frostbite or hypothermia on the way home because you've got no protection from the wind.

During the winter of 2008, a Utah couple got lost with their vehicle and was trapped in the snow in a remote area. Following their 12-day ordeal, they explained at a news conference that they had seen one of my shows, in which I explained how to cut the stuffing out of car seats to make "snowshoes." They did exactly that and walked through the deep snow to safety without losing their toes or feet to frostbite. They had had a decision to make: keep their car seats intact or survive. They chose life.

Tools You Can Make

One of the most often ignored but significant benefits of making your own survival tools is not the purpose they are meant to serve, but how the act of creating them prepares you psychologically for your ordeal. The creative process will keep your mind focused, distract you from the misery of your circumstances, and generally improve your mental state. Sure, you may make a snare or a trap and not be successful with it at first, but making the effort is much better than doing nothing at all, because doing something, *anything*, gives you hope that your efforts may bear fruit. This all ties into the all-important will to live: if you have a reason to survive, you likely will make it through alive.

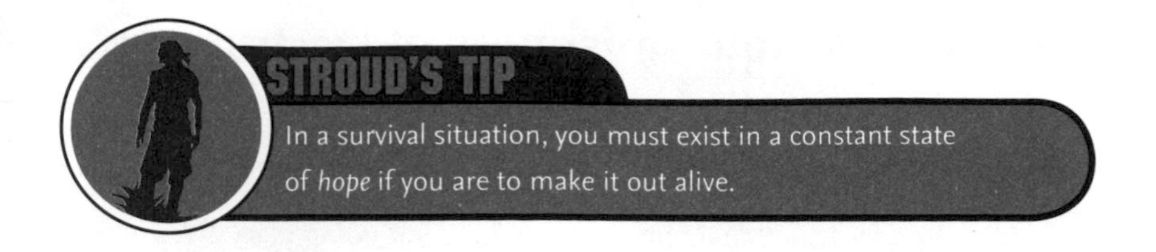

Making Rope

Making your own rope from natural materials may sound complex, but it's easier than you think. And having rope will greatly improve your chance of survival because it can be used in so many different ways.

Rope helps build traps. It fixes clothing, ties off wounds, holds shelters together, and binds your stuff together when the time to travel comes. My favorite rope-making materials are milkweed stem, evening primrose bark, spruce roots, and cedar bark. Rope from trees is typically made from the shredded inner bark. As with finding plants to use for tinder, your efforts here will helped immensely if you understand characteristics rather than memorize names. Quite simply, you are looking for anything *fibrous.*

The problem with rope making is that it's not always easy to find the right materials, especially because they are seasonally dependent. In other words, some plants become most fibrous in late fall or early winter, when they have dried to the point that they're no longer green. For others, such as tree bark, the best time is early spring.

If you are fortunate enough to have caught a large game animal, sinew and rawhide work well as rope (particularly for binding and lashing things together), although these are fairly involved undertakings. Sinew is the product of the tendons (strands lying flat against the leg bones). To make sinew, first dry the tendons, then rub them on a rough surface (or smash them with a club or rock) so they separate into fibers. These fibers can then be used as rope; they work better when moistened.

Rawhide is thin strips cut from the animal's hide and can be used even if the fur is still on.

Twisting Rope

1. It may sound complicated, but basic rope twisting is simple. Start with fibrous material, such as husks from the yucca plant. Separate the husks into strands.

2. Gather sufficient strands to be able to build a rope as thick as you need it. Roll or rough up strands together to get separate pieces.

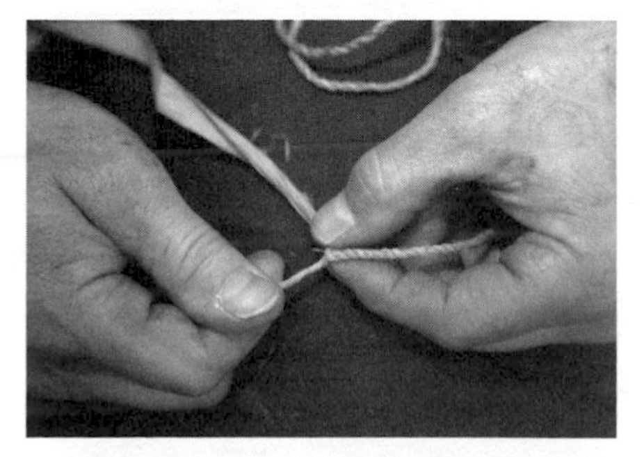

3. Twist each piece between two fingers in a clockwise motion. Then, wrap the two pieces together in a counter-clockwise motion.

4. This simple method works with many different types of materials.

5. Once you've completed winding the pieces together, you will have a strong rope to use for many purposes.

Making Rope from Sinew

1. Rub the sinew on a rough surface to separate it into strands.

2. These fibers can be woven together to form a durable rope.

Making Knots

A NATURAL PARTNER TO ROPE MAKING is the ability to tie knots. Like many survival skills, this one can be *over*learned, because there are hundreds of different types of knots, some of which have very specific uses.

You don't need to learn hundreds. I've found that knowing just a few simple knots will help you through almost any survival situation, enabling you to make more effective shelters, fishing implements, snares, and traps.

Les's Top Three Knots

Bowline: The bowline is a perfect survival knot because of its great strength and the ease with which it can be tied. It forms a loop (though not a noose) at the end of a rope, and it is typically used for securing a rope to an object.

To tie a bowline, start by making a loop a short distance from the end of the rope. Pass the working end of the rope *up* through the loop, wrap it around the base, and pull it back *down* through the loop to finish the bowline.

Clove Hitch: The clove hitch is nothing more than two loops "stacked" on each other. It's a great simple knot for securing rope between trees or poles, and for hanging things from a horizontal pole. Be aware, though, that to be

A bowline knot is a simple one to learn, and it's very strong.

effective it requires a load on each end, and it has been known to slip.

To tie a clove hitch, work from left to right. Make a loop somewhere along the length of the rope. Then make a second identical loop to the immediate right of the first. Stack the second (right) loop on top of the first. Place both loops over the pole and pull the free ends of the rope to tighten.

If you're tying a clove hitch to a standing object such as a tree, begin by wrapping the rope once around the tree. After the working end of the rope passes around the tree, it should cross *over* the main stem of the rope. Wrap the working end of the rope around the tree again, this time passing it through the loop you've just created. Pull both ends of the rope taut to finish the knot.

Figure Eight (and Double Figure Eight): Though traditionally used in climbing, the figure eight and double figure eight are also great for tying rope to other objects. They bind so well, though, that untying them can be a real chore. Make a long loop by passing the working end of the rope back *under* the main rope stem. Cross the working end *over* the main rope stem and pass it *up* through the loop from the bottom. Repeat this procedure for the double figure eight.

Clove Hitch

1. Form two loops as shown.

2. Stack one on top of the other.

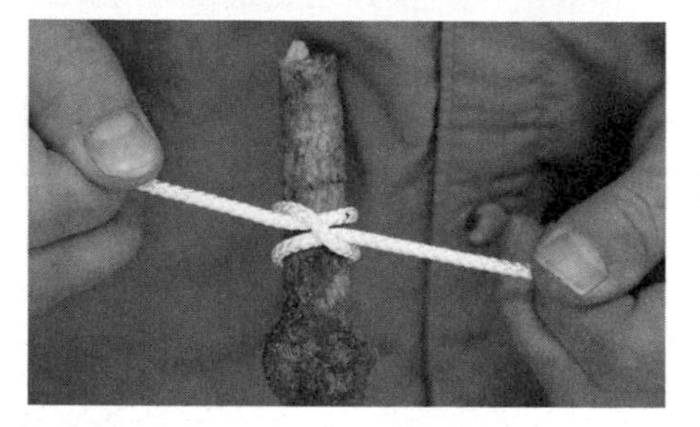

3. When tied properly around a tree or pole, this knot will self-tighten.

4. Here I used a clove hitch and a small stone to secure a tarp corner.

Figure Eight

To make a figure eight knot, the string goes around the tree and then follows its own path back.

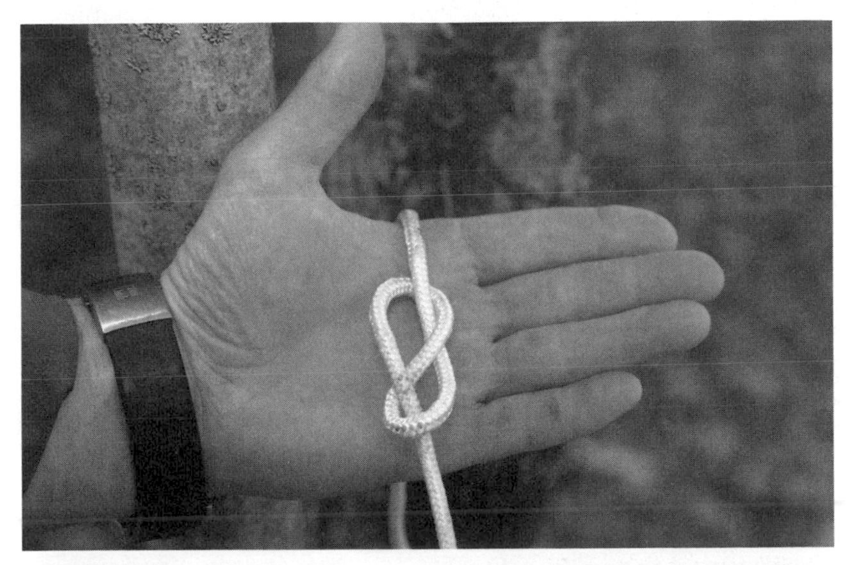

1. The figure eight: first stage.

2. The double figure eight: second stage.

Making Knives

KNIVES COME INTO PLAY in almost every aspect of survival. If you're without a knife, there are ways of making basic knives that will do the job. All you need is a semi-sharp edge. That edge can be made from a number of materials, including rock, metal, bone, or even wood.

Knives from Rock

One of the oldest skills known to humankind is taking a piece of solid rock and breaking it to form a cutting edge. Over time this became a complicated and refined skill, now referred to as flint knapping. The good news is that you need only learn the basics to fashion a knife edge sharp enough to get you through most situations. No, it won't be as sharp as a steel knife, but a survival blade will give you a rough, serrated edge for cutting or scraping.

The most useful blades I have made while surviving have come from throwing a rock—one I *hoped* would break—against another rock (while carefully protecting my eyes) until I had sheared-off edges sharp enough to cut into wood.

Refined flint knapping is a useful primitive living skill, but too advanced for the survival situations to which this book is dedicated. Like bow making, flint knapping takes much time and mentored practice to master. With that in mind, the following pictures illustrate the most rudimentary methods for breaking a rock down to a usable edge.

Knives from Metal

When making survival knives, there is simply no substitute for metal. The biggest challenge is finding a piece that's roughly the right size and shape. Rub the metal against a hard surface to sharpen the point and blade (this will take a long time, so sit down and be patient). Unlike most survival knives, a metal blade will require a handle to protect your hands. Tape, cloth, or rope can all be used as knife handles.

Knives from Bone

Bone knives work better for puncturing than for cutting or scraping because they don't hold an edge very well. To make this type of knife, you need to start with a decent-size bone, such as a leg bone from a large mammal.

Splitting a Rock to Make an Edge

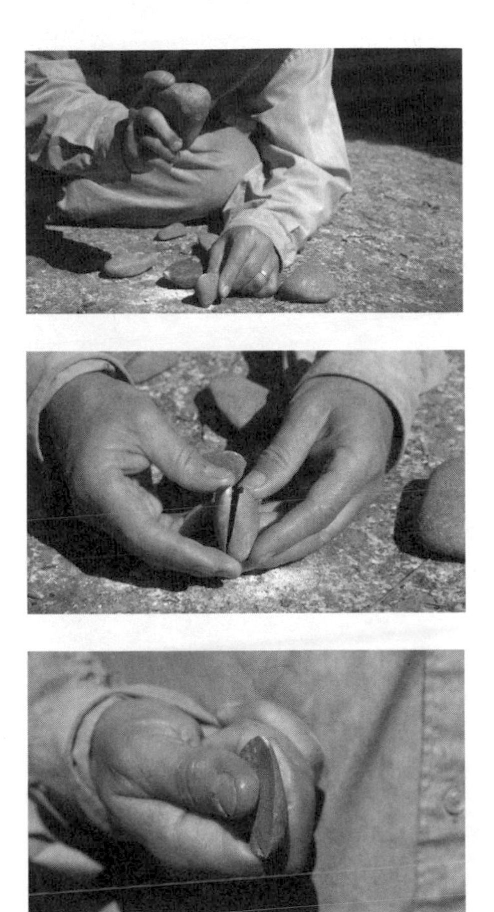

1. Splitting a rock in two can be a relatively easy undertaking, provided you find the right rock. Use a larger rock to hammer the smaller one.

2. Here, I've made a perfect split.

3. Given the right material, a split rock can be used effectively as a cutting or scraping edge, and can be further sharpened by rubbing it against another rock.

4. Your rudimentary rock knife has many uses, so keep it safe. Here, I'm making tinder by cutting into a dry branch.

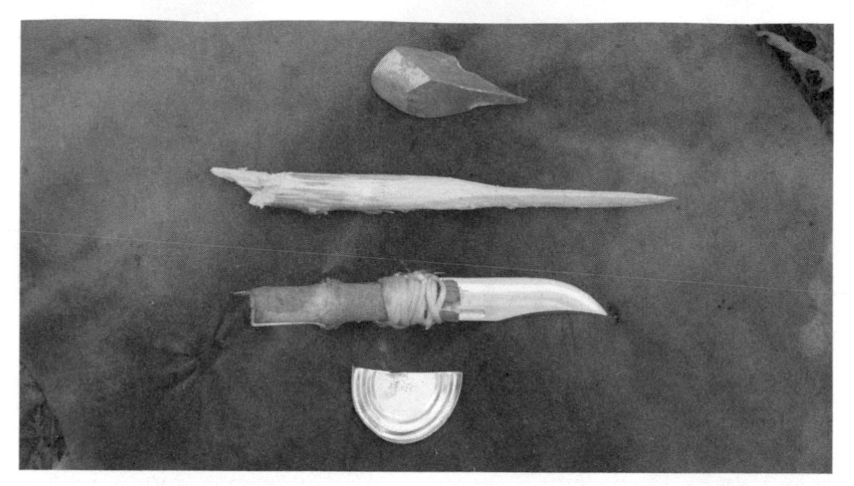

You can use a variety of materials to make cutting edges and knives, as well as handles for any metal blades you are lucky enough to salvage.

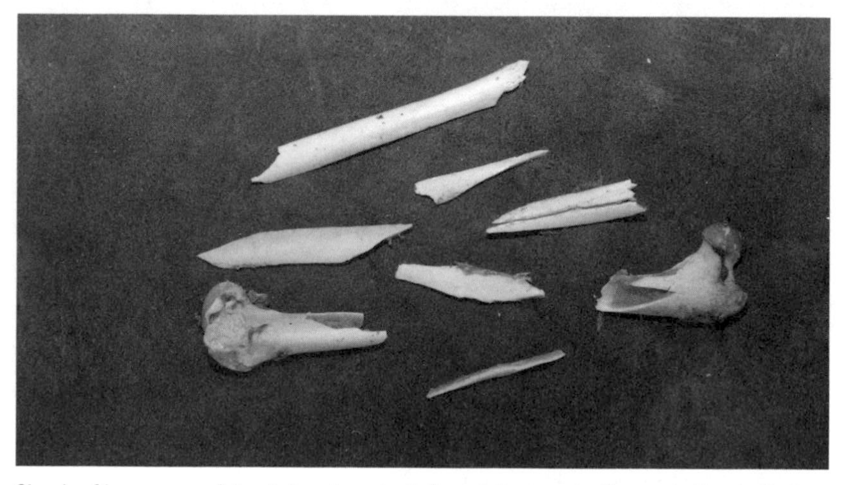

Shards of bone are useful as knives in a pinch, though they need refinement after shattering.

Lay the bone on a hard object and shatter it by striking it with a heavy object. Chances are you'll find a suitably pointy piece among the shattered bits. You can refine its shape by rubbing the bone piece on a rough rock. If you have only small bones or shards to work with, before rubbing, tie one to a piece of wood or other similar object.

You can also make a bone blade by scoring the bone along its length until you can insert a chisel of sorts and split the bone lengthwise.

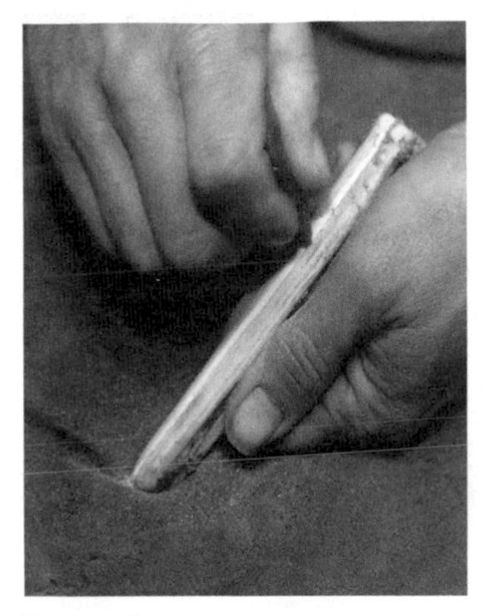

Scoring a bone.

Bone blades of various shapes and sizes made by scoring.

Knives from Wood

As with bone, it is difficult to get a sharp edge from wood, so wood knives are best suited for puncturing and scraping. This is certainly a last-ditch knife-making method, as it requires time, patience, and diligence. To make a wood knife, start with a piece of hardwood about 12 inches (30 cm) long and 2 inches (5 cm) in diameter; the blade should be 6 inches (15 cm) long. Shave the wood down to a point by rubbing it against a rough, hard surface, such as a rock.

You can further harden the blade by drying it over a fire until it's slightly charred. The drier the wood, the harder the point will become.

STROUD'S TIP

To sharpen a real knife, use a clockwise circular motion and push the blade away from you across the stone while applying consistent pressure on the blade. Try to keep it at a constant angle, say, 45 degrees. Do not drag the knife toward you under pressure, as this may create burrs on the blade. Regularly add water to the stone, if you have it. Reducing pressure gradually while you work will produce a finer edge.

My Favorite MacGyverisms

As many of you know, the hit TV show *MacGyver* (1985–1992) was based on the exploits of secret agent Angus MacGyver, whose claim to fame was his uncanny ability to use common items (and a Swiss Army knife) to improvise often-complex devices. During the many survival ordeals I've experienced, I've often tried to emulate MacGyver, with varying levels of success. Here is a short list of MacGyverisms I've managed in the field.

Using Underwear as a Hunting Tool

Desperate to catch fish, I cut the elastic strap from my underwear, combined it with a common ballpoint pen and a found piece of bamboo to make a Hawaiian sling spear.

Fishing with Gum

In the swamps of Georgia, I made a fishing lure out of a credit card that I cut into pieces. Then I used bubble gum to make a very thick bubble, pinched it off at the bottom, and used it as my fishing float. Had I been successful—there are 100-pound (45-kg) catfish in those swamps!—I could have enjoyed a very substantial meal.

Making Goggles out of a Snowmobile Cushion

One of the most insidious dangers in the Arctic is snowblindness. While surviving there, I cut a strip off my snowmobile's seat cushion to make goggles. All I needed was a knife to make the cut. In that survival situation, the goggles saved my eyes.

Purifying Water with a Plastic Bottle

In Africa, I suspended a plastic water bottle over a fire, letting the flames just lick the bottom of the bottle but not consume it. I was able to boil water without significantly melting the plastic.

Making a Flashlight from Car Parts

Use wire to connect the battery directly to the leads on the headlamps.

Making Rope from Car Parts

Wire from any vehicle's engine makes great rope.

Making Signals from Reflective Objects

Anything shiny is enough to flash sunlight at a passing airplane to attract rescue.

Making Knives from Glass

Broken glass can be used as an effective cutting tool.

Using Hand Sanitizer as a Fire Starter

Just about anything with a high percentage of alcohol can be used to make a fire.

Making a Throwing Stick

A THROWING STICK is a solid chunk of hardwood, approximately 18 inches (45 cm) long, that you can grip and throw efficiently, much the way you would a boomerang. Your purpose is to aim it well enough to stun or kill a rabbit, squirrel, or bird that's within range. It can be very effective when thrown at a group of roosting songbirds (see "Food," Chapter 8).

Making Clubs and Spears

ALTHOUGH SPEARS AND CLUBS were used by our prehistoric ancestors for hunting and warring, you'll likely find that they are most useful for protection and reassurance when you're in a place where there might be dangerous or predatory animals around. If you are surviving in a jungle, for example, and you know there might be 7-foot (2-m) cobras underfoot, a long piece of wood feels mighty good in your hands. You can make the tip of the spear itself quite sharp, or tie a handmade blade to the end.

But the usefulness of spears and clubs doesn't end there. Like ropes and knives, these are versatile items that can be used for just about anything, from digging holes to knocking fruit from nearby trees to pounding

To put a little distance between me and possible predators in Africa, I attached a handmade spear to a hunting knife.

stakes in the ground. So go ahead and make one even if you don't think you have a use for it at the time. Eventually, you will.

Like the throwing stick, a club is simply a tree branch. Size matters. Too long and you won't be able to swing it easily or quickly. Too short and it won't do any damage to whatever you're trying to hit. Hardwood is the best material, if you can find it. You can make a club more effective (especially for killing newly caught small game in your snare) by weighting one end. Tying a rock or similar heavy object to the end is the most common way to do this.

Making Eye Protection

SUNGLASSES ARE MORE THAN A FASHION STATEMENT. In the wild, exposure to the elements wreaks havoc not only on your body but also on your eyes. Unfortunately, sunglasses are not particularly robust items, and even if you bring a pair along with you, chances are they will get broken or lost during your survival ordeal.

You must protect your eyes against sunblindness (when you're on open water), and snowblindness (when you're surrounded by snow). In essence, both of these conditions are sunburns on your retina, causing discomfort and blindness for up to three days. Worse yet, being blind in an emergency—no matter how long the episode lasts—can mean the difference between life and death.

The Inuit protected their eyes by making sun goggles from caribou or walrus bone. When I was in the Arctic, I didn't have the luxury of these materials, so I made my own from a slit cut in a strip of vinyl. You can use almost anything for sun goggles as long as it limits the amount of sun beating against your eyes (see page 247).

Making Packs

WHEN YOU'RE ON THE MOVE, there is nothing worse than trying to carry all your vital survival materials in your hands or arms. It's not only slow, cumbersome, and frustrating, it's also dangerous because it impedes your ability to use your hands at a moment's notice.

You can use almost anything to make a pack on the fly, including plant fibers and bark, wood, rope, animal skins, or any other type of material you may have on hand.

To make a pack, lay a piece of square material on the ground, with your relevant items on one edge. Roll the material and the items toward the opposite edge. Once the bundle is cylindrical, securely tie off each end with one long piece of rope, about 6 feet (1.8 m) long. You can now use the long rope to drape the pack over your shoulder. Add extra ties along the length of the bundle to prevent contents from falling out (see page 221).

Making Snowshoes

Good for a multitude of uses, spruce boughs also make great snowshoes. Clump them together into the approximate size and shape you need, then tie the bundle together with some rope or cord. Lash the shoes to your feet, and you're off (see page 339).

Making Torches

As you may suspect, in a wilderness emergency there are many times when you will need to see in the dark but don't have a flashlight. As long as you have a fire, you will have light. Although there are many different ways to make a survival torch, the bark torch is one of the simplest yet most effective. You'll need a stick for the handle and a fairly thick strip of flexible bark (birch bark works very well) about 2 feet (60 cm) long and 6 inches (15 cm) wide.

Wrap the bark around the stick, and tie the base of the bark coil to the stick to secure it. Now wrap some cord or rope around the bark coil to prevent it from opening. You can burn the bark itself, but the torch will burn better if you fill the coil with flammable material, such as grass, small sticks, or small pieces of bark. Once you've lit the material inside the coil, it should last a good, long time (see page 339).

Here, I'm wearing snowboots and spruce-bough snowshoes, which make walking on top of snow a lot easier.

You could simply light some cloth on fire, but a correctly made torch will last much longer, increasing your chances of nighttime survival.

Group Versus Solo Survival

BEING IN A GROUP CAN BE A REAL BENEFIT when it comes to creating and sharing tools. You will have not only the benefit of a wider range of expertise and skills, but more people on hand to make the tools you need to survive. Your group will likely need only one good knife, for example, but three people can make it more easily than one!

Chapter Fifteen

WHEN DISASTER STRIKES CLOSE TO HOME

If you think about it, your chances of finding yourself in a true wilderness survival situation are slim, even if you're an avid outdoors person. In fact, you have a greater chance of getting caught in a natural disaster close to home. From hurricanes and earthquakes to tsunamis, from fires and floods and blackouts to extreme heat and cold spells, there are many ways that things can go dangerously wrong right in your own backyard.

Mental and Psychological Attitude

When facing a natural disaster, you should call on the same psychological strength that is so critical in wilderness survival. Do not panic; stop and assess the situation. Recognize that you will go through a range of emotions. Prioritize your needs.

Where natural disaster survival differs from true wilderness survival is in your ability, in most cases, to stay in touch with the outside world during the ordeal. If possible, stay connected through the media (for example, using a rechargeable hand-crank radio), if only to find out what else might be coming at you and how and when rescue/relief efforts may arrive.

Planning and Preparation

You need to get past the "It can't happen to me" attitude and understand that disasters *can* occur anywhere, anytime. The best way to prepare is to keep a few key items handy, just in case, in your home survival kit.

Like any survival kit, the one for your home must be tailored to your region and the events that are most likely to occur there. I live in Ontario, Canada, where earthquakes are rare. However, there's a good chance we could be struck by a blizzard and suffer a subsequent blackout, which could mean I'd be out of power, out of water (since I'm on a pump system), and out of heat. And if it was a prolonged blackout, I could eventually run out of food.

I recommend that you keep in your survival kit a *one-week supply* of everything you need to live. Refer to the checklist in the back of this book for everything you'll need to include.

Signaling

The ability to make an effective signal is important in disasters at or close to home. People are often trapped after natural disasters and need to signal for rescue, which is bound to come eventually. But if you're trapped, you will definitely need to let people know where you are and how you are.

Water

If you have the luxury of knowing in advance that a disaster will occur, fill your bathtub, as well as any other sink or receptacle you have available, with tap water. This is routine at our house when bad weather is on the way, and has paid off more than once. A water filter (not the cheap one that sits in a pitcher in your refrigerator) is useful if your supply becomes tainted or if you're getting your water from a nearby river or lake.

Remember that the water in the back tank of your toilet is perfectly drinkable, as it comes right from the tap and never contacts the bowl itself. Ice cubes that you've left in your freezer are another potential (though admittedly limited) source.

Fire

IF YOU LIVE IN A COLD CLIMATE, or disaster occurs during winter weather, you may need a fire source to keep yourself warm and to cook. Making a fire will not be an issue, since there should be fire-starting materials on hand; the trick comes in building and maintaining the fire in a safe place. The only safe places to make a fire that will keep the inside of a house warm are a wood stove or a fireplace. Fuel-based space heaters are also good backups. An electric stove can be used for heat, but you need to be extremely careful, particularly if there are small children around. Don't *ever* use your gas stove to heat your home.

Shelter

MOST NATURAL DISASTERS LEAVE YOUR HOME INTACT, which is a good thing. If that's not the case, you need to look at your situation through a different lens and try to improvise shelter, perhaps by moving to your car or setting up a tent. If you don't have either of these on hand, you're back to finding or creating shelter the same way you would in a wilderness survival situation. You need a shelter to keep warm and dry, and protected from the elements.

Food

IN MOST CASES WHEN DISASTER STRIKES, you will have a refrigerator full of food, all of which begins to spoil once the power goes out. Be sure to eat the most perishable foods first. You can preserve meats by using the drying methods described in "Food," Chapter 8. You can also place fish such as salmon in a dish or Ziploc bag and cover it with lemon juice (the process used to make *ceviche*). The citric acid "cooks" the fish through a process called naturation and preserves it for at least a few days.

Travel and Navigation

THE DECISION WHETHER OR NOT TO TRAVEL after a natural disaster is as critical when you are at home as when you're in the wilderness. If you are considering moving, the first thing to do is make sure the route is free of hazards. Listen to the radio before heading to the next community, so that you know, for example, whether a river has broken its banks upstream and is flooding the highway.

When it comes to navigation, GPS units are invaluable for locating street addresses. After Hurricane Katrina, I flew down to New Orleans to meet a woman and talk to her about her experience, but she had given me only her street address, not terribly useful because all the street signs had been wiped out. Luckily, the GPS unit in my car led me right to her house.

Don't think it can't happen to you! New Orleans and other parts of southern Louisiana were ravaged by Hurricane Katrina in August 2005.

Dangers and Hazards

WHEN DEALING WITH A NATURAL DISASTER it helps to recognize that the central event may have spawned other dangers around you, both seen and unseen. Think like a firefighter and address the risks of "gas, glass, fire, and wire."

Gas: Check to see whether there's any gas leaking in your house, such as natural gas or propane. Try to shut off the main valve into the house only if you have experience or training in doing so. If you suspect a gas leak, do not start a fire in your house, and leave the house if possible. If staying inside is safer than going out, keep the windows open for maximum ventilation.

Glass: Check for broken glass throughout the house and clean up as necessary. This will help prevent accidental cuts and potential infections in what might be unsanitary conditions.

Fire: This is one of the greatest dangers you'll face. Check for gas leaks, oil tank ruptures, and other types of leaks that can cause fire.

Wire: Electrical problems can result in fire. Also, check for exposed, live wires in the home, particularly if you have small children.

Unfortunately, most people give little thought to so-called urban disasters, even though many people will experience at least one in their lifetime. Be prepared, be ingenious, play it safe, and you will likely live to tell the tale. Remember that when all is said and done, everything is replaceable . . . except life.

Weather

SINCE WEATHER MAY WELL BE THE CAUSE of the natural disaster, stay in touch with the outside world for updates. Weather will dictate the extent of your survival activities; you also need to know if and when bad weather is going to exacerbate your problems, and when it is expected to subside.

First Aid

EVERYONE—NOT JUST THOSE TRAVELING IN THE WILDERNESS—should have a basic first-aid course under his or her belt. First aid can make the difference between life and death. Check with your local college for programs.

Essential Survival Skills

RELY ON YOUR INGENUITY AND ADAPTABILITY! Look at everyday objects around you and decide if, say, your couch would be better used as a survival tool than as furniture. In the case of any cherished memorabilia that may be used in an emergency, you need to get over the squeamishness of destruction. If it's a choice between your life and protecting a keepsake, the keepsake has to go.

Author's Note

In writing *Survive!*, I have tried to pull as much wilderness survival information from my memory as I can. Given that the past eight years have seen me survive in some of the most challenging environments on earth, much is still fresh in my mind.

Before I started producing *Survivorman*, I figured that my survival skills, all learned in North America, were pretty well honed. However, surviving alone in the jungles, deserts, oceans, and mountains of this planet have taught me how much I *didn't* know. And I'm still learning.

From the herbal remedies of the Waorani to the hunting skills of the Inuit, there are many wonderful survival skills that exist only within disappearing cultures. When I spent time in the Amazon, for example, I was amazed to learn that there were still 70 confirmed *uncontacted* tribes living in its jungles. Call me naive, but I had been convinced that everyone who *could have* been discovered *had been* discovered. Clearly that isn't so.

At the other extreme, new technologies are making survival easier and involve little more than pushing a button and waiting for rescue. PLBs and EPIRBs, cell phones and BlackBerries, and the new SPOT messenger technology have all made wilderness travel safer than ever.

In my research, I discovered that many survival publications are filled with outdated or untested skills and methods that may not help at all if you are in real jeopardy. Throughout the writing process, I always put myself in the position of an inexperienced person, lost and alone, and in need of basic survival knowledge that would keep him or her alive.

In my TV show, I like to throw in the occasional advanced survival skill. But that's just for fun, and this book is not about having fun. It's about surviving. That's why I have stuck to the most essential, trusted, and universal skills—skills that have kept me alive in the far-flung corners of the globe.

So, if this book is in your hands because you are in trouble, don't panic: calm down and assess your situation. Skim the book to the chapters that pertain to you. Make a plan. I sincerely hope there is something here that will improve your knowledge base and provide you with some practical ideas . . . even if it means ripping out some of the pages to start a fire!

You *will* survive. And perhaps like mine, your story can be told someday.

CHECKLISTS

Personal Survival Kit Checklist

Please see pages 19 to 21 for a detailed description of the elements of this survival kit.

❍ bandana
❍ compass
❍ flashlight (small, LED)
❍ garbage bags (2, preferably orange, large)
❍ lighter (my preference is a butane lighter that works like a little blowtorch)
❍ matches (strike-anywhere type) in a waterproof metal case (with a striker, just in case)
❍ magnesium flint striker (hey, I like fires!)
❍ metal cup (folding, for boiling water)
❍ multi-tool or Swiss Army–style knife (make sure it has a small saw blade)
❍ painkillers (a few)
❍ parachute cord or similar rope (about 25 feet [7.5 m] of 1/4-inch [0.6-cm] cord)
❍ protein bar
❍ sharp belt knife
❍ solar, or "space," blanket (small)
❍ whistle
❍ Ziploc bag (medium or large)
❍ coffee can or similar receptacle (in which to place all items)

Complete Survival Kit Checklist

Please see pages 21 to 30 for a detailed description of the elements of this survival kit.

- ❍ bandana
- ❍ belt knife (with sharpening stone)
- ❍ candle
- ❍ cup (metal, collapsible; for boiling water)
- ❍ dried food
- ❍ duct tape
- ❍ fire-starting devices: lighter and/or magnesium flint striker and strike-anywhere matches in a waterproof case (with a striker)
- ❍ fire-starting tinder
- ❍ first-aid kit: See checklist on page 356
- ❍ fishing lures (3), hooks, sinkers, and fishing line
- ❍ flares
- ❍ flashlight (small, LED)
- ❍ GPS (Global Positioning System)
- ❍ garbage bags (2, preferably orange)
- ❍ hand lens (small)
- ❍ map and compass
- ❍ marker or "surveyor's" tape
- ❍ money
- ❍ multi-tool or Swiss Army–style knife (with a small saw blade)
- ❍ needle and thread
- ❍ parachute cord or similar rope (about 25 feet [15 m] of 1/4-inch [0.6-cm] cord)
- ❍ pencil and notebook
- ❍ protein bars
- ❍ safety pins
- ❍ saw (folding)
- ❍ signal mirror
- ❍ snare wire
- ❍ solar, or "space," blanket
- ❍ SPOT satellite messenger/ EPIRB/PLB
- ❍ water purification tablets
- ❍ water-purifying straw
- ❍ whistle
- ❍ Ziploc bags (large)

Vehicle Survival Kit Checklist

Please see pages 33 to 36 for a detailed description of the elements of this survival kit. *In addition to* the complete survival kit, you should keep the following in your vehicle:

- ❍ cell phone
- ❍ clothing (warm) and blankets
- ❍ cook set (pots/pans)
- ❍ cook stove and fuel
- ❍ drinking water
- ❍ flares
- ❍ flashlight
- ❍ food, including MREs (Meals Ready to Eat)
- ❍ road maps (local)
- ❍ snow shovel (collapsible or folding) and tire chains
- ❍ tarp
- ❍ toilet paper
- ❍ tools

First-Aid Kit Checklist

Please see pages 24 and 25 for a detailed description of the elements of this first-aid kit.

- ❍ antidiarrheal tablets
- ❍ antihistamines
- ❍ antiseptic ointment
- ❍ bandages
- ❍ butterfly sutures
- ❍ painkillers
- ❍ prescription medicines (if applicable)
- ❍ surgical blades
- ❍ triangle bandages

Home Survival Kit Checklist

When assembling this survival kit, keep in mind that the size of your household will affect the quantity needed for several kit items.

Essential Items

❍ axe or saw
❍ basic tool box (hammer, nails, screwdriver, pliers, adjustable wrench, screw-in hooks, etc.)
❍ belt knife (with sharpening stone)
❍ camp stove (one burner) with all necessary supplies
❍ cash
❍ child-care items, if applicable (diapers, formula, bottles, etc.)
❍ clothing and footwear suitable for outdoor temperatures
❍ cooking container(s)
❍ duct tape
❍ emergency candles
❍ fire extinguisher
❍ first-aid kit and extra prescription medicines
❍ flashlight
❍ garbage bags (2, preferably orange, large)
❍ lighter (butane is best)
❍ matches (strike-anywhere type) in a waterproof metal case
❍ meal-replacement drinks (7-day supply per person)
❍ multi-tool or Swiss Army–style knife
❍ non-perishable food (7-day supply per person)
❍ pencil/pen and paper
❍ portable toilet and sanitation supplies
❍ rope or parachute cord
❍ rubber gloves
❍ shovel
❍ sleeping bags
❍ solar or hand-crank powered light, radio, and cell phone charger
❍ thermal blankets
❍ tissue packs and wet wipes
❍ tube tent and/or tarp >>

Home Survival Kit Checklist (continued)

- ❍ water purification tablets
- ❍ water, for drinking, cooking, and washing (7-day supply of 7.5 gallons [28L] per person)
- ❍ waterless soap or hand sanitizer

Other Useful Items:

- ❍ emergency plans, contact lists, meeting place information, etc.
- ❍ eyewear (extra glasses, contact lenses, cleaning solution)
- ❍ fishing and/or hunting equipment
- ❍ generator with extension cord
- ❍ light sticks
- ❍ pet-care items, if applicable (litter, carriers, bags, leashes, etc.)
- ❍ portable heater
- ❍ rain ponchos with hood
- ❍ recreational items (board games, cards, books, harmonica)
- ❍ siphon hose (rubber)
- ❍ smoke/carbon monoxide detector (for stove/heater use)
- ❍ spare gasoline for vehicle
- ❍ wash basin
- ❍ water filter

ACKNOWLEDGMENTS

I am greatly and deeply indebted to those who have helped me make this book happen.

Mike Vlessides is the ghostwriter, or perhaps more appropriately the editor, of this book. He spent hundreds of hours talking long-distance on the phone with me, pulling from my memory everything he could, to put down on these pages. Without Mike, and his tremendous patience, creative skill, and diligence, this book would never have been possible.

Laura Bombier is the photographer for this book. She is also the stills photographer for the TV series *Survivorman* and as such has traveled the globe with me, trying to capture the essence of what I do. And capture it she has! Her creative skill is second to none, and her partnership with me on this book has brought it to heights I could never have achieved without her.

Beverley Hawksley is the illustrator for *Survive!* I did not want the same old line drawings; I wanted the technical aspects to be combined with artistic beauty. Beverley captured that vision fantastically. Beverley's work is inspired, beautiful, and powerful. She is an artist in the purest sense of the title.

I enlisted the help of a group of survival-instructor friends to read every word and throw their comments back to me, challenging anything thought to be not quite right. To Doug Getgood, Dave Arama, and Douw Kruger, thank you so very much. You saved me from a couple of blunders and some forgetfulness, helping to make this book the best it can be.

Along the way, I have learned so much from some great people in the field and often had my preconceived notions changed forever. Thank you to "Desert" David Holladay, Mike Kiraly, Allan "Bow" Beauchamp, Brian Brewster, Charlie Ford, Belly John, Frank Gagliano, Belize Sailing Charters, Lee Gutteridge, Koos Moorecroft, Raphael Gunduza, Douw Kruger, Ngaa Kitai, Dave Reid, Sam Omik, Jim Yost, Tomo, Kinta, Anna, Ippa, and Duey (from the Amazon rain forest), Ron Durheim of Alaska Aquatics, Fred Rowe and Frank Yamick (my very first teachers), Matt Graham, John and Geri McPherson, Robert J. Wilson, Gino Ferri, Ernie and Donna Nichols of Huron Air, Wes Werbowy, and Dr. Gordon Giesbrecht.

Sue, Raylan and Logan: You have put up with my absence, which was a hard sacrifice. You have feared for my safety. You have created an environment that nurtured and cared for me greatly during many times of stress and challenge. Raylan and Logan, I know it's really hard to understand a dad who is away on adventures so much, but I miss you every single moment. You are the lights of my life, and I love you more than anything.

A special thanks to my "team." Wendy Turner: I am there for you and you are there for me—it's a beautiful thing; Beth Cavanagh, Andy Peterson, Max Attwood, Andrew Sheppard, Parres Allen, Barry Farrell, and Dan Larade: I have constantly felt bolstered and supported by you all and am very proud to call you my friends. Now "get back to work!"

Luke Despatie, for cover design and so much more—thank you so very much.

Also a nod of thanks to the *Survivorman* gang, who have fought hard through the challenges of making that series: Dave Brady, Seaghan Hancocks, Barry Clark, and Dan Reynolds. And none of it would have happened were it not for the first acceptance by Jane Mingay and Jane Gilbert of Discovery Canada and Anna Stambolic of OLN. Thank you, Patrice Baillargeon.

As always, thanks, Mom. And thanks to my sister, Laura. A very special thank you to Peter Dale, whose faith in me got me into of all this in the first place.

Also a special thank you to Rick Broadhead, who came out of nowhere to quickly become a trusted literary agent and friend. Thank you for helping me navigate the waters of publishing, Rick.

Thank you Brad Wilson and Anne Cole, editors for HarperCollins. I am so very proud to become a member of the HarperCollins family. You have renewed my faith that large, successful corporations can also treat one lone person with integrity and respect, and I am very grateful for the incredible support, belief, and gentle advice you have given me.

—Les Stroud, from somewhere out in the wilderness

ABOUT THE AUTHOR

Les Stroud, expert survivalist, is also a filmmaker, singer-songwriter, and creator of the television show *Survivorman*. A member of the prestigious Explorers Club, Les has produced, hosted, and appeared in many television specials, including *Shark Week*, *Surviving Alaska*, and *Off the Grid with Les Stroud*. He has been guest on *The Ellen DeGeneres Show*, *Larry King Live*, *The Late Late Show*, *The Hour*, and been featured in *Men's Journal*, *Entertainment Weekly*, and numerous other publications. Visit him at **www.lesstroudonline.com.**

INDEX

FIRE STARTER

FIRE STARTER

FIRE STARTER

FIRE STARTER